CAIAPHAS

To my darling Keith
With all my love

CAIAPHAS
Friend of Rome and Judge of Jesus?

Helen K. Bond

Westminster John Knox Press
LOUISVILLE • LONDON

Book design by Sharon Adams
Cover design by Night & Day Design
Cover art: Christ in Front of Caiaphas *by Francesco Ubertini Bacchiacca, II (1494–1557).*
  Courtesy of Galleria degli Uffizi, Florence, Italy / Bridgeman Art Library

First edition
Published by Westminster John Knox Press
Louisville, Kentucky

This book is printed on acid-free paper that meets the American National Standards Institute Z39.48 standard. ∞

PRINTED IN THE UNITED STATES OF AMERICA

04 05 06 07 08 09 10 11 12 13 — 10 9 8 7 6 5 4 3 2 1

Library of Congress Cataloging-in-Publication Data is on file at the Library of Congress, Washington, D.C.

ISBN 0-664-22332-X

Contents

Foreword

This is a book about Joseph Caiaphas, the longest serving Jewish high priest of the first century and, along with Pontius Pilate, one of the men who sent Jesus of Nazareth to his death. It is an attempt to piece together the story of his life from the fragments in the ancient sources: his early career, his role as high priest, his involvement in the politics of first-century Judea, his actions against Jesus and early Christianity, and his removal from office. It will also consider the way in which he was perceived afterwards by the earliest Christian Gospel writers.

The book is designed for the nonspecialist. After a lengthy process of sifting through often conflicting pieces of evidence, I have presented the image of Caiaphas that has emerged to me in as clear a way as possible. I am aware, however, that a nonspecialist, just as much as an academic, needs to know where the evidence comes from, where there are gaps in our knowledge, and where to find further literature. So there are notes, but these have been kept to a minimum and have been relegated to the book's end. Anyone not interested in the sources or more detailed arguments may ignore them. Greek and Hebrew have been transliterated and kept to a minimum.

A final word of orientation concerns dates. Following what has become modern scholarly convention, I have used B.C.E. (Before the Common Era) and C.E.

(Common Era) in place of B.C. (Before Christ) and A.D. (Anno Domini = Year of Our Lord). The dates themselves, however, are the same. For example, 37 C.E. (the year Caiaphas lost his post as high priest) can also be written A.D. 37. There is a time chart in Appendix 1 and a map on p. 27 for anyone not familiar with the history and geography of first-century Israel.

Some of the ideas in this book were tried out at a number of academic meetings: the New Testament/Hebrew and Old Testament Studies Research Seminar at Edinburgh University; the Early Judaism Seminar at Durham University; and the Jesus Seminar at the British New Testament Society. Thanks to the participants of all these learned gatherings for their ideas and criticisms. I would also like to thank the participants in my Historical Jesus course at the School of Divinity at Edinburgh in the academic years 2000/2001 and 2001/2002. Their lively questions and discussion helped my own understandings enormously.

On a more personal level I would like to thank Philip Law, formerly director of Westminster John Knox Press (UK), who had faith in the project when it was nothing more than a sheet of A4 paper, and Don McKim and Dan Braden, who saw it through the press. I am grateful too to my generous former doctoral supervisor, Professor Jimmy Dunn, and my dear friend, Professor Jack Hershbell, both of whom read the entire manuscript and provided me with helpful comments and suggestions. Thanks are due also to Crispin Fletcher Louis (for his helpful response to my paper at the British NT Conference), Henriett McFarlane (for translating Spanish), Professor Vladimir Zakharov and Lisa Bage (for help with Dostoevsky), and to Fighting Dog Murphy. I would also like to thank my Mum for her proofreading of the entire manuscript (often done under less than easy circumstances) and my Dad for the maps and diagrams. Most of all, though, I would like to thank my husband Keith Raffan, who, with his good humor and generosity, consented to share our first two years of married life with a rather demanding oriental priest. To him this book is dedicated.

Abbreviations

JSOT	*Journal for the Study of the Old Testament*
JTS	*Journal of Theological Studies*
LCL	Loeb Classical Library
LXX	The Septuagint
m.	Mishnah
NovT	*Novum Testamentum*
NTS	*New Testament Studies*
OUP	Oxford University Press
PEQ	*Palestine Exploration Quarterly*
RB	*Revue biblique*
RevQ	*Revue de Qumran*
RTL	*Revue théologique de Louvain*
ST	*Studia theologica*
TDNT	*Theological Dictionary of the New Testament,* eds. G. Friedrich (G. Kittel), Grand Rapids: Eerdmans, 1964–76. 10 vols. ET.
TLZ	*Theologische Literaturzeitung*
Tos.	Tosefta
War	Josephus, *Jewish War*
y.	Jerusalem (or Palestinian) Talmud
ZNW	*Zeitschrift für die neutestamentliche Wissenschaft*
ZTK	*Zeitschrift für Theologie und Kirche*

The Tomb

Toward the end of November 1990, park and road development in the Peace Forest to the south of Jerusalem led to an unexpected discovery. As the ground was cleared and leveled, a tractor suddenly plunged into the roof of what appeared to be a cave. The matter was reported to the Israeli Antiquities Authority, who sent a team of archaeologists to investigate.[1]

The cave proved to be a first-century tomb. This in itself was not particularly remarkable. The site lies just over two kilometers to the south of the Dome of the Rock, in an area that long ago formed part of Jerusalem's large necropolis. Archaeologists have uncovered hundreds of tombs here—some elaborate, others quite simple—all hewn into the soft limestone of the hills surrounding the city. Like other tombs, it was not reserved for an individual, but for a whole family. It would have been in continual use over a number of generations and the deceased would have been laid to rest with his or her grandparents and great-grandparents (in Old Testament terms, the dead were, quite literally, "gathered to their fathers"). What *would* prove to be remarkable, however, was the possible identity of one of the tomb's occupants.

The Tomb and Jewish Burial Practices

Entry to the tomb was from the southeast. A visiting family member would have arrived first at some kind of vestibule or courtyard. Straight ahead was the entrance, sealed with a large stone or with mud bricks and small stones. Once this had been cleared, it would be possible to crawl through the low, narrow entranceway into the tomb itself. Inside was a pit, half a meter deep, in which a person could stand upright. As the visitor's eyes became accustomed to the gloom, the irregular shape of the burial chamber would have come into view. On the opposite side of the chamber from the entrance, three smaller burial caves (known as *kokhim* or *loculi*) branched off towards the west. These *kokhim* were long and narrow, each measuring approximately two meters long by half a meter wide—the size of a human body—and sealed with a stone slab. In earlier times they had been used for permanent burial; the deceased would have been laid to rest within the narrow chamber in a wooden coffin or wrapped in a simple shroud. When all the *kokhim* were full, new chambers would be cut into the rock. However, some time in the late first century B.C.E., burial customs around Jerusalem underwent a significant change.

Over the preceding centuries, Israel had gradually but inexorably come under the influence of the dominant pagan cultures of the day. First came Hellenism, the syncretistic blend of Greek and Near Eastern culture that swept through the whole of the East in the wake of the victorious campaigns of Alexander the Great in the fourth century B.C.E. Then, as the Hellenistic empire waned, it was the turn of imperial Rome to assert its authority in the East. The Greco-Roman culture established by these empires was to leave its mark not only on Jewish life, but also in death. The wealthy upper classes were particularly keen to embrace Greco-Roman practices. Some of their tombs have splendid facades showing strong Hellenistic influences behind their use of ionic columns and doric friezes. Another pagan custom was the practice of putting coins on the mouth (or the eyes) of the corpse as payment for Charon, the ferryman who would take the soul on its final journey across the River Styx. Although not common, the number of coins found in Jewish tombs in Jerusalem steadily increases, suggesting that at least some of the more heavily Hellenized occupants of the city found nothing wrong with incorporating such a blatantly pagan practice into their burial customs.[2]

By far the most widespread example of pagan influence was the use of stone ossuaries, or "bone-boxes," for secondary burial. These ossuaries were rectangular chests made of soft local limestone. They had to be long enough for the thigh bone, wide enough for the pelvis, and high enough for the skull. Some ossuaries were plain while others were ornamented—the designs were chip-carved manually with a mallet and chisel in the flourishing local stone workshops. The use of these ossuaries was probably inspired by Roman practice: Romans cremated the bodies of their loved ones before gathering up their ashes into a box or urn. Cremation was forbidden by Jewish law, so Roman customs had to be adapted and modified, providing a new, essentially Jewish custom.[3]

When a person died, close friends and relatives would have carried the body to the family tomb. After being washed, anointed, and wrapped in a shroud, the body would have been laid out in one of the narrow burial chambers. A year later, when the flesh had decomposed, the family would return to the tomb. Standing in the pit in the middle of the burial chamber, lit by the flickering glow of oil lamps, they would systematically gather up the bones and place them in a stone ossuary. The long bones would be put in first, right to the bottom of the box, then the bones of the arms and hands to one side, those of the legs and feet to the other. The remaining bones, including the skull, would be carefully placed on top. The bones might be anointed with wine and oil before the heavy stone lid of the ossuary was lifted into place and the whole thing was slid into one of the *kokhim*. One last service needed to be performed. Using an iron nail, one of the relatives would scratch the name of the deceased into the soft limestone of the ossuary. This served to identify the occupant and, perhaps more importantly, ensured that the name of the deceased would never be forgotten.

The Main Chamber

The tomb in the Peace Forest had suffered at the hands of grave robbers in antiquity, on the lookout for anything of value that might have been buried with the dead. The floors of the main chamber and the three smaller burial chambers

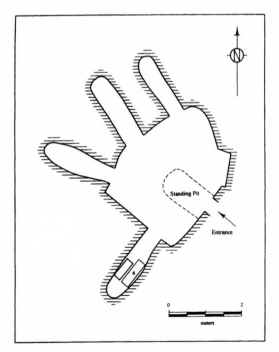

Plan of the tomb (adapted from Z. Greenhut, *Atiqot* 21 [1992] 64).

were littered with broken bones, shattered ossuaries, and smashed pottery. Yet, despite the destruction, it was possible to tell something of the family that had occupied the tomb. The small number of *kokhim* suggested that the family was not large, while the fairly high number of ossuaries suggested that it was in use for a relatively long time. An analysis of the pottery confirmed that the tomb had been in use from the first century B.C.E. to the first century C.E.

Four ossuaries were still intact, though they had been moved from their original position. They were decorated with typical first-century designs: rosettes, zigzags, floral and architectural motifs. Three of them bore inscriptions, etched in Aramaic in the Jewish cursive script typical of the first century C.E. Two of these had names very common in first-century Palestine: Shem (which is perhaps an abbreviation of Shim'on or Simon) and Miriam daughter of Shim'on. A coin from the sixth year of King Agrippa I was found in Miriam's skull, indicating that she was buried some time after 42/43 C.E. The third inscription, however, was extremely uncommon and reads *qp'*. Since Aramaic uses only consonants, we have to supply the vowels; a possible reading of this strange name is Qapha (though Qepha, Qopha, or Qupha would also work). Inside this third ossuary were the remains of one adult woman, a youth, and three children. Multiple burials among relatives were quite common (in fact, all the ossuaries found in the tomb contained the remains of between four and eleven people). But to whom does the enigmatic inscription refer? To the adult woman, or to the youth?

In all probability, Qapha was not a proper name at all but a nickname. First-century Jews tended to restrict themselves to a small number of names, often those reminiscent of great figures from the past, particularly the Maccabean freedom fighters of the second century B.C.E. Simon, John, and Judas were particularly popular for men, while Mary (sometimes spelled Maria, Mariamme, or Miriam) and Salomezion (or Shlomzion, meaning "Peace over Zion") were favorites among women.[4] To avoid confusion, it was common to use nicknames to distinguish between them. Sometimes these derived from a person's origin, sometimes their occupation, characteristics, or even a physical defect. Examples are "the Weaver," "the Wine Merchant," "Goliath," or, less flatteringly, "the Stupid," or "the Fool."[5] Nicknames are also found in the New Testament: Peter the Rock, the Sons of Thunder, or Thomas, meaning a twin. Sometimes these nicknames (even the derogatory ones) stuck and became attached to the names of sons and daughters, eventually becoming family names. "Qapha," then, was probably a family nickname belonging to all the occupants of this ossuary. So far, then, the tomb appeared to contain the remains of a number of people, some of whom could be identified: Shem, Miriam, and the family of Qapha. It was on the south side of the chamber, however, that archaeologists made their most exciting discovery.

The Caiaphas Ossuary

On the southern side of the tomb was another burial cave, one that the robbers had missed. Inside were two ossuaries that had escaped damage and were still in their original position. The smaller one on the right was inscribed with the word "Shalom," probably the Aramaic equivalent of the Greek Salome or a shortened version of the common Jewish name Shlomzion. It was the second, larger ossuary (known as ossuary 6), however, that was particularly interesting. This was the largest ossuary in the whole tomb and was much more richly decorated than the others. The front panel was graced by a leaf pattern enclosing two large circles, separated by a symmetrical floral motif. Each circle contained six small rosettes, an inner one surrounded by five others of various designs, some of which were painted orange. The ossuary was covered by a vaulted lid that was similarly decorated and painted orange.

The Caiaphas Ossuary (ossuary 6). (Photograph reproduced courtesy of the Israel Antiquities Authority.)

Inside, the ossuary contained partial remains of six people: a sixty-year-old male, an adult woman, two infants, and two children. Presumably this was the family of the sixty-year-old male; the woman was perhaps his wife, or unmarried daughter, the children his children or grandchildren. The large number of child deaths here testifies to the high infant mortality rates and short life expectancies even within what must have been a wealthy family.[6]

Outside, the ossuary bore two roughly carved inscriptions, written vertically, from bottom upwards. They seem to have been made after the ossuary had already been placed in its final position—the scribe had to force his hand down the narrow gap between the ossuary and the wall and the resulting scrawl is difficult to decipher. On the narrow side the inscription reads *Yehosef bar* (son of) *Qp'*, on the longer side *Yehosef bar* (son of) *Qyp'*. The man's first name was Joseph, a popular Jewish name that was found among all social levels. But what was his family name? The shorter inscription was the same as the earlier one: Qapha. The longer inscription might well have an extra syllable and could have been pronounced Qayyapha.

The shorter inscription, "Yehosef bar Qp.'" (Photograph reproduced courtesy of the Israel Antiquities Authority.)

Who was the man in this ornate ossuary? The unusual surname or nickname rendered into Greek would be something like "Kaïapha," giving the man's full name as "Joseph bar Kaïapha." This might be "Joseph *son of* Kaïapha," or "Joseph *of the family of* Kaïapha."[7] The Jewish writer Josephus refers to a high priest Joseph "who is called (or 'surnamed') Caiaphas" (*Kaïaphas* in Greek; *Antiq* 18.35, 95). The New Testament gives only his nickname: Caiaphas. He was the man, along with Pontius Pilate, who sent Jesus to his death and who, it is claimed in the Acts of the Apostles, persecuted the early Christian community. Could ossuary 6 be the final resting place of this high priest? Were the remains of the sixty-year-old man those of Joseph Caiaphas?

Objections

All the archaeologists and other epigraphical experts who worked on the tomb stated without hesitation that this was indeed the tomb of Joseph Caiaphas; and a great many scholars have accepted this identification. But archaeology is rarely the exact science we would like it to be, and there have been doubts raised about this identification. Four of these in particular need to be examined.

1. If this really was Caiaphas's tomb, why is there no reference to his high priestly status? Why did his family not record—with some pride—that he had held the supreme pontificate? Other ossuaries do occasionally have references to the status of their occupants. One such ossuary turned up on the Jerusalem antiquities market in the summer of 1983. It is inscribed in a beautiful, formal style with the words

> Yehohanah daughter of Yehohanan,
> Son of Theophilus the High Priest

(an incription which makes her Caiaphas's great-niece).[8] What is interesting here is that her status as granddaughter of a high priest is emphasized. Clearly her relatives (and perhaps Yehohanah herself when she was alive) thought that this enhanced their own prestige.

In general, however, specific references to religious (or even civic) offices are extremely rare. Most inscriptions are tantalizingly brief, mentioning only the person's name, along with perhaps the name of a father, a family name, or a husband; there are no long eulogies in the manner of Greek and Roman epitaphs. The reason for this is quite simple. The roughly etched names were never designed for outsiders, proclaiming the status of the occupant to the world in general. They were for insiders, the family of the deceased, who hardly needed elaborate inscriptions to tell them of their loved ones. The absence of an elaborate inscription referring to his status as high priest, then, is not a bar to identifying the occupant of this tomb as Caiaphas.

2. Is the tomb grand enough for a high priest? The Caiaphas *ossuary* is extravagantly ornate and clearly belonged to someone of great wealth, but the rest of the *tomb* is quite ordinary. Would we not expect a high priest to have an elaborate tomb? Something perhaps like that of Caiaphas's father-in-law, Annas, who had a tomb large enough to serve as a local landmark?[9]

Again, this objection is inconclusive. Annas (as we shall see later in this book) was the founder of a high priestly dynasty; five of his sons and probably his grandson held the position after him. We would expect such a man to have an ostentatious tomb. But Caiaphas was different. No one else from his family became high priest, nor do we know anything about his circumstances and those of his family at the time he died. It is probably not safe then to assume anything from the tomb's lack of grandeur.

3. Another uncertainty revolves around the presence of a coin in another ossuary in the family tomb. Joseph Caiaphas belonged to the Sadducees, an aristo-

cratic group that, among other things, denied that there was any kind of afterlife. (In this they were at variance with the majority of the people, who by the first century, had begun to believe in something beyond the grave.) How then do we account for the fact that one of his family—Miriam—was buried along with a coin that, in pagan mythology, was used to pay the ferryman who would take her to the underworld? Does the very presence of this coin suggest that Miriam and her family believed in an afterlife?

Perhaps not. Even if Caiaphas was a Sadducee, there is no reason to assume that *all* his family had a similar outlook. Furthermore, we need to be very careful about assuming that a coin meant exactly the same thing in a Jewish context as it did in its original pagan setting. We have already seen that when Jews borrowed pagan customs they adapted them to suit their own outlook. Miriam's family may have hoped that the coin would ensure that she arrived in Hades, which for them was not a place of life after death, but simply the eternal resting place of the dead.[10] Miriam's coin, then, does not preclude the possibility that one of her family was a Sadducee.

4. A final, and more significant, doubt regarding the identification of the tomb relates to the inscriptions themselves. The reading that corresponds most closely to Caiaphas is the longer one, Qayyapha (there is, in fact, a possible reference to Caiaphas in rabbinic literature that corresponds fairly closely to this reading).[11] The difficulty is the shorter reading, Qapha. Ossuary 6 bears both readings, and it is likely that these are both the same name and are to be pronounced in the same way. The only way that qp' and qyp' could be pronounced the same way is if the name were Qopha.[12]

This is the strongest argument against the identification of the tomb with Caiaphas, but, again, we need to be cautious. The inscriptions on this particular ossuary are extremely careless, and spelling mistakes and abbreviations are not uncommon in ossuary inscriptions generally.[13] In fact, a shortened version, Caiphas, appears in some texts of the New Testament, and it is possible that both a shorter and longer version of the name were in circulation.[14] None of the objections raised against the tomb, then, is conclusive.

Was this tomb the final resting place of Joseph Caiaphas? Were these the bones of the high priest, back from the dead to command the respect he was once given in life? Were those buried with him his wife and family? It is certainly *possible*. The tomb has now been sealed up and the bones reinterred in the Jewish cemetery on the Mount of Olives, a cemetery reserved for human remains unearthed by the archaeologist's spade. We will never know for sure, but the bones of the sixty-year-old male may well have been our one tangible link with a man who played a crucial part in the history of humankind: Joseph Caiaphas.

Perceptions of Caiaphas

All four Gospels agree that Jesus of Nazareth was interrogated twice: first in the house of the Jewish high priest and subsequently at the headquarters of the Roman prefect. Despite the historical difficulties with these accounts (and we shall see later that there are many of them!), most scholars are confident that two men were involved in the fateful events which led up to Jesus' execution: the Jewish high priest Joseph Caiaphas and the Roman prefect Pontius Pilate.

Of these two men, it is Pontius Pilate who has captured popular imagination. Pilate's struggle with "the Truth" has spoken to every generation—the apocryphal writers of antiquity, early Christian artists, medieval folklorists and dramatists, modern novelists and politicians. Yet perceptions of Pilate have varied enormously. In the first few centuries, Eastern Christianity tended to be sympathetic towards Pilate, focusing on his attempts to acquit Jesus and elevating him (in the Coptic church) to sainthood. At the same time, Western Christianity judged him harshly, blaming him for his weakness and delighting in devising gruesome accounts of his untimely demise.

More recent treatments of Pilate have been somewhere between these two extremes. Anatole France imagined the aged governor, years later, unable to remember Jesus; Mikhail Bulgakov pictured a tortured soul struggling to make the right decision in an impossible trial; while the creators of Monty Python presented Pilate (or a governor very like him) as a lisping, petulant fop.[1] Guidebooks in Scotland, Spain, and Germany gleefully claim the birthplace of Pilate, while his spirit is still believed to haunt certain lakes and rivers of Switzerland, France, Germany, and Italy. Estimates of Pilate often say as much about their authors and their own time as they tell us about the historical Pilate and the Roman province of Judea; yet the abundance of them testifies to the Roman governor's enduring dramatic appeal.[2]

But what about Jesus' other judge, Caiaphas? Two distinct processes seem to have been at work with regard to the high priest: (1) on one hand, Caiaphas's identity has been subsumed into that of "the Jews"; (2) on the other, history has tended to judge him extremely harshly.

Caiaphas and "the Jews"

Unlike Pilate, Caiaphas never really captured popular imagination. Today, few people outside church or academic circles would even recognize his name. Why did the Roman knight with the provincial command excite a great deal of interest while the oriental priest did not? Why has Caiaphas become such a shadowy figure?

We shall see in the second half of this book that the answer to this lies in the rhetoric of the Gospels. The so-called Synoptic Gospels (those of Mark, Matthew, and Luke) give Caiaphas remarkably little prominence in their trial narratives (Mark and Luke do not even mention his name). Writing at a time when Judaism and Christianity were beginning to emerge as separate faiths, the Gospels reflect the pain, anger, and bitterness between the two groups at the end of the first century. It was not enough for the evangelists to pin Jewish rejection of Jesus on one historical high priest. Instead, they preferred to blame the entire Jewish leadership (so Mark and Luke), or even the Jewish people (so Matthew). As far as the Synoptic writers were concerned, the precise identity of the high priest was irrelevant: those who delivered Jesus to Rome were "the Jews." And although John gives Caiaphas a certain amount of prominence, his Gospel ultimately shares the same outlook.

Later Christian speculation, taking its lead from the Gospels, reveled in seeing the destruction of Jerusalem as the punishment of "the Jews." Caiaphas was subsumed under a bevy of hostile chief priests, a kind of ancient mafia, who acted in murderous unison against an innocent Jesus. Discussions about the death of Jesus—even in academic circles—revolved around whether Jesus was put to death by Pilate or "the Jews," as if the latter operated as a united front.[3] This process, of course, had disastrous results for subsequent generations of Jews, but it also meant that interest in Caiaphas as an individual was diminished.

History's Harsh Judgment

Both John and Matthew did at least mention Caiaphas by name, a fact which ensured that the high priest's involvement in Jesus' death lived on, and prompted a certain amount of Christian speculation on his character.

Our earliest reflections on Caiaphas come from the church fathers. Origen, in the early third century, for example, was worried by the Fourth Gospel's assertion that Caiaphas prophesied Jesus' salvific death (11.51). After a rather lengthy discussion, he contented himself with the thought that "even a wicked soul is capable of prophesying sometimes" and that, in any case, Caiaphas's prophecy was not inspired by the Holy Spirit but by an inferior, satanic power.[4] Jerome, in the fourth century, speculated on the meaning of Caiaphas's name. He knew of some who took it to mean "investigator" or even "wise." He, however, preferred to derive it from the word "vomit" or "mouth" (perhaps because he acted as the spokesman of the Jews).[5]

As we might expect, early Christians had some interest in Caiaphas's death, though these traditions were never as fully developed as those recording Pilate's end. The late fourth-century *Apostolic Constitutions* preserved a tradition according to which Caiaphas killed himself (though it refrained from supplying any details).[6] And the eleventh-century *Letter of Tiberius to Pilate* imagined that Caiaphas, Pilate, and other Jewish rulers were arrested on Tiberius's orders and taken to Rome. On the way, Caiaphas died in Crete and, as the earth would not receive his body, was covered with a cairn of stones. (Until the nineteenth century there was a site near Knossos known as the tomb of Caiaphas.)[7]

Very few ancient works had any sympathy for Caiaphas. One fifth-century composition that had a particular interest in the conduct of the Jewish leaders was the popular, if highly fanciful, *Acts of Pilate*. Throughout Jesus' trial, Caiaphas and his father-in-law Annas act as the chief prosecutors in front of Pilate. Yet, after a series of miraculous events prove Jesus' divinity, they too begin to have faith, and the work ends with the entire Jewish people glorifying God. The *Acts of Pilate* was not intended as a positive account of Caiaphas but as a demonstration that even Jesus' enemies had to believe in him in the end.[8] A more extreme development of this view was held by the Syrian Jacobites who believed that Caiaphas had actually converted to Christianity. *The Book of Joseph Caiaphas* (also known as *The Arabic Infancy Gospel*) may well have originated in their circles in the fifth or sixth centuries. (Unfortunately, only the opening chapter of this curious work mentions Caiaphas; the rest is simply a collection of infancy stories.)[9] Such positive representations of Caiaphas, however, never really gained much momentum.

By medieval times, Caiaphas had become a well-established character of the mystery plays, yet the high priest was often little more than a caricature, a villainous and verbose example of worldly pomp and arrogance.[10] These characteristics were developed pictorially by Renaissance artists who painted a plump, smug, self-satisfied aristocrat, sitting in judgment against Jesus (often with his father-in-law Annas). If Pilate's most characteristic gesture was washing his hands, Caiaphas's was tearing his robes. Yet when this act was portrayed by Renaissance artists, it became a sign not of horror or grief, but of the high priest's rage and uncontrollable anger. The Florentine painter Giotto, for example, in his series on the seven vices represents Rage as a woman tearing the dress from her breast in exactly the same gesture used by Caiaphas in the artist's painting of

Christ before Caiaphas. Giotto's friend Dante, the great fourteenth-century poet, imagined Caiaphas in the eighth circle of Hell, crucified and transfixed to the ground with three stakes, destined to be trampled upon for all eternity by weeping hypocrites weighed down by long, golden robes.[11] And Dostoevsky, in the late nineteenth century, developed Caiaphas's nighttime trial of Jesus in the Gospels into the legend of the Grand Inquisitor, a critique of Catholicism and, in his stark contrast to Christ, a symbol of the antichrist.[12]

Caiaphas has not fared much better in recent treatments. Steven Berkoff's *Messiah: Scenes from a Crucifixion* (1978) presented Caiaphas as a corrupt representative of "organized religion": a self-righteous, smug priest reveling in the outward show of religiosity, luxuriating in his robes and gaudy jewelry, and with more than an eye for altar boys. Gordon Thomas, in his historical novel *The Trial* (1987), imagined Caiaphas as a man who "placated Romans and Jewish civil administration through fawning and manipulation"; physically, "there was a serpent-like quality about his puny body and narrow head."[13] (The serpent seems to be a natural image for Caiaphas, perhaps because of Jesus' invectives against the Jewish leaders as "serpents and vipers" in Matthew 12:34 and 23:33.) Modern films tend to present Caiaphas as a flat character, intent only on destroying Jesus; often he is swathed in black robes and the dark scheming of the council contrasts strongly with the joyful acceptance of Jesus by the Passover crowds.[14] In all these interpretations, Caiaphas is, at best, a representative of the lowest side of religion; at worst, a representative of evil, a symbol of the depths to which humanity can sink when pitted against its God.

The fullest discussions of Caiaphas, of course, are found in the works of biblical scholars. Yet here again Caiaphas has been judged extremely harshly. He and his high priestly colleagues are routinely labeled as "collaborators" and accused of bribery, corruption, nepotism, violence, greed, and oppression. They are generally assumed to have been self-serving, lacking in any true religious sentiment, and—naturally enough—hated and distrusted by ordinary people. Caiaphas, it is often argued, wanted Jesus out of the way because he exposed his own corruption and threatened his privileged status.[15] The language may be less harsh, but modern scholarly assessments of Caiaphas have, on the whole, been just as negative as previous centuries of Christian reflection.

Why has Christian history been so uniform in its condemnation of Caiaphas? Why has he—in contrast to both Pilate and Judas—never been treated with any kind of sympathy? And why has he never—again, in contrast to the others—been held up as an important agent in human redemption? On one level, Caiaphas's story is not attractive: a religious leader who handed over one of his own compatriots to a foreign power could hardly expect to earn sympathy from subsequent generations. Furthermore, his story does not have the dramatic possibilities of other characters in the Passion Narrative. We can ask whether Pilate perhaps had some inkling of the man in front of him: did he realize that the silent prisoner was, in fact, the Son of God? We can speculate on Judas's reasons for betraying his friend and teacher: was he perhaps a disillusioned revolutionary? Did he hope to force Jesus into an open acknowledgment of his messiahship? Or was he, perhaps reluctantly, obeying Jesus' orders?[16] But the Gospel writers portrayed the high priest in such villainous colors that there was no room for such speculation; for the leader of "the Jews" there could be no extenuating circumstances, and no redemption.

Less explicitly, perhaps, some of the negativity surrounding Caiaphas may be due to a modern distaste for cultic worship, an activity that was essentially the high priest's raison d'etre. The Jerusalem temple was a center of animal sacrifice, ritual, and outward show, and could be maintained only by the vast revenues that flowed into it through taxation. All of this was a perfectly ordinary part of religion in the ancient world, but we moderns may find it difficult to imagine sacrifice as a meaningful religious expression, and (particularly in Protestant circles) often imagine attention to ritual as the very opposite of heartfelt devotion. The high priest symbolizes an alien world, outside many people's religious experiences. We can admire Pilate's Rome, sympathize with Judas's humanity, but Caiaphas's cultic world is outside our comprehension.

In a similar vein, Caiaphas has also suffered for his connection with the Sadducees, the aristocratic group who concerned themselves with the operation of the Jerusalem temple and who had, by common consent, little to do with "true religion."[17] One of the difficulties here is that the Sadducees left no written records, and we are forced to rely instead on the negative parodies penned by their opponents. The Sadducees' own words would, no doubt, have told a quite different story. Another Jewish group, the Pharisees, were similarly caricatured in earlier scholarship (in their case as hypocrites, legalists, petty bourgeoisie); it is only in recent decades that historians, drawing on the work of generations of Jewish scholars who understood Pharisees as the correct and trustworthy side of Judaism, have now begun to understand the Pharisees in a more positive light.[18] Unlike the Pharisees, however, the Sadducees have no modern successors with an interest in rehabilitating them. It is perhaps for this reason that both Jewish and Christian scholars can lay the blame for the death of Jesus on an unrepresentative, corrupt, self-seeking, priestly aristocracy.[19]

Finally, the high priest has also suffered through anticlericalism. This was a common feature of the mystery plays and, as we have seen, found explicit expression in such diverse works as Dostoevsky and Berkoff. Divesting himself of his high priestly robes and donning instead a bishop's stole and miter, Caiaphas could readily be called upon to embody all that people of any age found wanting in "the church." In the modern Western world, where many people are disaffected with "organized religion," trendy presentations of Jesus as a liberal free spirit taking the side of the little people derive some attraction and power from contrasting him with the pampered fat cats of "the establishment": Caiaphas and his clerical cronies.[20]

Outline of the Present Study

The task of this book is, quite simply, to reevaluate the prevalent view of the historical Caiaphas and to see how he fared as a literary character in a number of writings from the early church.

Part 1 reconstructs what we know of the historical man. All people are shaped by their background and education, and so it is here that we shall start our investigation. We often forget that Caiaphas had a history before he met Jesus, and that this would have played as decisive a part in his life as Jesus' Galilean upbringing did in his. We shall look at major political events during Caiaphas's lifetime, his experience of messiahs and insurrectionists, his life as a priest, and his role in the temple. We shall also look at the relationship between Caiaphas and Pilate, and the crucial role that the high priest played in keeping Roman troops away from his people. Finally, I shall try to determine what it was about Jesus and his preaching that so troubled Caiaphas and his high priestly colleagues, evaluate how he reacted to other leading figures in the new movement, and attempt to piece together the reasons for his dismissal.

Part 2 turns to Caiaphas's afterlife—his presentation in early Christian reflection. We shall look at each of the canonical Gospels and Acts and see how the evangelists' particular historical contexts have influenced their portrayals of Caiaphas. We shall look at how the high priest is used as a *literary character* in these works; the way in which the evangelists have modified their traditions; and what these presentations of Caiaphas tell us about the relationship between a number of Christian communities and their Jewish neighbors in the late first century. By the end of this study, we shall be in a position to compare the negative caricature of Christian reflection with an evaluation of the historical man who condemned Jesus to death.

PART 1
THE HISTORICAL
CAIAPHAS

1

Sources

It is impossible to write a biography of Caiaphas in the modern sense of the word. Records relating to him are scanty in the extreme. We have no physical description, no letters, no reports, not even concrete records of his birth or death. We know nothing of his home life or of his relationship with his parents, wife, or children. We do, of course, have several descriptions of one event in his life—the trial of Jesus—but even here the evidence is shakier than we might think. The historical accuracy of the trial narratives in the Gospels is highly questionable, and few New Testament scholars would maintain that the Gospel reports are transcripts of the actual proceedings. There is, then, very little that gives us an insight into "the real man," his inner feelings, psychological motivations, or private emotions.

In this, however, Caiaphas is not unique. The same could be said of any number of characters associated with the story of Jesus of Nazareth: from John the Baptist and James the brother of the Lord to Mary Magdalene and Simon Peter. All we have to go on is a range of traditions and interpretations, some more historically likely than others. This does not mean that a biography is impossible, rather, that we need to modify our expectations a little. We may begin to understand what role and function Caiaphas played within his society, and perhaps something of the values and aspirations he held, but we will never know what food he liked or even his wife's name.

In the following chapters, I shall attempt to sketch Caiaphas's life. This sketch will be based on the most reliable written sources. I shall also draw on comparative material from the lives of other Jewish high priests and aristocrats, sociological studies of first-century Palestine, archaeological excavations, and a certain amount of imagination. We cannot hope for too much precision, but it *will* be possible to provide a reasonably rounded picture of Caiaphas's life. First, though, we need to turn our attention to the sources. Which are "the most reliable" historical sources? And how can we use them most effectively?

Flavius Josephus

Our most valuable source for Caiaphas is the Jewish writer Flavius Josephus. Born the year Caiaphas was deposed from office (37 C.E.), Josephus was a Jewish aristocrat of priestly descent. In 66 C.E., the ill-fated Jewish revolt broke out against Rome, and the young Josephus played a leading part in Galilee. But his abilities as a military commander were limited, and when his city had virtually fallen to the Romans, the wily nobleman managed to save his life by prophesying to the general Vespasian that he would become emperor. When this prediction came true, Josephus was taken to Rome and given Vespasian's old quarters in the city. He was allowed an imperial pension and devoted his remaining years to literary endeavors. Ambitious, egotistical, and vain, Josephus's many personal failings have been highlighted by generations of scholars. Yet what also shines through his work is his intense devotion to Judaism, his deep sense of the tragedy that befell his people as a consequence of the revolt, and his ardent desire to restore the political and religious standing of his people within the Roman world.[1]

His first work, *The Jewish War*, was written in the 70s and attempted to explain the causes of the revolt that had ended so tragically in the defeat of his compatriots. By about 93 C.E. he had a new work ready for the literary circles of Rome: *The Antiquities of the Jews*. This immense work (written in twenty books) chronicled the great and glorious history of the Jews from creation to the reign of Nero. To this work he appended a copy of his *Life*. In this—the oldest autobiography in existence—he attempted to explain his rather embarrassing desertion to Rome. The *Antiquities*, however, does not seem to have gone down well in the often anti-Jewish literary circles of late first-century Rome, populated as it was by such anti-Semites as Tacitus and Juvenal. Soon afterwards Josephus took up his pen once again and composed a defensive treatise known as *Against Apion*. Here he emphasized once more the antiquity of the Jewish people and countered a number of highly offensive anti-Jewish slanders circulating at the time.

Josephus's works provide a unique historical record. If it were not for him, we would know very little of first-century Jewish history and society. He was a careful historian, working from written sources (both Jewish and Roman), oral traditions, and his own recollections. Where his descriptions of places and buildings have been checked against archaeological excavations, they have often proved remarkably reliable. In fact, many medieval crusaders had such a high regard for Josephus's geographical and historical information that they marched to the Holy Land armed with Latin translations of his works! Yet modern scholars have pressed on us a greater sense of caution. When it comes to *facts,* Josephus is reasonably reliable, but less so in his *interpretation* of those facts and the motives he ascribes to individual characters. We need also to be aware of the larger rhetorical aims of his works, and to attempt to see beyond his rhetoric and bias. We must, then, treat everything Josephus says with a certain amount of healthy suspicion, but this should not detract from the fact that the Jewish aristocrat will be a witness of paramount importance in our quest for the historical Caiaphas.

With Josephus's help we can reconstruct the political dynamics at work within first-century Judea, and the relationship between Caiaphas and the Roman governor, Pontius Pilate. His works also help us to pick up something of the economic, social, and regional factors influencing Judean society. He provides us with dates for Caiaphas's tenure of the high priesthood, accounts of other high priests, and a coherent picture of their responsibilities.[2] As a priest, Josephus presents evidence relating to the temple and the sacrificial cult that is second to none. As an aristocrat, Josephus has views and opinions that may not have been very far removed from those of Caiaphas.

Other Jewish Writings

Along with Josephus there are a number of other Jewish writers whose work may illuminate parts of Caiaphas's story. An example is Philo of Alexandria, one of the most prolific writers of ancient times. A contemporary of Caiaphas (his dates are roughly 15 B.C.E.–50 C.E.), like Josephus he was born into a wealthy and distinguished family. Most of his works are philosophical and allegorical expositions of the Jewish law, but he does occasionally provide us with important historical information, particularly regarding the office of high priest. Two centuries earlier than Philo, Ben Sira wrote a book of wisdom, designed for the education of well-to-do young men. It was written in Hebrew, then translated into Greek by the author's grandson in the early second century B.C.E., and can be found nowadays in the Apocrypha (where it is sometimes called Ecclesiasticus). Ben Sira had a keen interest in the priesthood (he may well have been a priest himself) and provides a glowing description of a high priest wearing his vestments (chapter 50).

Further snippets of information can be gleaned from both the Dead Sea Scrolls, the writings of a group of Essenes who took themselves away from the Jerusalem temple and made their home in the desert at a place called Qumran, and the works collectively known as the Old Testament Pseudepigrapha. This includes texts such as the *Testament* (or *Assumption*) *of Moses,* the eighteen *Psalms of Solomon,* and the *Letter of Aristeas.* The last gives, among other things, an eyewitness account of the ritual in the Jerusalem temple.[3]

Later Jewish Writings

Another group of sources that can provide some help is rabbinic writings, the records of the schools of Jewish rabbis that flourished from the late first century onward. This group includes the Mishnah (which was written down around 200 C.E.), the Tosefta (ca. 300 C.E.), the Jerusalem Talmud (ca. 400 C.E.) and the Babylonian Talmud (ca. 600 C.E.), and comprises a diverse collection of teaching (halakah) and stories (haggadah). Individual collections are rather late, but it is possible that they preserve material from a much earlier period, though dating individual elements is extremely difficult. As we shall see, there may be some references to Caiaphas and members of his family in these texts. There are also detailed discussions of all aspects of Jewish law, from Sabbath observance to temple purity, and a clear outline of the way in which a capital trial should be conducted. Yet the problems surrounding these texts—in terms of their late date, the reliability of their transmission, and the degree of idealization in the minds of later authors looking back on first-century practices—mean that we have to be very wary of relying too heavily on rabbinic texts. Where rabbinic evidence ties in with what we know from other first-century sources, it is probably safe to use it. Otherwise, much more caution is necessary.[4]

Archaeological Sources

One unexpected outcome of the reunification of Jerusalem after the Six-Day War in 1967 was the dramatic increase in archaeological activity in the city. New building work gave archaeologists a chance—often for the first time—to dig in the old city's densely crowded streets. A series of excavations has provided a fascinating insight into the Jerusalem of Caiaphas's day. Several homes belonging to wealthy aristocrats have been uncovered, showing us the type of house Caiaphas would have owned. Remains of ritual baths, imported wine jars, and Hellenistic decorations give some impression of Caiaphas's probable lifestyle. The precise location of Caiaphas's house is uncertain (and in Appendix D we shall look at traditions associated with its whereabouts), but these palatial mansions give us some idea of Caiaphas's home life. Outside Jerusalem, excavations in Galilee and Judea have supplemented what we know of these regions from literary sources.[5]

Christian Writings

The most obvious place to look for historical information about Caiaphas within Christian writings is the canonical Gospels, particularly the later chapters, where we appear to have four relatively detailed accounts of Jesus' trial before the Jewish leaders. But, as hinted earlier, it would be a mistake to assume that the Gospels are straightforward historical documents. Three factors need to be taken into account.

First, all the Gospels were written much later than the events which they describe. Most modern scholars would set them at roughly 70–100 C.E., that is, *forty to seventy years* after the death of Jesus. Of course, the evangelists were work-ing with historical traditions, and these traditions had been carefully passed down orally from one generation of believers to the next. But the evangelists were theo-logians and pastors more than they were "historians" in the sense in which we would use the word. We do not know who any of the evangelists were—the tra-ditions linking them to individual disciples were later additions in the second-century fight against heretics—but clearly they were men of genius and vision. Each one had obviously reflected deeply for many years on the story he had to tell. When he came to write his Gospel, each one used his traditional material creatively. He selected, arranged, and adapted material so that it expressed his own particular theology and added irony, drama, and Old Testament allusions to underline the significance of his story. Individual Gospels might also have gone through several "editions" as they were repeatedly read out and reflected upon by the evangelists' congregations. The Gospels are, in effect, theological, post-Easter reflections on the life and death of Jesus of Nazareth. Each one reflects its author's conviction that Jesus was indeed the long-awaited Messiah, the royal Son of David, and the unique Son of God.

The second difficulty which needs to be taken into account is that the Gospels do not present four independent witnesses. Three of them are linked by a com-mon literary tradition and are known for this reason as the "Synoptic Gospels" (because their similarities can be seen most easily side by side in a synopsis). Both Matthew and Luke used Mark as the basis for their account. Although they have made considerable alterations to their source, they present basically the same tra-dition. John, however, is generally thought not to be dependent upon Mark and to present an independent witness. This means that we do not have four accounts of the trial of Jesus but two—that of the Synoptics and that of John.

A third and final consideration has a particular bearing on Caiaphas. This regards the Gospels' presentation of Jewish participants. Although early Chris-tianity developed from Judaism, the Gospels were written at a time of growing Jewish-Christian hostility. By the late first century, Jewish synagogues had begun to take firm measures against the new messianic sect and were expelling follow-ers of Jesus from their membership. We should not underestimate how traumatic this process was, and the deep sense of hurt, betrayal, and hostility felt by Chris-tian groups who now began to define themselves over against Judaism. This his-torical process has left its mark in the Gospels, both on a general level and in the shape of some ugly characterizations of Jesus' Jewish opponents (something we shall return to in more detail in the opening chapter of part 2 of this book).

Each of these three factors needs to be taken into consideration when we ask historical questions of the Gospels. The Gospels do contain a large amount of traditional historical material, but they are post-Easter theological reflections on this material, reflecting the turbulent Jewish-Christian relations at the end of the first century. This means that we need to be *very* cautious about accepting their presentations as straightforward historical data. The same is true for the Acts of the Apostles, which was written by the same author as the Gospel of Luke. Acts contains a great deal of information relating to the relationship between the Jewish priestly leaders and the early church in the years immediately following the crucifixion. Luke may have been dependent on a number of sources here, but even if this were the case, it is reasonable to assume that he tailored them to his own purposes, just as he did in his earlier work with Mark's Gospel. I shall draw on a reasonable amount of information contained within the early chapters of Acts, though always with the above considerations firmly in mind.[6]

The following discussion of Caiaphas, then, is largely dependent upon Josephus, snippets from other ancient Jewish authors, material from the early chapters of Acts, and archaeological data. For the trial of Jesus, I have used only the very general outline of events in the Gospel records (fuller investigations into each Gospel will be left until part 2).

The world of first-century Judea was far removed from that of the modern West. It was a world of foreign occupation, of fragile peace agreements, and deep-seated resentments. It was a world in which religion permeated every aspect of existence, in which politics and religion were inextricably intertwined, and in which many would rather die than see God's laws trampled under foot. It was a world, too, that placed great emphasis on the family, ancestral traditions, and men's honor. In the next few chapters, with the help of the sources outlined above, I shall attempt to recreate this world and to locate Caiaphas within it.

2

Caiaphas the Young Priest

Origins

There are no longer any records of Joseph Caiaphas's birth or early years. All that we know for sure is that he was born sometime during the long reign of Herod the Great (37–4 B.C.E.). After several years of civil war, the nation was once again enjoying a period of prolonged (if repressive) peace, security, and economic prosperity.

We might have hoped to glean some clues to the family's origins from their nickname: Caiaphas. Although a number of derivations have been suggested—from "basket" or "carrying," to "pole," "mute" and even "ape"!— none of these is entirely persuasive. It is *possible* that his family had been basket makers at one time, or worked with pack asses, but any reconstruction is clearly speculative.[1] Whatever the origins of Caiaphas's family, it is probably safe to assume that by the first century B.C.E. they were aristocratic and wealthy, deriving their wealth most probably from large estates in and around Jerusalem.[2] One of these estates may well have encompassed the village of Beth Meqoshesh, a settlement traditionally associated with Caiaphas and his family.[3] Like other aristocrats, they would have left the oversight of these estates to bailiffs, allowing the family to take up residence in the vibrant and cosmopolitan capital city of Jerusalem.

We can assume, too, that Caiaphas's family would have been intensely proud of their priestly ancestry. The hereditary priesthood was one of the defining characteristics of Judean society, and priests enjoyed considerable status and honor. All priests were believed to be descendants of Aaron, Moses' brother; they were divided into twenty-four divisions (or "courses"). Some of these divisions were more prestigious than others. Josephus, for example, took great pride in belonging to the course of Jehoiarib.[4] In all probability, the Caiaphas family belonged to the most illustrious branch of all: their ancestors were not just priests, but part of the high priestly line of Zadok. The mysterious Zadok had been high priest under both David and Solomon, and his descendants had held the high priesthood until the early second century B.C.E. The house was highly esteemed, and many in Israel believed that the high priest could be drawn from no other line.[5]

Since the family's authority and prestige derived from their descent, they would have kept detailed records, proving the purity of their lineage. These were meticulously copied and passed down from one generation to the next. So important were these priestly genealogies that duplicates were kept in the public archives in Jerusalem.[6] They would be brought out and consulted whenever a member of the family was due to enter the priesthood, wanted to marry, or wished to enter public office.

Education

As a boy, Caiaphas's earliest lessons would have been from his parents. As time went by, tutors would have come to his home to give the young aristocrat a thorough grounding in the Jewish Scriptures and their interpretations. He learned to read and write in Hebrew and committed large portions of the sacred text to memory.[7]

In outlook, Caiaphas and his family were Sadducees, members of a small yet prestigious, aristocratic priestly group. Taking their name from Zadok, they seem to have been particularly concerned with the *temple, its purity, and the maintenance of its cult.*[8] It is one of the great tragedies of this period that we have no surviving Sadducean literature; all we have to draw on are the often hostile caricatures of outsiders or opponents.

Most of our information comes from Josephus, who provides us with two brief descriptions (though very little material is common to both!). In the first (*War* 2.164–66) he claims that Sadducees rejected fate in favor of free will. They believed that a person had free choice whether to do good or evil, a belief that meant that God was not responsible for the presence of evil in the world. In his second account (*Antiq* 18.16–17) Josephus asserts that the Sadducees accepted only the written law (a claim also found in 13.297). Both accounts report that they rejected any kind of afterlife (a claim backed up by Mark 12:18 and Acts 4:2, 23:6–10). Later, in *Antiq* 20.199 he claims that the Sadducees "are indeed more heartless than any other Jews when they sit in judgment" (a claim also found in 13.294). Overall, Josephus presents the Sadducees as unpopular, "rather boorish," and "rude."

No doubt there are some grains of truth in Josephus's description, but we need to exercise caution. The Sadducees' own literature would certainly have cast their views in a more generous light and provided the all-important contexts in which they were to be understood. Most problematic is the claim that the Sadducees followed only the written law. It would have been impossible for anyone in first-century Judea to follow the biblical law without *any* interpretation and updating whatsoever. They may well have rejected Pharisaic interpretations, but that did not mean that they had none of their own. In fact, this is confirmed by rabbinic references to Sadducees that record several disagreements between Sadducees and Pharisees, mostly over questions of purity.[9] Given their association with the temple and its cult, it is highly likely that they had their own body of traditions associated with accurate observance of the daily liturgy and the great feasts, traditions that had been passed down from one generation to the next.[10]

Modern scholars have often assumed that the Sadducees embraced Greco-Roman culture at the expense of religion, and that they were more interested in safeguarding their own privileged position than the institutions of Judaism. Yet there is simply no evidence for this. As G. Stemberger notes: "The widespread characterization of the Sadducees as a party that was assimilated, hellenized, and oriented primarily toward realistic politics (*Realpolitik*) is . . . not substantiated."[11] As aristocrats, they no doubt came in frequent contact with Greco-Roman customs and may well have adopted some as their own, but there is no indication that their devotion to the temple was anything but central. Given Caiaphas's prominent priestly connections, it is likely that Sadducean interpretations, ideas, and views would have impressed themselves on the young priest from an early age.

The education of a young man from a good family, however, was not complete until he had also mastered Greek. The native language of most Jews at the time was Aramaic (though Hebrew was widely used as the "religious" language). But it was Greek—the language of Alexander and his successors—that became the lingua franca of the upper classes and wealthy traders of the eastern Roman Empire. In this respect, Jerusalem was no different from any other city of its day. Greek was the language of the magnificent Herodian court; Greek was the language of Gentile tourists and traders; and Greek was the language of Jews settled outside Palestine (in what was known as the Diaspora), many of whom would flock to the city during festivals.[12] There would, therefore, have been every incentive for an ambitious family to teach its son Greek and a wealth of potential Greek tutors around Jerusalem. Caiaphas would have developed his conversational skills and may well have acquired some basic proficiency in rhetoric. Perhaps, like Josephus, he spoke with a regional accent, but we can probably assume that his Greek was fairly fluent.[13]

Caiaphas's family would have brought him up to have a sense of his own position as an aristocrat and a member of a distinguished priestly clan. In a society where everything was conducted on a face-to-face basis, he would have been taught to recognize the importance of reputation, honor, and the family name. As he grew to maturity, he would have expected to be treated with a certain amount of respect, even by his social equals.

Political Events

Education then, as now, was not confined to books, and the young man's studies would have been furthered by observing political events around him. By the first century B.C.E. a new world power was sweeping through the lands of the East: Rome, its generals intent on territorial expansion and conquest. Inexorably, Rome tightened its grip on the Jewish homeland: by 63 B.C.E. Jews were forced to pay tribute; by 40 B.C.E. the new overlords had installed their own man—Herod the Great—as vassal king; and by 6 C.E. the southern part of the land would become the Roman province of Judea.[14] Caiaphas and his friends must have spent many hours discussing the impact of Rome on their land. What could anyone do against so powerful an empire? How could they keep the peace? And—most importantly—protect their temple?

Caiaphas had firsthand experience of the reign of Herod. He would have observed the king's attempts to "Romanize" his realm; his extravagant building projects; his dedication of temples to the goddess Roma (the patron goddess of Rome) and the divine Augustus; and his introduction of games and Roman forms of entertainment—theaters, racetracks, and amphitheaters. Caiaphas would not have needed Josephus to remind him that "one can mention no suitable spot within his realm, which [Herod] left destitute of some mark of homage to Caesar."[15] The young priest would have been only too aware of the king's shortcomings: he was unpopular at home, paranoid, oppressive, and had a disastrous family life. And yet, for all that, Herod's pro-Roman policies succeeded in protecting the temple cult and safeguarding Jewish rights both at home and outside Palestine. Throughout his long reign he kept the land free from Roman troops and the temple free from the threat of foreign pollution. To that extent at least, his reign could be said to have been a success.

As soon as the old king died in 4 B.C.E., however, the country was plunged into insurrection. After decades of Herod's iron rule, the people's suppressed frustrations broke out in demonstrations against both Herod and the Roman regime of which he was a part. Rome's response was swift and brutal. The Syrian legate Varus swept through Galilee with a large body of troops, routing out all those who were in revolt. The city of Sepphoris was captured and burned to the ground, and the inhabitants sent away as slaves.[16] Varus continued on to the city of Samaria, sacking and burning villages as he went until "the whole district became a scene of fire and blood."[17] The country must have been full of tales of Jewish heroism, Roman atrocities, and the terror inspired among rebels and pacifists alike. Whether Caiaphas had any sympathies with the insurrectionists is impossible to say, but the Roman reprisals must have been a sharp reminder of the way in which the Roman Empire dealt with opposition.

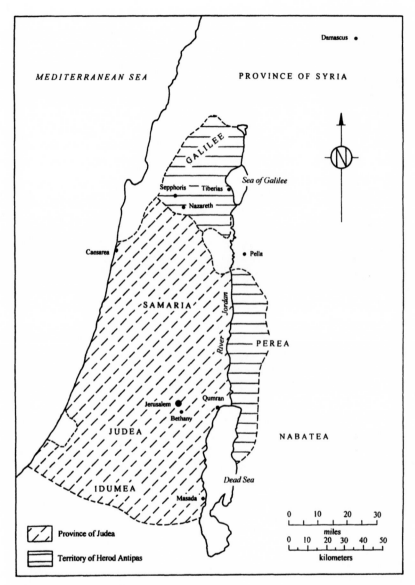

The Roman province of Judea, 6–41 C.E.

Still the land was in turmoil. All over the country kingly pretenders enlisted bands of supporters and tried to seize power. A slave called Simon made a claim to kingship across the Jordan in Perea; others did the same along the Jordan River itself; and a shepherd named Athronges and his four brothers staked their claim in Judea. Although each enjoyed some initial success, it was short-lived, and all were quickly executed by Rome. Again, we have no idea how Caiaphas viewed these kingly pretenders, but Rome's reaction showed that however great his popular support, no "king" could ever have any success without Roman backing.

One of the greatest horrors from Caiaphas's point of view must have been the bloody battle in the temple towards the end of the revolt. In the course of the conflict many Jews lost their lives, parts of the temple were burned, and the treasury was plundered. Further destruction was averted only by the surrender of the city. Perhaps Caiaphas witnessed these terrible events. If not, he would surely have heard numerous accounts of the atrocities, and seen for himself the charred remains of the temple porticoes. He knew that this time they had been lucky: Rome had stopped short of desecrating the temple's holiest area—or destroying it totally. But who could know what might happen if Rome chose to send its troops against the temple again?

As a final measure against the insurrectionists, Varus sent part of his army to scour the country and root out rebels. These men were no match against trained Roman legions and quickly capitulated. Some were imprisoned, two thousand were crucified. As another opponent of Rome was to remark some decades later, "they create a desolation and call it peace."[18] For the time being, the country was quiet.

The revolt and its suppression must have had a profound influence on everyone in Judea, fostering a variety of responses. Some continued their opposition, resisting a Roman census in 6 C.E. and making the most of any opportunity to rid their land of the hated Gentiles. Underpinning these anti-Roman feelings was a powerful national mythology that yearned for the glorious days of David and Solomon when Israel had been a great nation and, more recently, when the Maccabean brothers had shaken off their foreign overlords and established the Hasmonean dynasty in the second century B.C.E. Others would have more stoically reminded themselves that God was the sole author of history, that he was the one who had raised up Rome in the first place, and that their own Scriptures contained a long tradition of acceptance of and, to some extent, accommodation toward foreign rulers. That did not, of course, stop them from dreaming of a Davidic messiah who would shake off the hated foreigners and restore the fortunes of Israel, but until that took place, they were resigned to their present situation. For still others, the despair of the present was too great to bear: the recent upheavals convinced them that they were living at the end of the ages, and it was only a matter of time before God himself would intervene and end his people's sufferings.[19]

As far as aristocratic Sadducees like Caiaphas and his family were concerned, it must have been only too apparent that the single way to keep Rome out of the temple was to maintain peace, even if it meant acquiescing to Roman rule and paying tribute. They were realistic enough to know that in the political climate of the time nothing could be achieved without the help and favor of Rome. As far as they were concerned, Rome could occupy their land as long as they could run the temple unhindered.

Caiaphas and the Priesthood

From an early age, Caiaphas would have held the Jerusalem temple in the greatest respect and devotion. It was the holiest place in Israel, the center of the Jewish cult, and the place where God's presence was strongest. It also had immense political significance: it was a visual reminder of the might of Israel's God, the focus of Israel's national hopes, and the symbol of God's election of the nation. The temple known by Caiaphas was actually the second temple: it had been founded in Persian times, refurbished by the Hasmoneans, and dramatically expanded and remodeled by Herod the Great. Caiaphas had perhaps watched with boyish fascination as it was transformed before his eyes into one of the wonders of the ancient world.

Caiaphas and his family would have visited the temple many times. He would have known the route well. From the intoxicating smells and raucous shouts of the Lower City bazaars, worshipers entered the temple through its high southern doors, climbed a monumental stairway and emerged into the outermost of the temple courts: the court of the Gentiles. The whole temple reflected Jewish ideas of holiness. Just as the land of Israel was holier than the surrounding lands, and Jerusalem was holier than elsewhere in Israel, a pilgrim at the temple found himself or herself passing through ever-increasing layers of holiness. Different people had different levels of holiness, and each of the temple courts represented the furthermost point that members of particular groups could penetrate: Gentiles, women, Israelites, priests, and, finally, the high priest.[20]

As its name suggests, the outermost court of the Gentiles was open to everyone, including non-Jews. Stern warning signs, however, advised that the penalty for any Gentile trying to go beyond this court was death. The court itself, with its porticoes and white marble columns, was not only elegant, but immense—it was easily the largest sacred precinct in the ancient world. As was the case with all ancient temples, this outer court also functioned as an agora or forum. Everywhere people were deep in conversation, concluding business deals, or just passing the time of day. Stalls sold birds suitable for sacrifice, artisans advertised their glass souvenirs to pilgrims and tourists alike, and beggars entreated alms from passersby. Here and there were teachers, sitting on a raised area with students at their feet; Gamaliel taught here, as did Jesus when he visited Jerusalem.[21] In the background was the constant noise of the builders who continued to work on the outer courts of the temple until the early 60s C.E.

Leaving the hustle and bustle of this outer court, a Jewish pilgrim could make his or her way into the inner courts. Passing through the court of the women, one arrived in the court of the Israelites. In stark contrast to the commotion of the outer areas, this court was marked by its tranquility and holiness. Around the outside were several rooms, mostly relating to the more mundane aspects of priestly service—dormitories, meeting places, and storerooms. One of particular importance, however, was the temple treasury. Like many ancient temples, the

View of Herod's temple from the east showing the entrance to the sanctuary and the inner courts. (Holyland Hotel model; photograph courtesy of D. J. Reimer.)

Jerusalem temple was fabulously wealthy. Huge sums of money were necessary to meet the constant demands for sacrificial victims. The money was raised by an annual half-shekel tax, payable by every adult male Jew, wherever he lived; convoys brought the money from as far afield as Babylonia.[22] Besides taxes, people also gave voluntary donations: the Emperor Augustus, for example, donated gifts to the temple and ordered that regular daily sacrifices be made to the "Most High God" at his own expense.[23] All went to swell the vast temple coffers, which were guarded by Levites, a lower rank of clergy, who acted as both temple musicians and police.[24]

Standing in the court of the Israelites, Caiaphas could have easily seen across a low stone parapet into the court of the priests. Most striking would have been the altar on which burned a perpetual fire. All around the altar, priests would have been going about their duties. The precise sequence of daily and seasonal sacrifices was carefully laid out in the law: burnt offerings were made every morning and evening, and further sacrifices were offered on the Sabbath, at new moon, and at festivals. A recent innovation was the twice-daily sacrifice on behalf of the emperor and people of Rome.[25] Besides these communal sacrifices was a range of individual offerings that together formed the bulk of sacrifices—sin offerings, guilt offerings, thank offerings, freewill offerings, votive offerings, and burnt offerings. The priests' precise duties were determined each day by lot, and each priest would have his own special responsibility: some would be accepting and inspecting sacrifices; others would be slaughtering animals, flaying them, or pouring blood around the altar; still others would be praying, burning incense, or washing away the blood. The air would have been thick with the smell of blood—the symbol of life and the only part of the animal powerful enough to purge sin. Everything was done quietly, with great reverence, and "in a manner befitting supreme divinity."[26]

The yearly round of sacrifices, feasts, and offerings was popularly believed to have been revealed to Moses directly from God.[27] (Some people even thought of the Jerusalem temple as a replica of a heavenly service carried out by God's angels.)[28] The offerings were in direct continuity with the sacrifices offered by Noah after the flood and symbolized God's covenant with God's people. The service expressed the people's thanks to God, obtained God's mercy and forgiveness, and ensured the stability of the seasons, the fertility of the soil, and the fruitfulness of the crops. Yet the significance of temple worship went beyond the land of Israel: the vast complex symbolized cosmic order and took on a universal significance; its correct ritual preserved and *guaranteed the continuing order of the entire world.*[29] It is small wonder, then, that during the revolt, when the Roman troops were about to break into the temple, the priests continued to go about their duties to the very last moment.

Rising out of the court of the priests was the sanctuary, where God was believed to be especially present. This must have been an awe-inspiring sight: the sanctuary was entered through immense gold doors, above which hung a magnificent golden vine with huge grape clusters, and in front of which was a Babylonian tapestry embroidered with a colorful panorama of the heavens. Only the very best quality materials could be used, but human creations could be only a pale reflection of the glory of the God who dwelt there. Inside the sanctuary, and separated by a curtain, was the holy of holies, where only the high priest might enter, and only once a year. What effect the inner courts of the temple had on Caiaphas we cannot know, but another Jewish observer remarked that "a man would think he had come out of this world into another one."[30]

Consecration

When he was about twenty years old, Caiaphas would have made a special journey to the temple for his consecration as a priest. Perhaps other members of his family and friends went with him and stayed for the seven-day series of sacrifices, symbolic actions, and anointing.[31] In the course of this ceremony he would have exchanged his own tunic, soiled by city grime, for the colorful robes of a priest. First, he put on a linen tunic; over this went an ankle-length bodice. This was bound tightly to his chest with a beautiful sash embroidered with flowers of blue, purple, and scarlet. Finally, he would have put on a linen turban surmounted by a cloth cap.[32] For the first time, Caiaphas would have emerged as a priest, entitled to enter the court of the priests and to take up his duties as a priest of Yahweh.

From now on, the young priest would have to maintain a high level of purity, particularly when he was due to serve in the temple. Any number of things might make a man impure—natural functions such as ejaculation, contact with

JERUSALEM

THE TEMPLE MOUNT

DURING THE SECOND TEMPLE PERIOD

A RECONSTRUCTION BASED ON ARCHAEOLOGICAL AND HISTORICAL EVIDENCE

The Jerusalem Temple. A reconstruction by Dr. Leen Ritmeyer.

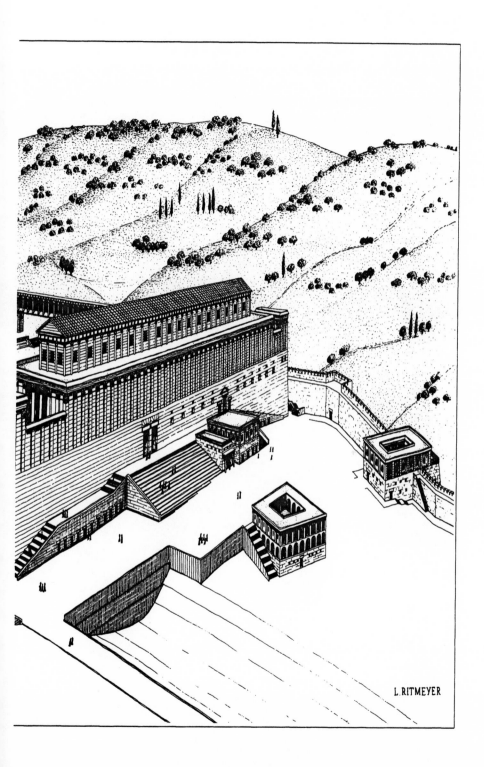

L.RITMEYER

a corpse, disease. There was nothing shameful about being impure—many people would have been unavoidably impure for large parts of their lives—but it was important to limit his impurity as much as possible. Most forms of impurity could be removed by washing in pure water that was specially stored in stone jars (pottery was unsuitable since, according to Lev 11:33, it absorbed impure liquids and would contaminate anything else that was put in it) or by immersion in a ritual bath, or *miqveh*.

Service in the temple, however, was not a full-time commitment. There were too many priests to serve in the Jerusalem temple at the same time.[33] Each of the twenty-four divisions took its turn to serve for one week, from Sabbath to Sabbath. Each of these divisions was further divided into "fathers' houses," which each served for only one day.[34] (An exception to this rotation system was Passover, when the large number of lambs to be slaughtered meant that all the priests had to be on duty together.) Caiaphas would probably have served in the temple for only a few weeks each year. When his service was over, he would go back to the family home, where he would devote himself to the activities of aristocrats. He might oversee the family's lands and properties, forge new business deals, or devote himself to leisure pursuits. It would have been at these times, too, that he took his first tentative steps in the world of public life and diplomacy.

3

Public and Private Life

The Jerusalem Aristocracy

The first few decades of Roman rule were a challenging, and yet perhaps exciting, time for Jerusalem aristocrats. The Roman presence in the country was small, consisting of only the Roman governor and a handful of administrative staff who chose to make their headquarters in the coastal city of Caesarea on Sea. These men devoted themselves to matters of national security and, in line with standard Roman policy, left the day-to-day running of the country in the hands of the indigenous local aristocracy. In Judea this meant the upper echelons of the temple priesthood and the lay nobility, men of wealth and status in the Jerusalem community.

Together these aristocrats formed the new government of Judea. Rome expected them to settle local disputes, to keep the peace, and to mediate between the governor and the people. They would be aided by an army of lesser officials, scribes, record keepers and secretaries, while the collection of taxes was probably overseen by an administrative council known as the *boule*.[1] It used to be assumed that the most important judicial, legislative, and executive decisions in Jerusalem were carried out by a fixed council of seventy-one elders known as the Sanhedrin.

Recent studies, however, suggest that no such council existed under Roman rule.[2] Instead, members of the nobility seem to have acted through ad hoc coalitions and alliances; the precise people involved would have varied according to the nature of the issue. In keeping with the spirit of the age, disputes were settled and deals were made through diplomacy, negotiation, and compromise.

There can be no doubt that Roman rule allowed the Jewish aristocracy much more freedom than it had experienced under Herod. Now a much wider group of men could take an active part in governing their country. Noblemen who had been forced to keep a low profile under Herod could assert themselves once again, and new families came to prominence.

The High Priest

Whatever role Caiaphas and his family took in the new government, we can be sure that, as members of a high priestly clan, they would have taken a particular interest in the high priesthood. The high priest was the supreme cultic official in the Jerusalem temple. He was the mediator between the Jewish people and God: only he could make atonement for the sins of the people, and only he could enter the innermost sanctum of the temple, the holy of holies, and come into the presence of God. Philo of Alexandria declared that the position of high priest was greater than that of the king, since kingship was concerned with the care of human beings, while the high priest was "concerned with the service of God."[3]

Before we can appreciate the position of the high priest under Rome, a brief historical survey is in order. In earlier times, the position had been hereditary and held for life, passing from father to son (it was believed) in an unbroken succession all the way back to Zadok.[4] Everything changed in the second century B.C.E., when the Hasmonean heirs of the Maccabees seized first the high priesthood and then kingship. Throughout most of their dynasty, one man was both king and high priest—the highest national leader and supreme head of the Jewish cult.[5] When Herod ascended the throne in 37 B.C.E., however, claiming the high priesthood for himself was not an option. Not only was the king not from a priestly family, but even his Jewishness was suspect in some quarters, since his mother had been an Arab. He seems rather shrewdly to have returned the post to Zadokites, but taken pains to keep the incumbent firmly under his thumb.[6] He took it upon himself to appoint and depose high priests at will, making it quite clear that he was the power behind the priesthood. He particularly favored little-known Diaspora Jews, and shared the office among a number of families so that no one family could become too powerful and no hereditary succession could develop. The king also kept the sacred high priestly vestments under his own control in the Antonia Fortress; when the high priest needed them for a festival, he had to collect them seven days in advance to allow time for their purification.

Herod's innovations were to have a profound effect on the priestly aristocracy. In particular, his deposition of high priests led to the formation of what the New

Testament and Josephus refer to as the "chief priests." This group included former high priests (who, due to the sanctity of their office, were often referred to as high priest even after they had technically been deposed) and the immediate families of present and former high priests.[7] His policies would also have introduced a stronger degree of competition among the nobility than ever before; the high priesthood could be given to another family at any time, and rival houses were constantly alert to opportunities for their own advancement.

With the arrival of Roman rule in 6 C.E., things changed again. The Romans appointed a new man, apparently from a new family: Ananus son of Sethi or, as the New Testament calls him, Annas. This man's origins are shrouded in mystery, though, given Rome's high regard for ancestral traditions, it is likely that he too was a Zadokite.[8] Like Herod, the Roman governors kept a watchful eye on the high priest and were not averse to replacing an incumbent from time to time. Yet, as the decades passed, two features of Roman policies would have become apparent.

First, until the brief rule of Herod Agrippa in the early 40s, Annas's family held a virtual monopoly on the high priestly office. Only two men were appointed from other families and the tenure of each was no more than a year. Later in the century, power was shared between four high priestly families—those of Annas, Boethus, Kathros, and Phiabi—and the 50s and 60s C.E. saw increasing struggles among these houses as each vied for power and prominence.[9] But, in this early phase, there was really only one house that mattered: the house of Annas. Second, Rome took a much less restrictive approach towards the high priesthood than Herod, and over the course of the next few decades many of Herod's innovations were gradually eroded, allowing Jewish authorities greater autonomy over religious affairs. For example, the high priestly vestments were returned to Jewish custody in 37 C.E., and Herodian rulers were allowed to appoint their own high priests from 41 C.E. onwards. The Roman governor and his entourage were content to concern themselves with matters of national security in Caesarea, while the high priest was allowed to preside over the temple in Jerusalem.[10] To the temple aristocracy, Rome's less intrusive approach must have been a welcome development.

The high priest's first duty now was to make sure that the temple cult ran smoothly and efficiently, and that the delicate compromise by which Rome allowed the vast temple complex to run unhindered was maintained. He may have also engaged in politics, particularly when issues concerning the temple were at stake. In such cases his authority made him the natural spokesperson for the rest of the nobility. Yet he was under no compulsion to be politically active, and the office itself did not automatically bestow leadership on its incumbent.[11] Writing several decades later, Josephus claimed that the constitution of the state was aristocratic under the leadership of the high priest—a claim that quite probably contains equal measures of exaggeration and wishful thinking.[12] Presumably some high priests were more interested, or better able, to engage in leadership roles than others.

Reactions to the Aristocrats

Jewish government, then, was in the hands of the chief priests, priestly aristocrats, lay nobility, and, when he chose, the high priest himself. We should not
underestimate the difficulty of the task entrusted to these men by Rome. It fell
to them to steer Judea through its first shaky years as a Roman province, to keep
the peace in a land recently ravaged by revolt, and to repair the broken structures
of government.

Despite these difficulties, it is fair to say that the Jewish aristocrats have not
fared well in many modern assessments. They are commonly condemned as "collaborators," "quislings," or puppets of the Roman regime.[13] There is, however,
no evidence that they were especially pro-Roman. They might well have urged
their compatriots to pay their taxes and not to rebel, but this may not have been
from any love of Rome. It was in everyone's interests to accept the situation, to
work out a way of living with their Roman overlords, and to safeguard Jewish
interests through diplomacy and compromise, rather than to lose ground
through violence and bloodshed. Years later, when revolt broke out in 66 C.E.,
these men could have sided with Rome (as the Jewish King Agrippa II and his
family chose to do). Instead, they advocated moderation, and when that proved
no longer possible, they threw in their lot with their rebellious compatriots.

But what did ordinary, first-century Judeans think of these men? It is notori-
ously difficult to know how "ordinary" people felt about anything in the ancient
world: those who kept records were almost exclusively the elite, and when they
wrote about "the masses" they often did so with little understanding or sympathy for their situation. However, although some people undoubtedly despised
any kind of compromise with foreign power and longed for a more confronta-
tional approach, it is likely that, in line with the cultural assumptions of the
ancient world, most Judeans would have held their nobility in honor and treated
them with respect. They were, quite literally, "the best people," "the great and the
good" as we might say (though without the irony), those to whom God had
shown favor. There was no sense of democracy in first-century Judea; the land
had always been governed by nobility of one sort or another and, as far as most
people were concerned, always would be. Furthermore, it was not only the aristocracy who had an interest in preserving the order of society; it was equally
important for those at the other end of the social spectrum to hold onto what little they had, from the farmer with a small holding to the tenant or the fisherman
with a small business. As long as they were allowed to go on living their lives as
they always had, with a reasonable degree of stability and harmony, most people
would have been content to put their trust in the Jerusalem aristocracy.[14]

Certainly in the first phase of direct Roman rule (6–41), the system seems to
have worked well. It is a tribute to the abilities of these aristocrats that Josephus
records very few disturbances during this period and that, commenting later on
the reign of Tiberius (14–37 C.E.), Tacitus could remark that "Judea was quiet."
These men must have been able to command—and maintain—the respect of
both Rome and the Jewish people.[15]

Married Life

Caiaphas married the daughter of Annas (whose name, like that of so many women in antiquity, has not been preserved).[16] Marriages at the time—particularly among the aristocracy—were very rarely the result of a romantic attachment. The match would have been arranged by both families, perhaps several years before it actually took place.

Aristocrats often married relatives—a practice that helped to keep wealth and property within the family.[17] It is possible, therefore, that there was already some family connection between the houses of Caiaphas and Annas. Alternatively, the marriage may have been an attempt to secure an alliance between the two families. The advantages from Caiaphas's point of view are self-evident: his future father-in-law would be one of the wealthiest, most prominent, and most respected men of his day. Annas too must have been assured that Caiaphas shared his own values and concerns, and would prove to be a loyal and supportive ally. Like Cicero, he may have hoped that "common blood forces men to help and care for one another."[18] If Annas's family were not originally from Jerusalem, an alliance with a Jerusalem family might have appeared advantageous.

Before the marriage could take place, both sets of family records would have been scrutinized, and every detail of descent noted. It was vitally important for both families to maintain the purity of their priestly line. Priests could choose their brides only from a restricted group of women: they were forbidden to marry a prostitute, a divorced woman, a prisoner of war (in case she had been raped by a foreigner), or a girl who had lost her virginity. Only virgins or widows of Israelite descent were regarded as suitable partners. The rules were stricter for a high priest, who could marry only a virgin.[19] Philo went even further and asserted that she had to be descended from priests herself, and although this requirement is not in Leviticus, it does seem to reflect actual practice.[20] Caiaphas would probably have been several years older than his wife; this was a common pattern and one that helped to enhance the superior status of the husband within the marriage. Younger women, it was believed, could be "molded" by an older, wiser husband.[21]

The newly married couple, along with Caiaphas's extended family (his parents, if they were still alive, and unmarried siblings), would have made their home in the wealthy and fashionable district of Jerusalem known as the Upper City. Located on the Western Hill, slightly higher than the Temple Mount, this densely constructed suburb housed Herod's royal palace and was a favorite among Jerusalem aristocrats and visiting foreign dignitaries.[22] From here an aristocratic priest on his way to the temple had no need to walk through the rowdy bazaars of the Lower City but could make his way across a bridge over the Tyropoeon Valley (known nowadays as "Wilson's Arch") straight into the court of the Gentiles.

The high priest's palace itself seems to have been large and spacious— the Gospels suggest that Caiaphas had a gatehouse and a fair number of male and female slaves.[23] Archaeological excavations in the Upper City have provided a vivid glimpse into the homes of the Jerusalem elite, several of which were

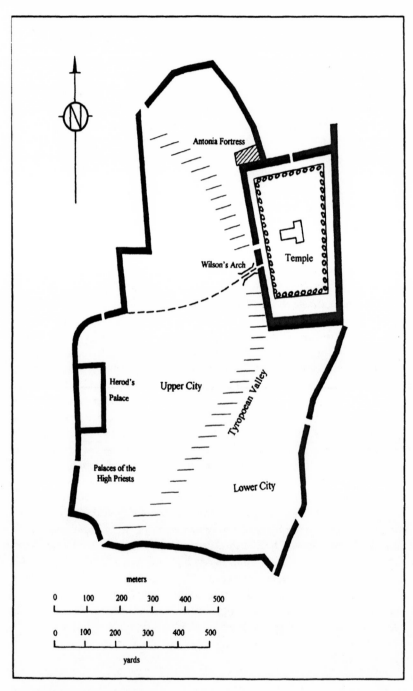

Jerusalem in the time of Caiaphas.

nothing short of mansions. Many were built in the style of Hellenistic or Roman villas with spacious reception halls, peristyle courtrooms, and even subfloor heating. The walls of the rooms were splendidly decorated with imitation marble, high-quality plastered frescoes, cornice work, and fine painting, while the floors were covered with beautifully colored mosaic pavements. Some rooms seem to have been periodically redecorated—presumably an indication that the wealthy occupants of this district were keen to keep up with changing fashions.

These houses were like those belonging to provincial aristocrats throughout the empire—from Pompeii to Alexandria—except for one thing: they all complied with the regulations of the Jewish law. This manifested itself most clearly in two ways. First, in keeping with the law that forbade the making of statues and graven images, the mansions in the Upper City contained no human or animal representations, but only geometric patterns.[24] Second, and perhaps more importantly, the archaeological evidence suggests a strong concern for Jewish *purity laws*. The inhabitants of this part of the city used stone vessels (which could not become ritually impure) and nearly every house had its own *miqveh*, or ritual bath.[25] Such a strong concern for purity would have been particularly important for temple priests, who needed to keep themselves as free from impurity as possible. If the occupants of these houses adhered to these laws, it is probably reasonable to suppose that their concern extended to other areas less accessible to the archaeologist's trowel. Despite their luxurious lifestyle, they presumably kept dietary laws and the Sabbath and instructed their children in Jewish traditions.

The household was the place where the private and public spheres met. Caiaphas's palace was not only his living quarters but also the place where he conducted his private business. Here he would have entertained other members of the Jerusalem nobility in his opulent public rooms. During these gatherings alliances would be formed, deals would be struck, and strategies would be formulated. The most important visitor to the house would have been Caiaphas's father-in-law, Annas. The high priest with his sons and son-in-law formed a tightly knit Sadducean clan, a force to be reckoned with in Jerusalem circles. The old man would probably have made sure that Caiaphas was quickly promoted up the temple hierarchy; after all, the higher the position Caiaphas held, the more useful he was to Annas.[26] As Caiaphas and his father-in-law sat in an evening discussing politics over glasses of imported wine, they could look down to the deep ravine of the Tyropoeon Valley below them and, further east, to the magnificent temple.[27] They could see the royal portico, glistening white, and the sanctuary itself rising above the walls, gold below and white above. From a distance it looked like a snow-clad mountain, gradually tinged with pink as it reflected the rays of the setting sun.

This was Caiaphas's life, punctuated by the rhythm of service in the temple. He probably had little expectation that he would become high priest himself. Annas seemed settled and, besides, had five sons to succeed him. Things, however, were about to change.

4

Caiaphas the High Priest

In 15 C.E. a Roman knight by the name of Valerius Gratus found himself sailing across the Mediterranean sea on a Roman ship, bound for the Judean port of Caesarea. Gratus was to take up his position as the fourth Roman prefect of the province of Judea.[1] It was perhaps not the most prestigious post in the empire, but it was, after all, a provincial command and for an ambitious man might prove a useful stepping-stone to greater things. Gratus had been personally selected by the Emperor Tiberius, perhaps on the basis of previous military accomplishments, and he would be determined to show that the emperor had made a good choice. Since Judea had only been a province for nine years, the governor's role was still primarily a military one; he was expected to maintain law and order and to oversee the collection of taxes. In all of this he would strive to exhibit to the newly subjected province the glory, valor, and superior civilization of Rome. And if he managed to make his own fame and fortune while he was about it, few would be in a position to complain.

As Gratus sailed into Caesarea he would have been impressed by its huge harbor, a legacy of Herod, apparently defying nature in its dimensions and grandeur. Soon the beautifully proportioned temple of Caesar would come into view, dominating a hill overlooking the harbor, and housing enormous statues of Augustus and Roma. Gratus would have felt quite at home here in this predominantly Gentile city with its little white houses laid out on a grid plan, its magnificent palaces, grand public buildings, and all the trappings of a Greco-Roman city: baths, a marble theater which could seat more than five thousand people, and one of the largest ampitheaters in the Roman world. It was here that Gratus, like his predecessors, would make his headquarters.

Caesarea had a number of advantages over the traditional capital of Jerusalem. Its position on the coast meant that communication with the emperor in Rome or the powerful legate of Syria stationed at Antioch was much easier than it would have been in landlocked Jerusalem. The Roman prefect needed to visit the holy city occasionally, particularly during festivals, to dampen any overzealous displays of Jewish nationalism, but there was no need for him to take up permanent residence in a city where his very presence would have been a source of friction. In Caesarea there would be no resentment at his public worship of his own Roman gods. Many of the Caesarean elite would have joined him, effortlessly absorbing Roman gods into the worship of their own native deities. The city's Gentile character made it much more congenial to the governor and his entourage than Jerusalem.

Gratus moved into Herod's splendid palace, along with a relatively small entourage of friends, advisers, scribes, translators, and messengers. Some of these might have been brought with him from Rome; others had already worked under earlier governors. Together, this skeletal administration would devote itself to matters of national security.

It was not, by any means, an easy posting. Although small, Judea's borders encompassed three different groups: Jews, Samaritans, and Gentiles. Despite the fact that each lived to a large extent in a clearly defined area, tensions between them were common. Gratus would have needed a system of reliable informants to keep him abreast of any potential tensions or uprisings. The need to strike quickly was particularly acute, since the governor had only a small military presence. The common picture of Roman soldiers marching up and down the province is mistaken. As a relatively junior officer, the Judean prefect had no Roman legions at his disposal—he had to make do with only auxiliary soldiers, amounting to five infantry cohorts and one cavalry regiment. Auxiliaries were usually drawn from the occupied country itself, but since Jews were exempt from military service (on account of diet and Sabbath regulations), only Gentiles could be used. In fact, the Roman governors seem to have simply inherited Herod's army of non-Jews drawn from the cities of Caesarea and Sebaste. Most of these men remained at headquarters in Caesarea; others were scattered throughout a number of Judean fortresses; while a permanent garrison was deployed in Jerusalem in case of unrest in the city. If things got out of hand, the prefect would have to appeal to the legate of Syria to intervene with his legions.

Apart from his regular trips to Jerusalem, Gratus passed his days in Caesarea, occupying himself with his troops and monitoring situations of potential unrest. He spent time checking that taxes had been paid, dealing with correspondence from Rome and Syria, and entertaining visitors to the province. His predecessor, Annius Rufus, would have left his records in order and perhaps a set of papers for the new governor, outlining procedures and policies, and arrangements in Jerusalem. Gratus's governorship seems to have been quite uneventful, except for a series of related incidents soon after his arrival.

Caiaphas's Meteoric Rise

Not long after taking up his post, Gratus deposed Annas from the high priesthood. At first sight, the precise reasons behind this are not clear. Under the Herods, high priests had lost their posts for a number of reasons: one was too popular with the festival crowds; another had failed to stop a demonstration against Herod in the temple; the people themselves overthrew Joazar, the high priest who persuaded them to accept the Roman census in 6 C.E.; and others were deposed at the whim of the king.[2] None of these reasons, however, fit the deposition of Annas. We have no indication that he was particularly popular (or unpopular) with the people, nor do we know of any rebellions at the time for which he might have been held responsible. We can also rule out the possibility that Gratus was being deliberately provocative toward the Jewish cult. Rome was generally tolerant and respectful towards native religions, particularly when they could boast an ancient heritage. Foreign gods might be inferior to those of Rome, but they were still gods, and there was no point in antagonizing them.[3]

A clue to Gratus's intentions, though, can be found in his subsequent actions. Annas was replaced by a man from another family, Ishmael ben Phiabi, who held office for a short time before being replaced by Annas's son Eleazar. After no more than a year Eleazar was replaced by Simon son of Camith, who not more than a year later was himself deposed. By 17/18 C.E. four men had held the high priesthood in as many years.[4] What was Gratus doing? Was he simply dissatisfied with four high priests in a row? Or was there some other reason for his actions? Is it a coincidence that priesthoods in other provinces, for example Asia Minor, were *yearly* appointments?[5] Did Gratus entertain the notion of modeling the high priesthood on priesthoods elsewhere in the empire and resolve to appoint a new man every year? The move would have stopped any one high priest gaining too much power and prestige and would have underlined the dependence of the post on the prefect. Whatever Gratus's intentions, his actions would have undoubtedly thrown the priestly aristocracy into some turmoil.

One man who seems to have done rather well out of the upheaval was Caiaphas, who found himself promoted rather more quickly than he might have expected. By 17/18 C.E. he probably held the post of captain of the temple (or *sagan*), in effect, the general manager of the temple and the next in line to the high priest. His remit included not only oversight of the cult and temple personnel, but also (with the aid of the temple police) the maintenance of law and order in and around the Temple Mount.[6] And only one or two years later, in 18 or 19 C.E., following the deposition of Simon son of Camith, Caiaphas was raised to the most highly esteemed position of all: the high priesthood.

A year came and went, and Caiaphas was not deposed. Several more years passed and still Caiaphas remained in position, outlasting not only Gratus but also his successor, Pilate. In fact, Caiaphas held the high priesthood for the next eighteen or nineteen years and was easily the longest serving high priest of the first century. What happened here? What caused Gratus to change his mind about the high priestly appointments? Why, after trying other men for only a year, did he allow Caiaphas to stay longer? It is often assumed that Caiaphas's long term of office was due to his ability to bribe the governor.[7] Not only is there no evidence for this, but it is inherently unlikely that an *incumbent* would offer the highest bribes for such a long time.[8] Surely, if the post were available to the highest bidder, there would have been opposition from other wealthy aristocrats over the course of eighteen or nineteen years. That is not to say that Caiaphas did not occasionally send Gratus gifts, lend him a few servants when the prefect was in Jerusalem, or send him an occasional amphora of wine. The giving of gifts to one's benefactors and patrons was part of how an ancient Mediterranean society worked. But it is unlikely that Caiaphas owed his long tenure to "bribery" alone.

There could be another reason for Caiaphas's long appointment. The aristocratic priests (and for that matter all other Jews) had a legitimate grievance against Gratus. He had gone further than anyone else—even Herod—in his high-handed treatment of the high priesthood. Yearly appointments might work in other provinces, but were unthinkable within the Jewish high priesthood. The Jewish aristocrats had two courses open to them: they could take their complaints to the prefect—either in Caesarea or during one of his visits to Jerusalem—or, if that course failed, they could try the Syrian legate. Although Gratus was the most senior Roman official in Judea, he was subordinate to the more powerful legate of Syria. When negotiations between Jewish delegations and the Roman governor reached deadlock, the Syrian legate was the normal route of appeal for both sides.

In the period 17–19 C.E., however, there was a third option. The great general and younger brother of Tiberius, Nero Claudius Drusus—or Germanicus as he was popularly known—was on a tour of the East. According to Tacitus, the provinces of Syria and Judea sent delegations to him, asking him for a reduction in tribute (*Annals* 2.42). Perhaps the Judean delegates took this opportunity to complain about Gratus's treatment of the high priestly office. Perhaps their grievances were heard, and Gratus (and his successors) was instructed by the Syrian legate (or Germanicus himself) not to meddle with the high priesthood any more than was strictly necessary. It is even possible that, given the sensitivity of the high priesthood, the right to appoint and depose high priests was now taken away from the prefects and restricted to the legates, men of higher status who generally commanded more respect.[9] This is, of course, speculation, but it is interesting that *no prefect ever appointed or deposed a high priest again.* Until the reign of Agrippa, every other change was made by the Syrian legate; after the reign of Agrippa, high priests were appointed by Herods. Such a move fits in well with what seems to be Rome's policy at this early period of gradually relinquishing control over the Jewish cult (see above, p. 35).

Perhaps, then, Caiaphas stayed in office so long not because of his ability to pay for the post, but because the governors had no authority to depose him. What is certain, though, is that his long tenure would have given the post an air of much needed stability.

The High Priesthood

What did Caiaphas *do* as high priest? What extra duties did the post entail beyond that of an ordinary priest? The high priest was the head of the vast temple complex. All its associated workers—bakers, weavers, purveyors of incense and ointments, goldsmiths, and bankers—although under the immediate control of the captain of the temple, came ultimately under Caiaphas's authority. But the high priest's most important responsibilities would have been *cultic*. According to Josephus, high priests officiated in the temple on Sabbaths, the new moon, New Year, the three pilgrimage feasts (Passover, Weeks, and Tabernacles), the Day of Atonement, and gatherings of the people.[10] We shall pause for a moment and look at just two of these—the Day of Atonement and Passover—to get a sense of Caiaphas's high priestly role, the intense commitment involved, and the demanding purity expectations associated with the office.

The high priest's most important role—and the only one stipulated by the law—was to officiate on the foremost day of the cultic year, the Day of Atonement (or Yom Kippur), held every year on the tenth day of the seventh month. This was not, strictly speaking, a festival but an annual fast, a day of self-examination, confession of sin, and communal worship. Preparations for the day would have begun early; it was vitally important that everything was performed properly. Seven days before the fast, the temple treasurers made their way to the Antonia Fortress to collect the high priestly vestments. Legend had it that they were the robes of Adam, passed down to Aaron, and through him to subsequent high priests.[11] The splendid robes were believed to possess special powers of their own (which is one of the reasons why Rome still kept them in custody) and were often the subject of theological speculation.[12] After inspecting the seal, the treasurers would receive the robes from the commander of the Roman garrison and carefully transport them to the temple for purification.[13]

Caiaphas himself needed to maintain an even higher level of purity than he had done as an ordinary priest. Not only was he precluded from touching a corpse; any form of outward mourning or taking part in a funeral procession—even for his own parents—would render him unclean.[14] The high priest had to be scrupulously honest about his own purity. Once, during Herod's reign, the high priest Matthias was made unclean by an erotic dream the night before he was due to serve on the Day of Atonement; a relative of his, Joseph the son of Ellemus, had to officiate instead.[15] Due to the strict purity regulations, Caiaphas might have confined himself to the temple for some days prior to the fast, so that he could not accidentally become defiled.[16]

The rituals for the Day of Atonement are laid out in Leviticus 16, a complex and composite piece of legislation in which several rites seem to have been combined.[17] What is clear, though, is that there were two stages. The first involved the cleansing of the sanctuary, the holy of holies, which Caiaphas would have entered wearing the ordinary linen garment of a priest. This was the only day of the year in which the high priest could enter the holiest part of the temple, and we can only imagine his sense of awe and trembling as he pushed the protecting veil to one side and carried the smoking censer of coal and incense into the inner sanctum. Three times he entered the holy of holies, coming as near as any mortal could to the presence of God. It was vitally important that the sacred rites were performed properly; any breach of the rules would incur God's judgment.

The second part of the rite was the atonement for the sins of the people. In recognition of the fact that he was now acting as the people's representative before God and the mediator between God and Israel, Caiaphas would change into his ceremonial robes. First, he would put on the long blue seamless tunic and tie it with the brightly colored sash. The tunic was decorated along its lower hem with tassels and bells that tinkled as he walked. Over this was a waistcoat (known as an ephod), which covered his chest and part of his back. This was attached at the shoulders by two sardonyxes, one on each side, which between them contained the names of the twelve tribes of Israel. The waistcoat itself was richly decorated with embroidery in gold and bright colors. At the front was a breastplate on which were four rows, each with three precious stones. Each contained the name of one of the twelve tribes of Israel and, by this means, brought Israel directly into God's presence. On his head Caiaphas would have worn the priestly turban and cap, above which was a "crown of gold in three tiers" on which was written the name of God.[18]

The overall effect of the high priest in his robes was dazzling. The brightness of the gold and precious stones was thought to reflect the heavenly radiance, the very glory of God. The sight assured onlookers of God's presence with Israel. Ben Sira even compared the vested high priest to divine wisdom, the principle upon which the universe was founded.[19] It is perhaps not surprising that it was popularly believed that the high priest in his robes might have direct access to God, and several high priests were said to have the gift of prophecy, a belief expressed (albeit ironically) in John's Gospel.[20]

Dressed in these splendid robes, Caiaphas would have stood between two goats and cast lots. He rested his hands upon one, confessed "all the iniquities of the people of Israel" and passed it to an assistant who drove it out into the wilderness, symbolically removing the nation's transgressions. The other goat was sacrificed on the altar along with a bull; together they constituted sin offerings for the people and himself. At the end of the service, the people prostrated themselves and prayed, while Caiaphas lifted his hands over them in the name of the Most High God. Afterwards, he would have gone home and feasted with his friends, giving thanks to God that he had come out of the sanctuary alive.[21]

Yom Kippur may have been the cultic highlight of the year, but Passover (or Pesach) was Caiaphas's busiest time. The feast was a national celebration, a commemoration of deliverance from Egyptian oppression. Thousands of pilgrims made their way to the holy city from all over the world—Syria, Asia Minor, North Africa, and Babylonia—until the city was crowded to bursting. Some found lodgings in inns, synagogues or with friends; others found places to stay in the surrounding villages of Bethphage and Bethany; those less fortunate had to pass the cold nights in tents.

People began to gather a week before the festival for the seven-day corpse purification ceremonies. High mortality levels meant that most people would have come in contact with death in some way, and even walking on a grave could cause corpse impurity (Num 9:9). Caiaphas knew the rituals well. He would have supervised the selection of an unblemished red heifer, which was then taken outside the city and slaughtered. The cow's ashes were mixed with spring water, and this "water of cleansing" was sprinkled on the people on the third and seventh day of the week. After the second sprinkling, people bathed and laundered their clothes and, that evening, were considered ritually pure once again.[22]

The festival itself had originally been two feasts—Passover and Unleavened Bread—but by the first century had merged to produce a single feast lasting eight days. As the Levites sang psalms of praise and thanksgiving to God for their deliverance from Egypt on the first day of the feast (Pss 113–18), pilgrims would come to the temple in their hundreds and thousands and slaughter their lambs. That night, families all over Jerusalem celebrated the Passover, the men with their loins girded, sandals on their feet, and staff in hand, to recall the haste with which their ancestors had left Egypt.

Festivals were joyous times, celebrations of God's covenant with Israel and the fertility of the land, times to catch up with friends and families, and welcome breaks from the monotony of work. But they could also have their darker sides. As Josephus noted, "It is on these festive occasions that sedition is most apt to break out" (War 1.88). These gatherings were natural arenas for tension and resentment to break out in the form of unrest or aggression. Nearly all the riots we know of took place at festivals, particularly Passover, when many would have been all too painfully aware of the irony of praising God for military and political deliverance (Ps 118:10) at a time when the nation was under Roman subjugation. A riot broke out in the temple at Passover under Herod's son Archelaus and again in the governorship of Cumanus (48–52 C.E.), when a Roman soldier made a rude gesture at the crowd. On both occasions, thousands lost their lives.[23] For these reasons Rome took measures to keep the peace; yet the sight of the Roman prefect riding into Jerusalem with his troops, and the presence of Roman soldiers mounting guard along the roofs of the temple porticoes, could only have fueled popular anger and resentment.

As Caiaphas went about his high priestly duties, particularly at the great festivals, a range of emotions must have passed through his mind. He would have been constantly alert to any threats to his own purity (particularly in the days running up to the festival). Once the temple rituals were underway, he had to make sure that every stipulation of the law was followed to the letter; there was no room for error. And lurking in the background was the constant worry that any disruption—however unintentional—could halt the sacred rites and bring down God's wrath, not just on the high priest, but on the whole nation. Caiaphas depended on the support of the entire temple personnel, who made sure that everything ran smoothly and remained vigilant throughout the feast for any signs of unrest. Acting as God's anointed high priest was an enormous privilege and honor, but it must also have been an incomprehensibly heavy responsibility.

Figurehead of the Jewish Faith

When Caiaphas was not officiating in the temple, there was still a great deal to be done. As high priest, he was the figurehead of the Jewish faith, the link with the scattered Jewish communities all over the Mediterranean world and as far away as Babylonia. Caiaphas would have kept in contact with these communities by commissioning letters. Sometimes these letters might transmit news; at other times they might discuss matters of law or observance. At certain times of the year, Caiaphas would have sent out "festal letters," calling for appropriate festal preparation and repentance in the form of prayer, fasting, and almsgiving. Just as importantly, these letters would have let people know the dates of the celebrations. Festivals were calculated according to a lunar calendar, but, because of the discrepancy between a lunar year and a solar year, a supplementary month had to be added every two or three years at the end of the year. If Jews from the Diaspora planned to come up to a feast—a journey which could take several weeks—it was vitally important that they knew the precise date well in advance.[24]

As high priest, Caiaphas would have continued to take some part in the politics of his day, particularly in matters concerning the temple. Yet his cultic activities would have prevented him taking on too many extra responsibilities. He would have continued to lend his support to Annas and his family. As a former high priest, Annas retained a large amount of influence; so too, perhaps, did his son Eleazar, despite his short incumbency. Scholars often talk of Annas "manipulating" Caiaphas and of his being "the power behind the throne." This is, however, rather misleading terminology. Presumably now that Annas was relieved of his cultic responsibilities, he had more time than Caiaphas to devote to other matters.

Whatever role Caiaphas and Annas chose to adopt, there were plenty of other important men in Jerusalem who may have been called on to debate matters of policy and to decide what course of action was best for the people: the heads of influential families (probably the "elders" of the New Testament), Joseph of Arimathaea (John 3:1, 7:50), Gamaliel (Acts 5:34) and his son Simon (*War* 4.159, *Life* 190–98, 216, 309), and perhaps Josephus's father Matthias and grandfather (*Life* 4–5).[25] These, and other men whose names are now lost, would have continued the difficult task of mediating between the people and the Roman governor. On occasion, and particularly when a matter related to the temple, they would have been joined by Caiaphas and his family.

Reactions to Caiaphas

What did the people think of Caiaphas as their high priest? The fact that Caiaphas was a *Roman* appointment may have demeaned both the man and the office to some extent (it is interesting that when the revolutionary Zealots elected a high priest during the revolt they declared that the choice would be *God's* through the drawing of lots [*War* 4.147–57]). But many Judeans must have been realistic enough to accept the situation. What mattered most was that a man of Zadokite lineage held the position and that he was, as far as possible, allowed to go about his duties with minimal interference by Rome. Not everyone would have gone along with the aristocratic Philo, who declared that the high priest stood midway between God and humans, but—as far as we know—the temple service never suffered neglect, and there were no requests for the removal of the high priest: most people continued to bring their offerings to the temple and were content that Caiaphas had successfully intervened with God on their behalf on the Day of Atonement.[26]

The supreme importance of the temple cult within Jewish life cannot be stressed enough. We have already seen that the accurate annual following of the divine liturgy guaranteed stability and fruitfulness not only for Jews, but for the whole cosmos. Because of this supreme importance, however, voices of dissent were often raised. Criticisms of the temple and its priesthood go as far back as the Old Testament prophets, particularly Jeremiah, Isaiah, and Micah.[27] In the second century B.C.E., the priestly founders of the Qumran community left Jerusalem in disgust at the assumption to the high priesthood of a man they called the "wicked priest" (probably either Jonathan Maccabee or his brother Simon). Far away from Jerusalem in their desert home, the Dead Sea Scrolls show that these men rejected the Jerusalem priesthood, followed a different calendar, and conceived of their own community as God's true temple.[28] Other texts from the time—such as the *Psalms of Solomon*, *The Testament of Levi* (which was later appropriated and edited by Christians), and the *Testament of Moses* (which probably reached its final form shortly after the death of Herod)—testify to an ongoing critique of the temple priesthood.[29]

Yet we need to treat all these texts with a certain amount of caution. As E. P. Sanders has pointed out, they are highly polemical in nature, drawing on the vice lists typical of both Jewish and pagan moral teaching of the time, and all derive from powerless (and therefore disaffected) religious groups who bitterly opposed the priestly establishment. The writers took issue with the ruling priests over their legitimacy, their interpretation of the law, and the way the law was followed in the cult. Such sectarian wrangling is only what we would expect, given the importance of the cult and the fragmented nature of the various strands that went to make up first-century "Judaism."[30]

No texts remain from Caiaphas's day, but we can assume that a healthy critique continued. The Essene community at Qumran was still thriving and their colleagues, the Essenes who lived in towns, no doubt persisted in spreading the sect's teaching to all who cared to listen. Some decades after Caiaphas, Josephus reports that some prophets led large numbers of people out of Jerusalem, promising that God would reveal himself to them in the wilderness. Josephus himself took a rather dim view of these prophets and tells us nothing about their teaching. Yet it may be possible to piece some things together from their actions. Theudas, for example, persuaded his followers to go with him to the Jordan, where at his command the river would part and allow them all to cross (unfortunately for Theudas, the Roman governor Fadus sent out his cavalry before his movement could get started). We cannot know whether Theudas *openly* criticized the temple and its priesthood, but the very fact that he led his followers out into the wilderness (the symbol of an earlier, closer relationship with God) and that he intended to reenact events from Israel's early history (Exod 12:29–14:30, Josh 3–4) suggests that in his view Israel had lost its way; it may well be an implicit assertion that holiness was no longer to be found in the Jerusalem temple but within his own movement. Perhaps he felt that the priesthood of his day (ca. 44–46), by accommodating with Rome and relinquishing God's claim on "the land," had demeaned the temple and its cult.[31]

Voices of dissent from Essenes or prophets like Theudas would quite probably have simply been a fact of life for Caiaphas and his colleagues. There were, after all, many different ways of making sense of Israel's past and many different opinions as to what course of action was most appropriate in the present. The Sadducees had compromised with Rome in exchange for the right to run the temple, but not everyone was happy about this, at least not all the time. The temple aroused strong emotions and was a natural focus for political and religious movements alike (and, more often than not, the two could not be separated). What is surprising is that the priests seem to have done nothing about their dissenters; as far as we know, there were never any attempts to silence the Essenes, nor do Josephus's accounts of the desert prophets give the slightest hint of any kind of priestly involvement. Caiaphas and the other chief priests appear to have been content to live with a certain amount of criticism. In the next few chapters we shall meet two prophets whose messages were more disturbing: John the Baptist and Jesus of Nazareth.

5

Caiaphas, Pilate, and John the Baptist

In 26 C.E., Gratus retired as prefect of Judea and was replaced by another Roman knight: Pontius Pilate. We know nothing of Pilate's early career, but he probably had a military background, like Gratus, and hoped that the provincial command would prove a useful stepping-stone to higher honors. Pilate would probably have known very little about Judea or the Jewish religion before taking up his appointment; any opinions he did have would probably have been colored by the substantial Jewish community in Rome, which had been expelled by Tiberius only a few years earlier.[1] As soon as he arrived in Caesarea, however, his advisers would have begun briefing him on the land and its defenses, the Jewish way of life, and—of course—the place of the temple and the high priest.

A crucial question in our study of Caiaphas is: What kind of relationship existed between him and Pilate? It is often supposed that the two men worked together closely in support of Roman interests and that the high priest was little more than the governor's henchman.[2] Yet, setting aside for the moment the incident with Jesus of Nazareth, there is very little evidence for this thesis. Three incidents from Pilate's term of office will enable us to look at the relationship between the two men in more detail.

Caiaphas and Pilate

The first incident occurred early on in Pilate's governorship, perhaps even during his first winter in the province. Josephus writes that Pilate brought a new cohort of troops into the Antonia Fortress in Jerusalem. This new cohort, perhaps as a sign of honor and military distinction, had standards decorated with busts of the emperor. As soon as they saw them, the people were outraged, regarding the busts as a violation of the laws against graven images in Exodus 20:4 and Deuteronomy 5:8, and proceeded en masse to Pilate at his headquarters in Caesarea, begging him to remove the offensive images. When Pilate refused, Josephus reports that the people "fell prostrate around his house and for five whole days remained motionless in that position." His account continues:

> On the ensuing day Pilate took his seat on his tribunal in the great stadium and summoning the multitude, with the apparent intention of answering them, gave the arranged signal to his armed soldiers to surround the Jews. Finding themselves in a ring of troops, three deep, the Jews were struck dumb at this unexpected sight. Pilate, after threatening to cut them down, if they refused to admit Caesar's images, signaled to the soldiers to draw their swords. Thereupon the Jews, as by concerted action, flung themselves in a body on the ground, extended their necks, and exclaimed that they were ready rather to die than to transgress the Law. Overcome with astonishment at such intense religious zeal, Pilate gave orders for the immediate removal of the standards from Jerusalem. (*War* 2.172–74)[3]

Did Caiaphas play a role in this demonstration? It is often supposed that Josephus's silence suggests that the high priest kept a low profile back in Jerusalem, unwilling to oppose Pilate openly.[4] But it would be unwise to conclude too much from Josephus's silence here. One of his major aims was to show Jewish readers that passive trust in God would succeed against Israel's enemies, while resort to armed rebellion would always fail.[5] He would like us to think that it was a mass movement, a spontaneous show of solidarity among the people; in all probability, though, the protest was neither as spontaneous nor as passive as he claims. A demonstration on this scale would certainly have needed leaders and organizers, but Josephus has no interest in telling us these details; the scene he wants to present is one of Jewish people confronting a Roman governor with nothing more to rely on than simple trust in God.

Who, then, *did* lead the people? The most obvious answer is the Jerusalem aristocrats. The people would naturally have turned to them to approach the governor on their behalf and to act as spokespersons and mediators. During the five days at Caesarea these men would have put the Jewish side to the governor. They might have pointed out that Jews had tolerated pagan standards for twenty years in silence, but these new standards with their busts of the emperor were just too much. It was bad enough to think that Caesarea was filled with such imperial images, but their presence in the Antonia Fortress—right on the Temple Mount—was utterly unacceptable! Pilate would presumably have countered this with his own point of view. Why should he allow the people of his province to dictate which squadron he deployed in Jerusalem? Did people in any other province make such demands? Coming at the beginning of Pilate's governorship, it was vitally important for both sides to take a firm line, to weigh up the resolve of their opponent, and not to back down too hastily.

Whether Caiaphas was one of the negotiators is difficult to say, though it is perhaps unlikely that he was there. His cultic responsibilities might have made it difficult for him to go to Caesarea for what could well be a prolonged period. There were plenty of other aristocrats (perhaps his father-in-law Annas was one of them) who could oversee the negotiations. Even if Caiaphas was not there, though, there is no reason to assume that he would be indifferent to a new governor's innovation; the high priest, perhaps more than anyone else, would have been anxious to maintain the sanctity of the Temple Mount and would have wanted to be kept informed of developments.

A second incident shows a closer working relationship between Pilate and Caiaphas. According once again to Josephus, Pilate decided to provide Jerusalem with a new aqueduct.[6] Superficially, this sounds like an excellent idea: Jerusalem's hilltop location meant that the city often had difficulties with its water supply. Perhaps Pilate thought that the aqueduct would help to foster and promote good relations between himself and the people. Caiaphas and the rest of the chief priests seem to have been happy with the proposal; it was in their interests to promote good Jewish-Roman relations and the water supply would be particularly beneficial for the temple. In fact, some of the money for the project seems to have come from the temple treasury (a passage in the Mishnah allows the use of surplus money from the treasury to be used for "all the city's needs") and was presumably handed over to Pilate (with Caiaphas's agreement) by the temple treasurers.[7]

What started off as an enterprising plan, however, seriously backfired. The precise cause of unrest is not entirely clear. The *Antiquities* records, rather enigmatically, that the people "did not acquiesce in the operations which this involved," leading some scholars to suggest that the problem concerned the construction of the aqueduct or that its route perhaps passed through a graveyard. The account in the *War*, though, suggests that the dispute centered on the financing of the project; Pilate is accused of "using up" or "completely draining" (the Greek here is *exanaliskon*) the sacred treasure known as *corbonas* (or what was "gifted" to the temple). While the *War*'s assertion that Pilate drained the account may be exaggerated, it is quite possible that disputes arose when Pilate began to ask for increasing amounts of money. Perhaps the aqueduct proved to be a larger undertaking than had initially been envisioned and began to require more money than had been originally expected. Perhaps Pilate began to demand more than the allowable surplus and threatened to drain the supplies for the daily sacrifices. Perhaps, too, the governor began to take this money for granted, demanding and expecting that the priests would hand it over to him and treating it as his own personal fiscus.

There was probably a range of responses among ordinary people to Pilate's use of temple money. Some may have been quite happy with the arrangement, feeling that it was better to use temple money than to be required to pay a new tax for the purpose; others may have gone along with the proposal initially and then become angry and disillusioned as Pilate demanded more money. Some may have been against the idea from the start, wanting Rome to have nothing to do with their temple; others may have jumped at any opportunity to engage in an anti-Roman protest. Gradually, many people seem to have become irritated at what appeared to be Pilate's continual use, even control, of their treasury. If his use of the money went so far as to use money reserved for sacrifices, this would have been a serious ground for complaint.

Next time Pilate came to Jerusalem, a riot broke out; the governor was surrounded by an angry mob, clamoring and baying against him. Having foreseen trouble, however, he had already interspersed among the crowd a number of undercover troops, who, at his command, beat the rioters with their cudgels. Large numbers of Jews perished, some from the blows of the soldiers, others trampled to death by the flight of their compatriots.

We cannot know how Caiaphas reacted to all of this. Pilate's presence in Jerusalem suggests that the riot took place at a *feast*. Caiaphas would presumably have been engaged with his cultic responsibilities and would not have been available, either to calm the protestors or to intercede with the governor. He must have gone along with the project initially, but there is no reason to assume that, as time went on, Caiaphas was any less scandalized by Pilate's continual appropriation of temple funds than his fellow Jews. His way of tackling the governor would have been more restrained: through letters, envoys, or face-to-face negotiations when Pilate came to Jerusalem. On this occasion, though, all of Caiaphas's probable diplomacy could not prevent a riot and the loss of many lives.

A third incident is reported by Philo of Alexandria in his *Embassy to Gaius*.[8] Philo tells how Pilate set up gilded shields in Herod's palace in Jerusalem. Unlike other honorific shields, they did not contain images, but they did contain both the name of Pilate and the official name of the emperor: Tiberius Caesar Augustus, son of the deified Augustus. Gradually, the fact that the shields had a reference to a pagan god (the "divine Augustus") became widely known. The people were scandalized that such a reference should be located in the holy city of Jerusalem and appealed to four Herodian princes who were in the city at the time to use their influence to have Pilate remove the shields. The princes did as the people asked, presumably stressing to the governor the sanctity of Jerusalem and how a reference to the divine Augustus was an insult to their God. Pilate, for his part, would have explained how he had set up the shields in honor of the emperor; how could he now remove them? In the resulting stalemate the Jewish spokespersons sent a letter to Tiberius, who ordered Pilate to remove the shields from Jerusalem and set them up instead in the altogether more appropriate setting of the temple of Augustus at Caesarea.

The fact that Philo, like Josephus earlier, makes no mention of Caiaphas, has again suggested to some that the high priest was not the natural spokesperson of the people. Yet three points need to be made here. First, the only time when four Herodian princes and the Roman governor would all be in Jerusalem would be for one of the three pilgrimage feasts (perhaps the best attended, that of the Passover). As was the case with the previous incident, Caiaphas's cultic responsibilities would have prevented him from engaging in diplomatic affairs. Second, the matter was rather sensitive, and the leaders of the protest may have felt that the Herodian princes (all of whom were Roman citizens) would have more clout with Pilate than the high priest. It was not, after all, as though the high priest *alone* was the central mediator in such matters. There would have been a range of aristocrats whose status enabled them to act as leaders and negotiators, and people would have appealed to whoever seemed best placed to succeed. Third, it is quite likely that not everyone was opposed to the shields. Pilate had at least taken care not to include the Emperor's *image* on the shields, and Herod's former palace (which was used as the governor's official Jerusalem residence, or *praetorium*) would have been the most appropriate place for them and presumably housed many other documents containing the emperor's official title. Pilate's offense here was simply not in the same league as his earlier introduction of standards. It may have seemed to Caiaphas and certain other aristocrats that it was better not to protest too much about small issues. Perhaps he advocated a certain amount of acceptance of minor infringements, if only to court Roman goodwill and to make Jewish bargaining power all the greater when it mattered most.

These three events stood out in the minds of Josephus and Philo from Pilate's time of office. It seems rather significant that *all three occurred at locations* (Caesarea) *or times* (during festivals) *that prevented Caiaphas's involvement*. Presumably many other potential incidents were dispelled by successful intercession by Caiaphas and his aristocratic colleagues. How then would we sum up the relationship between Caiaphas and Pilate? We can come to the following, admittedly tentative, conclusions.

Pilate must have found in Caiaphas a man with whom he could do business, a man who could be relied on to maintain law and order, and a man who instinctively knew where the boundaries lay between what was acceptable and what was unacceptable to Rome. If not, Pilate would have appealed to the legate of Syria and had him removed. There is, however, no evidence that Caiaphas was particularly pro-Roman, or that Pilate ever expected him to promote a particularly Roman point of view (unlike, for example, the high priest Joazar, who persuaded the people to accept the Roman census in 6 C.E. and was subsequently overthrown). Caiaphas, for his part, was probably wise enough to be considerate of Rome's expectations, but a hard negotiator for Jewish rights. Perhaps, secure in his own aristocratic lineage, he enjoyed letting the Roman knight know that he answered to none other than the legate of Syria. It is unlikely that the two men became friends—the religious and cultural gulf between them was probably too great to allow any degree of intimacy—but the eleven years that they worked together may well have produced a civil cordiality, a respect for one another's boundaries, and the development of a certain modus operandi.

In only one incident do we see Caiaphas and Pilate working together toward the same outcome—the execution of Jesus of Nazareth. Before turning to this, we need to look at one more event that may well have had a bearing on Caiaphas's treatment of Jesus—the execution of John the Baptist.

John the Baptist

By the late 20s C.E., Jerusalem would have been buzzing with stories about an ascetic holy man in Perea.[9] This region was not formally under the jurisdiction of either Pilate or Caiaphas but (along with Galilee) was part of the territory of Herod Antipas, a son of Herod the Great.[10] Both Pilate and Caiaphas, though, would have watched what happened in the neighboring region with some interest.

John based himself in the wilderness by the Jordan River. There was nothing accidental about this location: both the wilderness and the Jordan were powerful symbols of Israel's history and tapped into a longing to return to an idealized past, a time when people enjoyed a pristine relationship with God. Caravans from across the desert would have told excited Jerusalemites about John's message: his proclamation that the end was imminent and that it would be heralded by an eschatological judgment carried out by a mysterious "coming one." There was some confusion as to whether this "coming one" was God himself or God's agent. In any case, John was calling people to repent and to accept baptism as a symbol of God's forgiveness. All over Judea and Perea, John was held to be a prophet, people were flocking to him in the desert, and large numbers were coming forward to be baptized in the Jordan. Then more news came: John had been arrested by Antipas and was imprisoned in the fortress of Machaerus. Soon after came another report: John was dead.

Perhaps Caiaphas sought out Antipas when he next came to Jerusalem; the two men might have talked in the Hasmonean palace where Antipas stayed or in Caiaphas's own dwelling. Antipas might have stressed, for the benefit of the high priest, the affront that John's offer of forgiveness posed to the temple. How dare John claim that sins could be forgiven through baptism alone? Where did that leave the temple and its cult? But Caiaphas would have known that there was another motive behind Antipas's execution of John. Antipas had recently divorced the daughter of Aretas, king of Nabatea, in favor of his brother's wife Herodias. The divorce was a grave insult to Aretas and jeopardized the fragile peace agreement between the two kingdoms. Then John had turned up, pointing out that marriage to a brother's wife was unlawful (Lev 18:16). The last thing Antipas needed was a holy man preaching in Perea, only twenty kilometers from the Nabatean border, undermining his position. John could easily stir up discontent and constituted a political threat to the stability of Antipas's realm.

Executing him, Antipas perhaps admitted, was not a popular move with the people, but it had to be done. Persons like John could be dangerous. There was no predicting what the people might do, stirred up into an apocalyptic frenzy by such a man. It would not take much provocation for Aretas to avenge his daughter by declaring war on Antipas. Things could escalate, Rome could become involved; who knew to what disasters it might lead? Antipas's own brother, Archelaus, had been deposed by Roman intervention in 6 C.E.; the Jewish ruler would make certain that such a thing did not happen to him. Antipas was quite clear: better to nip a potential uprising in the bud than allow it to escalate. Who knew what might happen if Rome started to take an interest?

With all this, Caiaphas was probably in agreement. He knew that the best way to guarantee the safety of the temple was to keep Roman legions off Jewish soil. Better to deal with troublemakers ourselves, he might have reiterated, than allow Rome to intervene. Little could he know that he would very shortly have a troublemaker of his own with whom he would have to deal.

6

Caiaphas and Jesus

Soon after the death of John, Caiaphas would probably have become aware of another holy man: Jesus of Nazareth. News would have reached Jerusalem of a Galilean peasant who was preaching the imminent arrival of the kingdom of God —a kingdom in which the normal expectations of society would be radically reversed.[1] Galilean pilgrims and traders would have been full of the news back home; of the excitement stirred up by Jesus everywhere he went; of his clever sayings and memorable parables; and of his miraculous healings and exorcisms. Herod Antipas might have had a quiet word with the high priest about Jesus, explaining that he had been a follower of John the Baptist who branched out on his own after John's death. It would not have been long before everyone in Jerusalem had heard something of Jesus and his message.

We cannot be sure how often Jesus visited Jerusalem in the course of his mission. Mark's Gospel (followed by Matthew and Luke) suggests that he made only one visit to the capital city. John's Gospel, on the other hand, suggests a ministry of about three years, in the course of which Jesus visited Jerusalem on several occasions. Both accounts are theologically motivated, but many scholars think the longer ministry of John has greater plausibility.[2] If so, Caiaphas would have had a reasonably good knowledge of the Galilean holy man and his preaching. And quite probably he had already determined to keep a close eye on Jesus' activities before Jesus made his last, fateful visit to Jerusalem.

As the muddy roads began to dry in the warmer spring air of 30 C.E., Jesus would have joined the hundreds of thousands of people who made their annual Passover pilgrimage to the holy city.[3] Most pilgrims arrived a week in advance of the festival to take part in purification rites, to spend time in the holy city, and to prepare themselves spiritually. Jesus probably went up early, too, staying with friends outside Jerusalem in the village of Bethany, as he had probably done many times before.[4] Yet something about this final visit was different and would lead to Jesus' arrest and death. The next two chapters will explore the likeliest course of events that final week of Jesus' life, what the high priest made of the preacher from Galilee, and to what extent Caiaphas was involved in Jesus' arrest and execution.

Was Caiaphas Involved in Jesus' Death?

First, though, the most basic question needs to be addressed: Can we be absolutely sure that Caiaphas *was* involved in Jesus' death? Since Jesus died on a Roman cross, ought we not to conclude that there was no Jewish involvement and that Jesus went to his death purely on the orders of Pontius Pilate? Two pieces of evidence, however, go against this conclusion: (1) the tradition underlying the Gospels, and (2) a passage in Josephus commonly known as the *Testimonium Flavianum*.

1. The Tradition Underlying the Gospels

In their present form, the Gospel Passion Narratives are full of differences in detail: they disagree over the details of Jesus' arrest, over whether Jesus had a "formal" Jewish trial, and over what went on in the hearing before Pilate. And yet, for all their differences, it is striking that the same general sequence of events underlies all four accounts: Jesus (alone) is arrested in Gethsemane, brought before Caiaphas and other Jewish religious leaders, handed over to Pilate, and crucified on a charge of claiming to be the "king of the Jews." This sequence has convinced most scholars that behind the Gospels is a very early historical tradition, a tradition that outlined the events of Jesus' last few hours.[5]

One notable exception to this view is J. D. Crossan, emeritus professor at DePaul University.[6] Crossan puts a great deal of store on the flight of Jesus' disciples after his arrest (Mark 14:50) and concludes that none of his followers knew any of the details of Jesus' last few hours.[7] As the months and years passed, Christian scribes reflecting on Jesus' death and resurrection began to search through their own (Jewish) Scriptures, weaving together texts and allusions to create stories. Gradually these stories were put together to form what we now refer to as the "Passion Narratives."[8] For Crossan, then, there is no core of solid history behind the Gospel passion accounts; they are nothing more than "prophecy historicized."

It is fair to say that Crossan's views have not fared well with the majority of scholars.[9] It is true that Jesus' inner group of twelve disciples desert him in Mark's Gospel, but this flight is part of Mark's stark picture, in which everyone abandons Jesus as he makes his lonely way to the cross—even, apparently, God himself (15:34). The other evangelists tone down this bleak scene. Yet, even if Mark is historically correct here, the twelve were not the only possible witnesses to Jesus' last hours. It is clear from the rest of Mark's account that there were other followers of Jesus in Jerusalem: the owner of the colt, the owner of the upper room, Simon the Pharisee, Simon of Cyrene and his sons Alexander and Rufus (whose very presence in the narrative suggests they were known to Mark's church), the women at the cross, and Joseph of Arimathea. Paul too suggests that there were already many believers in Jerusalem by the time of Jesus' death (1 Cor 15:6). Even if the twelve *did* flee in terror of their lives, it is inconceivable that men who had invested everything they had in following Jesus would not have made strenuous efforts to find out what happened to him. Even in hiding, friends and supporters would have quickly pieced together what they could of Jesus' last few hours. It seems highly probable, then, that the basic sequence of events would have been quickly established.

Between the basic historical sequence of 30 C.E. and the accounts in the Gospels, however, we have to contend with two processes: (1) scriptural reflection and (2) oral transmission.

1. Crossan is right to underline the importance of *scriptural reflection* in the Passion Narratives (though few would go as far as he does). It is clear from Paul's letters that Jesus' death and resurrection were the central elements of Christian preaching from very early on; and yet the very fact that Jesus came to such a shameful end would have seemed like an insurmountable barrier to many (see 1 Cor 1:23). As the post-Easter community began to regard Jesus' death and vindication as part of God's plan for the salvation of humanity, they began to mine their Scriptures for passages that seemed appropriate. The death of the righteous sufferer of the Psalms (especially Ps 22) and Deutero-Isaiah's Suffering Servant (especially Isa 50:4–9, 52:13–53:12) were particularly apt. As the events of Jesus' last few hours were retold and reflected upon, scriptural echoes, allusions, and quotations gradually made their way into the stories. Some events in the Passion Narrative perhaps even grew out of Scripture: Jesus' silence in front of Pilate (Mark 15:5) may have been inspired by Isaiah 53:7, the casting of lots for his clothes (Mark 15:24) by Psalm 22:18, and the darkness at noon by Amos 8:9. The point of these details was to show that Jesus' death was *in accordance with Scripture* and so part of God's plan.

2. These passion traditions would have circulated *orally* for a long time. When they were first written down is impossible to say. Perhaps it was Mark; more likely, he drew on an existing written account. We can see the process of creative interpretation still going on in the way Matthew and Luke develop Mark (which was not yet regarded as "Scripture"). Each evangelist felt free to adapt Mark's material as he presented his own particular view of the life, death, and significance of Jesus.[10] The Gospels, then, contain a core of historical fact, but in their present

form they are theological reflections on Jesus' passion, seen through the lens of Old Testament prophecy.

How much, then, can we say about the hearing before Caiaphas and other Jewish religious leaders? When we look at the trial narratives in each Gospel, it is immediately apparent that there are many discrepancies in detail. In the Synoptic Gospels Jesus is arrested by Jews; in John, Roman troops are also involved. Mark and Matthew have a nighttime meeting of the whole council; Luke presents an informal meeting the following morning; and John (who has already described a meeting of the council in chapter 11) has only a brief interrogation, first in front of Annas, then Caiaphas. In Mark and Matthew the Jewish trial revolves around Jesus' words against the temple and his "messiahship"; in Luke it concerns only his "messiahship"; and in John only Jesus' teaching is discussed. In Mark and Matthew, Jesus is condemned for blasphemy; Luke does not give a specific charge in the Jewish trial; and in John, it is because Caiaphas fears Rome will intervene and destroy the temple. Quite clearly they cannot all be historically accurate. If Mark had reasonably good historical information, why did Matthew and Luke alter Mark's account? Did they each think (in completely different ways!) that they had more reliable sources? And why is John so different? The simplest explanation is that the evangelists knew the general sequence of events—the arrest, Jewish custody, Roman custody—but not what actually happened at each stage. It is also quite probable that the evangelists were primarily interested not in transmitting historical data in the manner of a modern historian, but rather in the theological significance of events.

The following reconstruction will accept the reliability of the broad outline of the Gospels, but not the details of each scene (the meeting of the whole council, the false witnesses, the charge of blasphemy, and the high priest's rending of his garments). We shall see later that these "details" are part of the theological constructs of the evangelists.

2. The Testimonium Flavianum

Our second piece of evidence for Caiaphas's involvement in Jesus' death is a famous passage in Josephus, known as the *Testimonium Flavianum*. The passage occurs toward the end of Josephus's *Antiquities of the Jews*, in the middle of a series of upheavals in the time of Pontius Pilate:

> About this time there lived Jesus, a wise man, *if indeed one ought to call him a man*. For he was one who wrought surprising feats and was a teacher of such people as accept the truth gladly. He won over many Jews and many of the Greeks. *He was the Messiah.* When Pilate, upon hearing him accused by men of the highest standing amongst us, had condemned him to be crucified, those who had in the first place come to love him did not give up their affection for him. *On the third day he appeared to them restored to life, for the prophets of God had prophesied these and countless other marvellous things about him.* And the tribe of the Christians, so called after him, has still to this day not disappeared. (*Antiquities* 18.63–64)[11]

The passage as it now stands presents a number of obvious difficulties. Josephus, as a loyal and devoted Jew, could hardly have referred to Jesus as "the Messiah" (or "Christ"); nor is it likely that he would question whether it was proper to call Jesus a man; or that he would happily declare that Jesus appeared to his disciples again on the third day "restored to life"! Quite clearly the passage in its present state has been worked over by Christian editors or scribes. This in itself is not unduly surprising. Although he celebrated Israel's long and glorious history, Josephus's works were not popular with his fellow Jews (who, due to his less than creditable military exploits, regarded him as a traitor). His works were preserved instead by Christians, who regarded his detailed description of the siege and fall of Jerusalem as a sign of God's wrath on Israel for its rejection of Jesus.

Not surprisingly, a large amount of scholarly attention has been devoted to this paragraph. While some earlier scholars tended to regard the entire paragraph as a forgery, recent scholarship has tended toward the view that Josephus did write something about Jesus, which was then tampered with by Christian copyists.[12] But what did Josephus write? If the three problematic phrases in italics are removed, we are left with a fairly neutral, detached reference. The paragraph flows well and there is nothing un-Josephan about the language and style. Removing the italicized sentences, then, may take us back fairly closely to what Josephus wrote:

> About this time there lived Jesus, a wise man. For he was one who wrought surprising feats and was a teacher of such people as accept the truth gladly. He won over many Jews and many of the Greeks. When Pilate, upon hearing him accused by men of the highest standing amongst us, had condemned him to be crucified, those who had in the first place come to love him did not give up their affection for him. And the tribe of the Christians, so called after him, has still to this day not disappeared.

What makes this passage particularly important is that it seems to have come from *outsiders*. The language is not typically Christian: Christians would not refer to Jesus as a "wise man," nor would they dream of referring to themselves as people who "accept the truth gladly" or as a "tribe" (*phylon*). Josephus's testimony, then, does not seem to be a secondhand reworking of the Gospels but in all probability comes from Jewish circles. But where did he get his information? While he was a young man in Palestine? Or when he visited Rome as part of an embassy in 64—the same year that saw Nero's brutal persecution of Christians? Or was it from his friend the Jewish King Agrippa II (before whom Paul was tried)? Or from the synagogues in Rome? Josephus's information could have come from any of these sources, and his brief note, therefore, may well preserve an independent and historically important strand of tradition.

What does Josephus tell us about Jewish involvement in Jesus' death? Only one sentence is relevant: "when Pilate, *upon hearing him accused by men of the highest standing amongst us,* had condemned him to be crucified . . ." Although the authenticity of this phrase has occasionally been challenged, the measured way in which the text refers to Jewish leaders contrasts strongly with later Christian references (which were all too often highly negative) and suggests that the text is original.[13] Unfortunately, Josephus's account is tantalizingly brief. Who are the "leading men" (*ton proton andron* in Greek)? Josephus uses this phrase often to refer to "men of the highest standing" or "influential persons."[14] They are clearly Jewish leaders and could easily be Caiaphas and his high priestly colleagues.

The text suggests a two-stage trial: the charges against Jesus were laid in front of Pilate by Jewish notables, but it was the Roman governor who pronounced the death sentence. We are not told why Jesus was killed (in contrast to John the Baptist in *Antiq* 18.117–19). Christian editors would have been capable of deleting offensive material as well as adding their own touches, and it is possible that the original had the charge, which was then deleted. It is equally possible, however, that Josephus felt no need to go into details. We in the twenty-first century might see the life and death of Jesus as crucial to world history. Josephus, writing in late first-century Rome, did not. Jesus, as far as he was concerned, deserved a short paragraph, but no more.

Taken together, the underlying narrative of the Gospels and the account of Josephus suggest that Jesus was handed over to Pilate at the instigation of leading members of the Jerusalem priesthood. Reconstructions (such as that by Israeli Supreme Court judge Haim Cohn) that attempt to remove the Jewish leaders from *any* complicity in Jesus' death are difficult to substantiate.[15] The question confronting us now is: Why? What was it about Jesus that made the chief priests want him out of the way?

Political Expediency?

One possible explanation is that the Jewish chief priests handed Jesus over not because they had any particular problem with him, but out of political expediency. This is the argument put forward by Paula Fredriksen in her *Jesus of Nazareth, King of the Jews* (1999). Fredriksen believes that there was no fundamental clash between Jesus and the Jewish religious leaders: Jesus kept the purity laws and held both the temple and the priesthood in high regard. The chief priests, for their part, knew that Jesus considered himself a prophet and that he proclaimed the imminent arrival of God's kingdom, but they did not see him as a threat either to their own position or to the stability of the city.

The event that led to Jesus' death, Fredriksen believes, was his triumphal entry into Jerusalem. Jesus had predicted that this would be the last Passover, that very soon his followers would finally see the dawn of the kingdom of God. Crowds of excited pilgrims flocked to welcome him into the city and, misunderstanding both Jesus and his message, hailed him as their Messiah, noisily proclaiming the coming kingdom throughout the city. Pilate heard of the situation but did nothing, knowing that Jesus himself was harmless. But the excitement grew, and the crowds became ever more restive and excitable, a fact that began to alarm the chief priests. They knew the overexuberant crowds had misinterpreted Jesus' message and in ordinary circumstances would not have intervened. But the crowded city was highly volatile and might erupt into sedition at any moment—for which Pilate might well hold the chief priests themselves responsible. Their only course of action was to have Jesus arrested. Jesus' death, then, resulted from a combination of misunderstanding (by the pilgrims) and political expediency (on the part of the chief priests and Pilate).[16]

Treated in isolation, Fredriksen's reconstruction is plausible. However, the problem with a theory that refuses to see *any* conflict between Jesus and Jewish leaders is that it becomes very difficult to understand why soon after his death the leaders of the early church continued to be engaged in a certain amount of controversy with the religious authorities. I shall argue in chapter 8 that this controversy was not as heated as Acts would have us believe; yet even so, the chief priests occasionally arrested the leading apostles, and doctrinal disputes erupted in certain synagogues. Would such events be likely if Jesus had met his death as a result of nothing more than political expediency?

In the light of these considerations, the majority of scholars think that there *was* a specific conflict between Jesus and the Jewish religious authorities, and that this conflict came to a head in Jesus' last week. More specifically, this conflict appears to have been over Jesus' attitude towards the temple and manifested itself in his actions in the temple shortly before his death. In fact, Mark's Gospel suggests that it was specifically Jesus' activities in the temple that led directly to the high priest's decision to arrest Jesus and to have him executed (Mark 11:18).[17] But what, exactly, did Jesus *do* in the temple? And, more importantly, what was the *significance* of his actions?

7

Execution of a Galilean
Holy Man

A Disturbance in the Temple

Although Jesus' actions in the temple are described somewhat differently by the four evangelists, most scholars take our earliest account, that of Mark, as the most historically plausible (Mark 11:15–18). According to this Gospel, Jesus entered the temple directly after his triumphal entry into Jerusalem, looked around, and left with his disciples to spend the night in Bethany. The following day, he came back to Jerusalem and entered the temple once again. This time he began to drive out those who sold or bought in the temple, overturned the tables of the money changers, upset the seats of the pigeon sellers, and prevented anyone from carrying anything through the temple. Jesus accompanied his actions with words drawn from Isaiah 56:7 and Jeremiah 7:11: "Is it not written, 'My house shall be called a house of prayer for all the nations'? But you have made it a den of robbers." On hearing this, Mark claims, the chief priests and scribes sought to kill him.[1]

One aspect that is not immediately apparent from Mark's account is the *scale* of the incident. We often imagine that Jesus' actions created a major disturbance, stopping trade in the temple for some time. But two features count against this.

First, the temple court was so huge—the size of twelve football stadia—that it would take a sizable protest before anyone would notice what was going on.[2] The actions of one man would probably have been noticed only by those immediately surrounding him. Second, Jesus was not arrested by either the Levitical police on duty throughout the whole temple complex or by the Roman soldiers posted above the temple porticoes. This suggests a relatively small incident, one that presumably was over almost as soon as it had begun. Jesus' action, then, was not in any sense an occupation—still less a failed political coup, as S. G. F. Brandon famously argued—or even a serious attempt to disrupt cultic activities.[3] It was, instead, meant to be understood in *symbolic* terms.

But what did Jesus' actions symbolize? How would a first-century Jewish observer have understood them? We can come to an answer here by considering a number of related issues: (1) Jesus' attitude towards the temple generally, (2) the parallels between Jesus and the Old Testament prophets, and (3) Jesus' prophecies of the temple's destruction.

1. There is no indication in any of the Gospels that Jesus shunned the temple and its cult or held them in low esteem. Like thousands of other Jews, he made his way to the Jerusalem temple for Passover (as, in John's Gospel, he had done several times before). He seems to have had every intention of fulfilling the rituals associated with the feast, and even made preparations to eat the paschal meal with his disciples (Mark 14:12–16).[4] His wish that the temple be a "house of prayer" (Mark 11:17) is not a criticism of the sacrificial system, but a common Jewish term that simply highlights one of the other functions of the temple. Later, after Jesus' death, his followers continued to worship in the temple with no indication that their leader had opposed the institution.[5] It seems, then, that for Jesus (as for most first-century Jews), the temple was an essential, God-given part of Jewish religious life.

It is also fairly safe to presume that Jesus would have seen nothing improper in the presence of the money changers and pigeon sellers in the outer court of the temple. The money changers traditionally set up their stalls at Passover time and would have been busily changing ordinary currency into the Tyrian shekels required for the annual temple tax (a tax demanded by God and enshrined in the sacred law).[6] The pigeon sellers would have been selling pure and unblemished birds for use in personal sacrifices; presumably people could have bought their sacrificial victims elsewhere, but by buying them in the temple precincts people could be sure of the purity of the birds. To claim, as a number of scholars still do, that Jesus' demonstration was an expression of disgust at improper commercial activity in the house of God is to read modern notions of the proper activities of a "religious institution" into the temple cult.[7] The money changers and pigeon sellers were necessary parts of the temple's proper function: there is no evidence that anyone was doing anything improper. Nor is there any indication that corruption was particularly rife amongst the temple traders or that Caiaphas and his family held some kind of "monopoly" on these activities.[8]

2. What then did Jesus' outburst symbolize? The image his actions would most immediately have evoked in his first-century onlookers would have been that of the Old Testament prophets—Isaiah, Hosea, and, particularly, Jeremiah. Each of these not only spoke in the name of God but also at times expressed their message through symbolic actions.[9] Furthermore, each of these prophets had occasion to speak out against the temple. They were not against sacrifices or the celebration of festivals, but they passionately believed that *these were not the most important things*. What God really wanted, they argued, was obedience, kindness, morality, and justice. Sacrifices were all very well, but no amount of purification could atone for an unjust and immoral society.[10]

Read against this background, Jesus' prophetic actions begin to make some sense. His mission in Galilee had been directed toward those at the receiving end of societies' injustices: those who were blind, lame, diseased, widowed, orphaned, penniless, and outcast. Such people, he promised, would be the first to enter the kingdom of God. Yet the social evils that struck Jesus so forcefully in the Galilean villages must have paled into insignificance compared to those of Jerusalem. Perhaps, as Jesus made his way through the capital city, he was all too painfully aware that most people had little time or inclination to help their neighbors, still less to care for the needy and distressed, or to provide for the beggars who flocked to the city in their hundreds. The Jerusalemites, as far as Jesus was concerned, were far from God's kingdom.

Things came to a head when Jesus entered the temple. Perhaps he was struck by the elaborate preparations for the Passover, a religiosity that contrasted strongly with what he saw as the ugliness of society at large. Perhaps he felt a sense of frustration that the people thought they were honoring God through their sacrifices, when what God really wanted was mercy and charity. Through their injustices, the people had made God's holy house no more than a "den of thieves." There would undoubtedly have been much in Jesus' critique with which Caiaphas would have agreed. The priestly leaders of Israel would also have called for righteousness and justice, and encouraged compassion among the people. But there was perhaps a difference of emphasis, a prophetic versus a priestly understanding of what was important. More than anyone else, the priests encouraged the people to think that the smooth running of the temple was an indication of God's presence and guaranteed the nation's security.[11] Like the prophet Jeremiah before him, however, Jesus passionately believed that this was not the case.[12] What the people could not see was that God was even now preparing to intervene in human affairs, to visit his people with judgment, and to establish his kingdom on earth.

What, then, did his activities symbolize? It is noteworthy that Jesus' outburst encompassed a wide range of temple activity, a microcosm of everything that went on in the holy place. Without the buying and selling of pigeons, there could be no individual sacrifice; without the annual tax, there could be no communal offerings; and without priests and Levites moving from one court to another, the vast machinery of the temple would grind to a halt. Whether his actions were premeditated or a spontaneous outburst is impossible to know, but their meaning must have been all too clear to his audience. His actions symbolically stopped the temple's functioning—if only for a moment—and powerfully symbolized its end.

3. If this was indeed the meaning of Jesus' sign, we should expect to find indications elsewhere in the Gospel record that Jesus predicted the end of the temple. In fact, a number of his sayings and actions do point this way: "Not one stone will be left here upon another; all will be thrown down" (Mark 13:2); "I will destroy this temple that is made with hands" (Mark 14:58);[13] the cursing of the fig tree, which, in Mark's presentation, frames the temple incident and symbolizes the destruction of the temple (Mark 11:12–14, 20–21); and, perhaps, "I shall destroy (this) house and no one will be able to build it" (*Gos. Thom.* 71). It seems highly likely, then, that Jesus expected the temple to be destroyed, perhaps as a vital first step in the establishment of God's kingdom. It was not that Jesus was *against* the temple or its cult, but that in the kingdom of God it would be transcended; there would be no further need for an earthly temple. Drawing on Jewish apocalyptic hopes, he probably imagined that the current temple would, in some way, be replaced by a perfect, eschatological temple, a temple of the messianic age.[14] It seems more than likely too that Jesus saw himself as God's agent, not only announcing the temple's destruction but in some ways bringing it about.

Jesus' actions, then, were a protest at what he saw as the injustices of Jerusalem, a lament that the people were far from God's kingdom, and a prophetic announcement that God was even now preparing to destroy the temple and to inaugurate God's kingdom. Such a message would have shocked and even scandalized many who heard it.[15] Our question now is, Why was this so offensive to Caiaphas and his colleagues that they wanted to have Jesus killed?

The Decision to Put Jesus to Death

Prophesying the destruction of the temple could get a person into serious trouble. Several centuries earlier, the prophet Jeremiah was threatened with death for speaking against the temple (Jer 26:1–15, 38:1–5). Four years before the Jewish revolt, a peasant named Jesus ben Ananias who was in Jerusalem for the autumn Feast of Tabernacles began the following lament:

> A voice from the east,
> A voice from the west,
> A voice from the four winds;
> A voice against the sanctuary,
> A voice against the bridegroom and the bride,
> A voice against all the people.

When he refused to be quiet, the leading Jews handed him over to the Roman governor, Albinus, who concluded that Jesus was a madman and had him scourged and released. Jesus continued his mournful dirge until he was hit by a stone hurled from the Roman camp, seven years and five months after he had begun—and only a few months short of seeing his prophecy against the temple come true in 70 C.E.[16]

Both Jeremiah and Jesus ben Ananias were *threatened* with death, but neither one was, in the end, executed. What was different about Jesus of Nazareth? Three features would have made him much more dangerous from Caiaphas's point of view. First, unlike Jeremiah and Jesus ben Ananias, he had a group of followers, some of whom had followed him from Galilee. Even if Jesus himself posed little threat, there was no telling what trouble his followers could stir up in the crowded city at Passover. Second, unlike Jesus ben Ananias, who only *spoke* against the temple, Jesus of Nazareth performed a symbolic action in the temple itself. Once words translated themselves into actions, the priestly aristocracy was bound to take more notice. Third, and perhaps most importantly, while both Jeremiah and Jesus ben Ananias predicted that God would destroy the temple through foreign adversaries (the Babylonians and Romans respectively), neither man fulfilled any role himself except that of prophet. Jesus of Nazareth, however, does seem to have spoken of his own role in the temple's destruction, a role that could only have been understood by his followers as messianic.

These three differences meant that Jesus of Nazareth was a much greater worry to the Jewish leaders than Jesus ben Ananias would be to their successors three decades later, and would quite probably have been enough to seal Jesus' fate. But there may have been something even more disturbing about Jesus and his message, something linked to his concept of the renewed temple.

It is remarkable that our earliest strands of tradition (some dating to before the fall of the temple) refer to the *Christian community* as if it were a temple. Already in the mid-50s C.E., Paul tells the Corinthians that they are God's temple—the place where God's Spirit dwells (1 Cor 3:16–17) and "the temple of the living God" (2 Cor 6:16)—and refers to the leaders of the Jerusalem church as "pillars" (Gal 2:9), a metaphor that fits in well with the image of the Christian community as a spiritual temple. Quite possibly this concept goes back to Jesus himself: it may lie behind the reference to a temple "not made with hands" in Mark 14:58, and Jesus' description of himself as the "cornerstone" in Matthew 21:42. Jesus was not opposed to the Jerusalem temple while it still stood, but saw that in the coming kingdom of God there would be no need for an earthly temple: those who belonged to the kingdom would permanently enjoy God's presence, obtain forgiveness for their sins, and receive assurance of God's blessings. Jesus expected God to break into human affairs very soon, but while they waited he and his followers may well have thought of their own movement as the embryonic form of the kingdom, and perhaps, in a sense, as a new, spiritual temple.[17]

If Jesus and his followers did conceive of their movement as a "new temple," they would not have been unique in first-century Palestine. We have already seen that the Qumran sectarians (and perhaps too some of the desert prophets) claimed that their own movement was a "new temple," a new center of holiness (pp. 48–49). Jesus, however, was significantly different. He brought his teaching into the temple itself, prophesied its destruction, and implied that a physical building would be rendered unnecessary in God's kingdom. And he did all this at the busiest and most potentially turbulent time of the year: Passover. Quite clearly, as far as Caiaphas was concerned, Jesus had to be eliminated, and quickly.

There is no need to assign cynical motives to Caiaphas. His whole upbringing would have told him that the temple had to be protected at all costs. He had seen with his own eyes what happened when Rome was provoked; and the memory of the burning temple porticoes in 4 B.C.E. was perhaps still all too vivid. Jesus was very different from the kingly pretenders who arose after Herod's death, but his movement was no less dangerous politically.[18] At the very least, he and his followers might disrupt the festival; at worst, he could bring about Roman intervention and pollution of the holy place. Caiaphas probably genuinely believed that in doing away with Jesus he was acting for the good of the nation. What was the life of a deluded peasant when the house of God was at stake?

Besides, Jesus was uneducated; he was not a priest, he claimed no learning in the law, and he was not part of the religious establishment. What credentials did he have for claiming to speak for God? How could he act with messianic authority over the temple? Would Caiaphas, with his high priestly lineage and all the benefits of the best education Jerusalem could offer, pay much attention to such a man? He and his Sadducean colleagues doubtless had their own ideas of what Israel's destiny would hold. Perhaps, as J. P. Meier suggests, they:

> cultivated an eschatological hope for the exaltation of Mount Zion in the last days . . . all the gentiles would come bearing gifts to the Temple, as indeed some gentiles already did in the first century A.D. A Davidic or Hasmonaean king could have been included in this scenario, but the priestly and lay aristocracy may have preferred to dispense with that particular hope.[19]

There was no room in such a view for the destruction of the temple and its replacement by a movement started by a Galilean peasant messiah. The idea would have been utterly ridiculous. If Caiaphas did spend more than a moment considering Jesus' message, it would only have been to pour scorn on it.

Quite clearly, as far as Caiaphas was concerned, Jesus was fundamentally misguided. Perhaps Caiaphas regarded Jesus' words and actions against the temple as blasphemous, though, as we shall see, the Gospels are probably anachronistic at this point (see below, p. 107). At any rate, there were two clear charges from the Jewish law that could be brought against him: leading Israel astray (Deut 13) and being a false prophet (Deut 18).[20] The penalty for both was death.

Whether Jewish courts had the power of capital punishment under Roman rule is a hotly debated issue.[21] While it is quite possible that the high priest retained some jurisdiction over religious matters, it might have seemed advisable to hand this particular prisoner over to Rome as a potential revolutionary, an aspiring "king of the Jews." Caiaphas and his colleagues were busy with preparations for the festival and may have been quite happy for Pilate to do their dirty work for them. Such a move might perhaps store up goodwill with the governor and could be useful at a later date.[22] Pilate had perhaps recently arrived in the city with a small body of troops, on the lookout for any insurrectionary activity. It would not have taken much persuasion to convince him to execute Jesus— anyone who worried the chief priests was a worry to him. Besides, if reports of Jesus' jubilant entry into the city had reached his ears, the governor may have been watching him already.

Arrest and Interrogation

All four Gospels suggest that the Jewish leaders called a meeting without Jesus some time before his arrest. Mark places it two days before the feast and gives it the air of a preliminary meeting (Mark 14:2); Matthew makes it more formal (Matt 26:3–5); and Luke gives no time indication (Luke 22:1–2). John 11:47–53, however, presents a formal meeting some time between the feast of Hannukah in December (10:22) and the Passover (11:55). The major difficulty is over the *timing* of this meeting: did the Jewish leaders gather just before the feast (as the Synoptics suggest) or several weeks earlier (as John implies)?

The difference here, however, may not be as significant as it first appears. Mark has telescoped events in Jerusalem into only a few days, while John has a fondness for placing events from Jesus' passion earlier in his story (for example, the incident in the temple is in chapter 2, and John's only eucharistic language is in chapter 6). If Jesus' demonstration in the temple took place soon after his arrival in the city (as the Synoptics suggest), there would still have been some time before the feast. Caiaphas probably called his priestly colleagues together as soon as he heard about Jesus' demonstration and decided at that first meeting that Jesus had to be eliminated.[23] Someone was presumably elected to take the matter to Pilate and enlist his support. Perhaps too the priests discussed the possibility of persuading one of Jesus' followers to betray him, and made preliminary arrangements with the temple police, perhaps under the leadership of the captain of the temple, so that, when an opportunity presented itself, Jesus' apprehension was swift and without problems. [24]

When did Jesus' arrest take place? This question is complicated by a discrepancy in the Gospels. Mark (followed by Matthew and Luke) suggests that it occurred on the day of the Passover, after Jesus had eaten the Passover meal with his disciples. John, however, suggests that it occurred a day earlier (and that Jesus died on the day of preparation—at precisely the time when the lambs were being slaughtered in the temple). Scholars have long debated the merits of each of these dates.[25] Is Mark correct? In which case, why were the chief priests holding a trial when they should have been celebrating the Passover at home with their families? Or is John correct? In which case, why did the chief priests hand Jesus over to Pilate at the very hour when their presence in the temple was most required? Both accounts are clearly theological: for Mark, the Christian Eucharist is the new Passover meal; for John, Jesus dies in place of the paschal lamb.[26] Both accounts, in their different ways, want to show Christian symbols as the replacement of Jewish ones; to show, in effect, that God's promises to

Israel are now fulfilled in the Christian movement. Both dates expressed a theological truth as the evangelists saw it, but in all probability neither dating is historically accurate.

The earliest Christian traditions probably passed on the basic fact that Jesus was arrested "around the time of" the Passover. In fact, some early Christian writings maintain that Jesus was arrested on the Tuesday evening.[27] It would not have taken long for popular religious memory to transform a death "around the time of" Passover to a death "at" Passover. Speculations on the parallels between Jesus' death and the significance of the feast would soon have produced at least two different traditions: one that associated the Christian meal inaugurated by Jesus with the Passover seder (Mark) and one that associated Jesus' death with that of the paschal lamb (John). Such theological conflations of time are not at all uncommon or unexpected. In a similar vein, some early church fathers were quite happy to regard the destruction of the temple as God's vengeance on the Jewish people for the death of Christ, even though the two events were separated by roughly forty years![28] Likewise, medieval Jews had no difficulties in dating the end of Jewish kingship to the destruction of the temple, even though the last king (Agrippa II) died a generation after the destruction of the temple![29] And in our own times we may speak of someone dying "at Christmas" without specifically meaning that the person died on December 25; somehow, though, the death is made more poignant by reference to a festival celebrating birth, light, and life. Religious memory has never confined itself to the straitjacket of precise historical remembrance but has always freely made connections in pursuit of deeper, theological truth.

The Gospel traditions, then, are no help in precisely dating Jesus' arrest. The historical likelihood, though, is that Jesus was arrested some time before the feast. Caiaphas and his colleagues probably arranged things so that their duties in the temple were not disrupted. Their request may also have carried more weight with the governor before the feast. They could stress the danger to public order Jesus might present if he were allowed to preach openly. Once the feast was underway and was progressing without incident, any impetus was lost. Although certainty is impossible, the likeliest reconstruction is that Caiaphas and his high priestly colleagues had Jesus arrested and brought to Caiaphas's house for questioning some days before the commencement of the festival.

What happened next is even more speculative. We shall see later that Mark's nighttime court scene is highly theological and cannot be taken as reliable history. A growing number of scholars regard John's narrative at this point as the most historically plausible.[30] That is not to say that John has drawn from a better historical tradition, but that he seems to have a better grasp of the realities of first-century Judea and that the historical sequence of events was something like the sequence he presents. John suggests that, after Jesus' arrest, both Annas and Caiaphas interrogated him. This is historically quite plausible; we know of very few instances where leading priests voluntarily handed another Jew over to Rome. It was not at all a common occurrence, and the two most important men in the temple hierarchy presumably wanted to satisfy themselves that Jesus was indeed as dangerous as they believed.

An odd feature of the Gospel narratives is the prominence given to Annas. Luke seems to think that Annas is the high priest, while John's only interrogation at this point takes place before Annas.[31] Scholars often dismiss this, suggesting that the Gospel writers were a little confused at this point. But two things need to be said. First, Annas was the head of the dynasty as a whole and, even though he was no longer high priest, would still have exerted a great deal of influence. Second, it is possible that Annas *did* play a significant role in the proceedings. Both men together presumably made the decision to do away with Jesus, but Caiaphas had Passover duties and needed to maintain his purity. It would make more sense if, after the decision was made, Annas was the one who took charge. Perhaps he enlisted Pilate's support in the first place, played the leading role in Jesus' brief interrogation, and handed the prisoner over to Rome.

Pilate, perhaps after a brief interrogation, sent Jesus to the cross.[32] Anyone claiming any kind of kingship was a potential threat to security in the crowded city. He does not seem to have been interested in rounding up Jesus' followers, perhaps because the movement, like that of John the Baptist, clearly centered on one man. Pilate presumably thought that once the leader had been executed, the messianic fervor associated with him would calm down. By the time Caiaphas and his family gathered for their Passover meal that year, Jesus was already in his grave. The threat to the temple had been removed, and the danger of unrest had—apparently—passed.

8

Caiaphas and the Earliest Christians

Jesus had been executed, his followers had gone into hiding, and the Passover pilgrims were beginning to disperse. Pilate and his entourage were winding up their affairs in Jerusalem, ready—and thankful—to be leaving a city where they were not welcome, and looking forward to their return to airy, Gentile Caesarea. Caiaphas and his colleagues probably congratulated themselves on their swift and adroit handling of a potentially difficult affair. They would have let it be known throughout the city that the prisoner had been condemned as a false prophet and a deceiver of the people. And, as far as many of Jesus' followers were concerned, that would have ended the matter. They had hoped that Jesus would be the one to redeem Israel, but his rejection by the nation's leaders and his deeply shameful death (Deut 21:22–23) convinced them that this could not be the case. The messianic fervor that seemed so dangerous before the festival had now all but abated, and the city was beginning to return to normality.

It would not have been long, however, before the name of Jesus of Nazareth was once more brought to the high priest's attention. According to Acts, Jesus' followers publicly proclaimed his resurrection at the feast of Pentecost, fifty days after Passover, and three thousand people were immediately baptized (2:1–47). Even allowing for some exaggeration in Luke's report, the news would have quickly spread throughout Jerusalem. Soon, one of Caiaphas's informers and retainers may have hurried to the high priest's house and told him of the latest news in the city. How did Caiaphas react? With scorn? With irritation? With fear? With dread? According to Acts, he and his colleagues had but one aim: to destroy the new movement. They are behind two formal trials of apostles (4:1–22, 5:17–40), the stoning of Stephen (6:8–7:60), and the outbreak of persecution (8:1b), and authorize Paul's persecuting activities in Damascus. In this chapter, we shall examine each of these incidents in turn, draw attention to Luke's theological tendencies, and examine whether the high priest and his family were really as antagonistic towards Jesus' followers as Luke (and many modern scholars) would have us believe.[1]

Trials of Apostles

Although originally a Galilean movement, Jesus' followers very quickly organized themselves under the leadership of the twelve apostles in Jerusalem.[2] This was not at all a surprising development: most Jews believed that their holy city was the center of the world, that the Jerusalem temple was the point where heaven and earth met, and that it would be here, at the close of the age, that God would gather his people.[3] What better place could there be, then, to await Christ's imminent return? And, while they waited, the continual flow of pilgrims and other visitors to the city meant that there was an abundant source of potential converts to the new way.

According to Acts, conflict soon broke out at the highest levels: between the leaders of the new movement and the high priests and representatives of Israel. In Acts 4, Peter and John are arrested while they preach and heal in the temple. The following day they are brought before a Jewish council comprised of rulers, elders, scribes, and the high priestly family, and after some debate they are released with a caution. In the following chapter, all the disciples are arrested, imprisoned, and miraculously released. Next day, the disciples are rearrested, brought before "the council and all the senate of Israel" and, after some debate, are flogged and sent away (5:17–42). The narrative suggests continual tension, with hostilities instigated by the highest Jewish authorities and cases heard before official representatives of the nation.

We need to treat Luke's narrative, however, with some caution. We shall see in part 2 that the author of Luke–Acts is not interested in historical details for their own sake but has carefully adapted and reworked historical traditions so that they conform to his theological outlook and address the needs of his readers.[4] At least four theological interests dominate Acts 4–5. First is the author's fondness for setting debates in formal, courtroom settings (the word *synedrion*, council, is used fourteen times in Acts). He presents this early history as a struggle for the hearts of the Jewish people: it is the disciples (who are clearly under divine protection) versus the high priests (who, for Luke, are opposed to God).[5] The ordinary people (and, of course, Luke's readers) have to choose between the two. Second, Luke presents an escalation of conflict in these early chapters: initially controversy involves only *two* disciples, then *all* the disciples, then all the "church in Jerusalem" (8:1). Similarly, the first trial ends with a warning, the next with a beating; Stephen is stoned (7:58–60); and finally opposition broadens into general persecution (8:1–3). Third, Luke highlights the boldness of the apostles in the face of adversity. Their demeanor shows his readers the truth of Jesus' prediction in Luke 21:12–15, that when they were delivered up to synagogues and prisons, Jesus himself would give them "words and a wisdom that none of (their) opponents (would) be able to withstand or contradict" (21:15).[6] Finally, and most importantly of all, Luke shows that no one can stop the growth of the new movement, since God is behind it (5:39). In fact, measures taken against the church always backfire and lead to its further miraculous growth (4:4). If Luke were writing for a community which had recently experienced persecution, as some scholars believe, his theological emphases would have been particularly appropriate and welcome.[7]

Luke's theology, then, may well account for the courtroom settings in Acts 4–5, the escalation of conflict, the boldness of the disciples, and the recurring chorus that the church's growth is unstoppable. These overriding theological interests mean that the new movement's adversaries become nothing more than stereotypical opponents or caricatures; they cannot discern what is truly from God and so are no longer capable of leading the people. It is impossible, then, to infer anything about their historical motives or actions. As if things were not difficult enough, further reasons for doubting the historical accuracy of Acts 4–5 stem from the narratives themselves. There are internal inconsistencies within the first account;[8] the second seems to be a doublet of the first scene;[9] and the language throughout is Lukan.[10] All this suggests that, while Luke is undoubtedly dependent upon genuine sources and traditions, he has reworked his material, perhaps to a considerable degree.

Is there, then, any hope of reconstructing the events behind Acts 4–5? One element in all of this may well go back to solid historical tradition, and that is the identity of the disciple's opponents. We need to look more carefully at Luke's description of them in 4:5–6: "The next day their rulers, elders, and scribes assembled in Jerusalem, with Annas the high priest, Caiaphas, John [Jonathan], and Alexander, and all who were of the high-priestly family." There is some redundancy here: the high priestly family were probably all included by the phrase "rulers, elders, and scribes," yet Luke painstakingly mentions each individually. Annas is named first and referred to as "high priest" (presumably a reflection of his prestige),[11] then Caiaphas (without reference to his office), then Jonathan (who succeeded Caiaphas and was probably captain of the temple at the time),[12] and finally Alexander (who must be another relative of Annas). In fact, as Luke emphasizes, the entire high priestly family of Annas was involved. How, then, are we to account for Luke's strange juxtaposition of the phrase "rulers, elders, and scribes" with his very specific list of chief priests? Given Luke's interest in formal, courtroom settings, the likeliest explanation is that he has added the rather vague "rulers, elders, and scribes" to a tradition that told of

disciples being brought before the high priestly family alone. This group of leading priests, then, dealt with Jesus' followers in precisely the same way that they
had done with Jesus himself.[13] Perhaps, as head of the family and retired from his
cultic activities, Annas once again took a leading role.

Our question now is, Why? What was it about the disciples that caused the
high priestly leaders to arrest them? Luke himself offers two reasons: in 4:2 he
tells us that, as Sadducees, the high priests were annoyed at the disciples' proclamation of the resurrection; and in 5:17 he claims that they acted out of jealousy.[14]
Neither, however, rings quite true. The Sadducees could hardly have arrested
everyone who openly preached resurrection, since by the first century a belief in
some kind of life after death was shared by most Jews. And Luke's claim that they
acted out of jealousy is bound up with his presentation of the miraculous growth
of the early church and the popularity of the disciples, both of which are surely
exaggerated.

What other reasons, then, might have led Caiaphas and his high priestly colleagues to take an interest in the early Christian community? Two aspects of the
new movement might well have caused tension. First, the early Christians were
engaging in vigorous missionary activity, proclaiming that the crucified Jesus had
been raised, that he was truly the messiah of Jewish expectation, and that he
would soon return in glory. Some seem to have sold their possessions as a sign of
their belief in the nearness of Christ's return (Acts 3:44–45, 4:32–5:11).[15] At certain times, perhaps particularly at festivals, apocalyptic hopes might well have got
out of control. Perhaps the excited atmosphere generated by Christians gathered
in the temple to await Christ's triumphant return (and their disappointment
when, yet again, he failed to arrive) led to minor incidents and clashes with other
pilgrims. Even if the numbers of converts to the new way were not as high as
Luke maintains, such intense eschatological excitement must have had a desta-
bilizing effect on the city and caused Caiaphas and his colleagues some concern.

Second, adherents of the new group were "breaking bread" together, sharing
their memories of Jesus, and reflecting on the meaning of his death and resurrection. The more these events were thought to have been prefigured in the Scriptures, the more Christian preaching had to represent Jesus' high priestly
opponents as ignorant of those Scriptures—as acting, in effect, not as the official
representatives of the Jewish faith, but as the enemies of God. As the months wore
on, the situation must have become ever more strained.

It would be quite understandable, then, if representatives of the twelve were
occasionally brought before Annas, Caiaphas, and their colleagues. The issues at
stake seem not to have been doctrinal: first-century Judaism embraced many different views and perspectives, and there was nothing "heretical" about earliest
Christianity (at least nothing more than any other Jewish group). Besides, Christian beliefs were themselves far from uniform at this early period. What would
have worried the chief priests was when Christian preaching stirred up trouble,
especially at festivals. They would have wanted to monitor the extent of the threat
and to make sure that nothing would attract the attention of Pilate. There was,

of course, nothing illegal or irregular about such interrogations; the high priestly leaders were merely fulfilling the role demanded by their position in the temple and status in the wider community.[16]

An interesting feature of these early clashes is that, unlike their leader, none of Jesus' closest followers lost their lives. The worst that happened was that disciples were sent away with a warning or were flogged—presumably the thirty-nine lashes that Paul later received from synagogue authorities (2 Cor 11:24). This suggests, once again, that the high priestly leaders were remarkably tolerant of the beliefs of other Jews, even criticism of themselves (see above, p. 49). It would be some years after Jesus' death before one of his followers would lose his life and this, as we shall see in the next section, had nothing to do with either Caiaphas or the family of Annas.

The Death of Stephen

Some time in the mid-30s C.E., a controversy broke out in a Jerusalem synagogue.[17] Luke sets events in the "synagogue of the Freedmen (as it was called), Cyrenians, Alexandrians, and others of those from Cilicia and Asia" (Acts 6:9).[18] What connected the people in this synagogue was the fact that they were Greek-speaking Diaspora Jews who had moved to the holy city. Some had formerly been slaves (and were now "Freedmen"); others might have been of higher status and perhaps of some wealth. Some were probably permanent residents in Jerusalem, while others were perhaps visitors. All would have read their Scriptures in Greek translation (the Septuagint), and presumably enjoyed worshiping and gathering together with people who had similar backgrounds and experiences to theirs.

One of the members of this synagogue was Stephen, a follower of Jesus and a prominent preacher and missionary.[19] According to Luke, Stephen's performance of "great wonders and signs among the people" (Acts 6:8) led to conflict with certain other members of the synagogue. When open argument failed to stop Stephen, his opponents spread rumors that he was blaspheming against Moses and God. Agitated by these claims, "the people as well as the elders and the scribes" brought Stephen before "the council" where false witnesses accused him of speaking against the temple and the law (6:12–13). The "high priest" (7:1) asked Stephen to answer the charges, a request that allowed him to launch into a long, eloquent speech, culminating in the counter-charge that the Jews had rejected their messiah. Stephen's defense so incensed his opponents that they attacked him with murderous rage and stoned him to death (6:8–7:60).[20]

Luke's account suggests that the high priest (either Caiaphas or Annas) and a formal Jewish council played a decisive part in the events which led to Stephen's death. But was this really the case? As usual, we need to exercise caution. One of the most striking features about Stephen's trial is its similarity to the trial of Jesus in Mark's Gospel. In both, we have a formal courtroom setting with elders, scribes, and a high priest. In both, we have false witnesses and charges of blasphemy and speaking against the temple. Just before Stephen dies, he sees a vision of "the Son of Man" at the "right hand of God" (7:56), a vision that clearly recalls

Jesus' prophecy to the high priest in Mark 14:62.[21] Luke's purpose here, however, is not to *parallel* the two trials, since (as we shall see in chapter 11) he abbreviates Jesus' trial in the Gospel quite considerably. Instead, the point is rather that in the same way Mark has Jesus' trial signal God's rejection of Judaism, so Luke uses Stephen's trial to signal the rejection of the people and city of Jerusalem. Until this point, Jerusalem has been the center of the Christian movement; now, with Stephen's death, the gospel will begin to move out into the Gentile world, and "the Jews" will become increasingly hostile.[22]

The important position Stephen's death occupies within Luke's narrative scheme should make us wary regarding historical events. But we do need to investigate two specific historical questions: (1) Did Stephen actually have a formal trial? (2) What was his offense?

1. Although Luke describes a solemn gathering of people, elders, and scribes, the proceedings descend into chaos: there is no verdict, no sentence; Stephen's death resembles a mob lynching rather than an official execution. Luke's reference to the high priest is also rather strange: the character is introduced abruptly in 7:1, but after his one question he disappears from the scene; furthermore, the vague and unspecified reference to "the high priest" jars oddly with the precise list of high priests in 4:6. These features suggest that the courtroom setting is largely a creation of Luke himself: the grand gathering of the council provides an appropriate context for Stephen's speech and, perhaps more importantly, emphasizes the rejection of Christianity by the Jerusalemites. If this is the case, the historical events presumably all occurred within the setting of the Greek-speaking synagogue. Christian preaching caused a dispute that got out of hand, and in the ensuing riot Stephen was stoned to death.[23]

2. But what caused the dispute? According to Luke, two points were at issue: Stephen's attitude towards the law and the temple. Yet again, some caution is needed here. Writing in the late first century, one of Luke's prime concerns within his two-volume work was to demonstrate the continuity between the Jewish Scriptures and the Christian church, and to show that through the church God's promises to Israel found their true expression. The law and the temple, of course, were the two most important institutions of Judaism, and the whole of Acts frequently demonstrates that Christianity is not hostile to either: Christians continue to hold the temple in high regard, regularly worshiping there and teaching in its outer courts, and are obedient to the law to the end.[24] It is not at all surprising, then, that in Luke's presentation the trial of the first Christian martyr revolves around these two central institutions, and that the evangelist makes it quite clear that Stephen (as a representative of Christianity in general) has spoken against neither. In fact, for Luke it is not Christians who are against the law, but their Jewish opponents (7:53). As A. Loisy put it, "The true representatives of the religion of Abraham, Moses and the prophets are not the Jews, ever stubborn and rebellious, but the Christians."[25]

Luke's narrative, then, is little help in reconstructing the nature of the dispute between Stephen and other members of his synagogue. It could have been over any number of things: his proclamation of Jesus as Messiah; his missionary zeal in the synagogue; his talk of Christ's imminent return. Or, despite Luke's denials, Stephen might have repeated Jesus' prophetic warnings that the temple was about to be destroyed. Perhaps, too, he suggested that his own community, the emerging kingdom of God, would replace the temple and that his signs and wonders were symbols of God's presence. A synagogue composed of Diaspora immigrants might well have taken particular offense at this: many would have believed strongly in God's special presence in the temple; some may have come to Jerusalem precisely because of a belief in the unique holiness of the city and its temple; and thus quite a few may have been offended by Stephen's words.[26]

We will probably never know the precise reasons behind Stephen's death. What is important for our purposes, though, is the recognition that, despite Luke's attempts to superimpose a reference to the high priest and a more formal setting on his tradition, the historical events behind Acts 6:8–7:60 were in all likelihood played out within one particular synagogue, and did not involve either Caiaphas or Annas.

Persecution (8:1b)

The result of the conflict between Stephen and the members of his synagogue was that the early church experienced its first wave of persecution: "That day a severe persecution began against the church in Jerusalem, and all except the apostles were scattered throughout the countryside of Judea and Samaria" (8:1b). Luke is keen to link this persecution with Stephen's death: he makes it clear that persecution began the very day of Stephen's death, and even delays telling us about Stephen's burial in 8:2, so that the notice about persecution follows directly on news of his death.[27] Luke does not say so explicitly, but the connection with Stephen suggests that the persecution was initiated by the highest levels of the Jewish establishment, the high priest and members of his council.

Again, there are problems with Luke's presentation. The death of Stephen represents a watershed in Acts: missionary activity will no longer be confined to Jerusalem but will spread throughout the Mediterranean world. Jesus' prophecy in 1:8b—"you will be my witnesses in Jerusalem, in all Judea and Samaria, and to the ends of the earth"—is about to be fulfilled. The attempt by the Jewish leaders to stamp out the new movement will lead directly to the Gentile mission and the spread of the gospel even to Rome. Acts 8:1b, then, has a clear literary purpose: to get the gospel out into the Roman world.[28]

If the persecution were as great as Luke suggests, however, it is very strange that the twelve apostles were able to withstand it—it would be an odd persecution that left the leaders unmolested.[29] Furthermore, it is strange that Josephus does not mention any kind of disturbance at this point; his record is relatively full for the period of Pilate's governorship (26–37 C.E.), yet nowhere is there any reference to this persecution. And would Pilate have allowed the Jewish leaders to embark on a "severe persecution" without intervening himself? It seems likely, then, that there is some exaggeration here. It is possible that tensions continued on a synagogue level, particularly within the Greek-speaking synagogues where conflict first arose. Perhaps there were further riots, and even violence, and perhaps some Christians decided it would be wise to leave the city. But a "great persecution," initiated by Caiaphas or any other member of his family, is a Lukan literary device rather than a historical reality.

Saul of Tarsus

We need to consider, finally, the man presented by Luke as the archpersecutor of the early church: Paul or, as he is known in the early chapters of Acts, Saul.

Luke introduces Saul in 7:58 and 8:1a, where we are told that he consented to Stephen's death. In 8:3 he embarks upon what seems to be a single-handed attack on the church, dragging Christians from their homes and throwing them into prison (looking back on this in 22:3–5, Paul adds that his persecution was "to the death," presumably indicating that some lost their lives). Not until 9:1–2, however, is any connection made between Saul and Caiaphas (or Annas): Saul went to "the high priest" and asked for letters for the synagogues at Damascus, "so that if he found any who belonged to the Way, men or women, he might bring them bound to Jerusalem." When the apostle reflects on this in his trial before King Agrippa II, he goes further, suggesting that his activities were actually *commissioned* by the high priest (26:12). Two historical questions need to be resolved: (1) What was the nature of Paul's role as persecutor? (2) Was he really acting with the authority of the high priest?

1. Paul's letters openly admit that he persecuted the church (1 Cor 15:9, Gal 1:13, 23, Phil 3:6), though there is no indication that anyone died as a result of his actions. Quite probably there is some exaggeration here; by highlighting Paul's role as persecutor, Luke can make his acceptance of Christianity all the more remarkable and dramatic. Two aspects of Paul's activities, however, remain unclear. His letters do not tell us *where* his persecutions took place; an odd fact, though, is that Galatians 1:22 suggests that after his Damascus road experience, Paul was "still unknown by sight to the churches of Judea," a reference that, in its context, clearly includes the church of Jerusalem. Second, it is impossible to know *when* Paul began persecuting the church; as J. D. G. Dunn suggests, it is quite possible that he began persecuting only once the church opened its doors to Gentiles, a development that was still in the future.[30] In all probability, Luke knew only that Saul engaged in some kind of persecution and, in the interests of a tidy and dramatic narrative, simply inserted what he knew of this activity alongside his reference to the "great persecution" of 8:1b.

2. The lack of clarity as to Paul's persecuting activities makes it difficult to assess Caiaphas's role in the affair. There are two possibilities here. First, Caiaphas *did* lend some authority to Paul's activities. He and his colleagues would have known what was happening in Jerusalem: the stoning of Stephen would have come to their attention very quickly (and would perhaps have been a rather difficult matter to explain to Pilate); and any continuing troubles in the syna-

gogues would have caused concern. It is possible that Caiaphas supplied Saul with letters of recommendation to Diaspora synagogues (rather like those of 2 Cor 3:1), introducing him to their leaders, asking for help to root out troublemakers, and perhaps even adding a brief comment on Jesus himself. Writing letters to Diaspora communities was one of the high priest's duties (see above, p. 47). Such letters would have had no formal weight (the high priest had no legal jurisdiction in Damascus, situated as it was in the Roman province of Syria), but his position as high priest would have conferred authority on his requests.[31] Second, and more probably, the rather vague reference to "the high priest" in 9:1–2 and in the flashbacks of 22:5 and 26:12 may be simply another example of Luke's attempt to give opposition to Christians official backing.

Whichever was the case, Paul never finished his mission. If there was a letter from Caiaphas, it was never read, and any contact between Paul and the high priest was well and truly broken by the events that overtook him on the Damascus road.

Early Christianity and the House of Annas

Having reviewed the evidence of Acts, a summary of the relationship between early Christianity and the leading priests is now in order. We have seen that the existence of sustained opposition towards the new movement owes more to Lukan theology than historical reality. Reading between the Lukan lines, what is perhaps most striking is the *lack of any formal measures* taken against the new movement. It is likely that Christian leaders were occasionally arrested and interrogated by Caiaphas and his family, yet none of them suffered the same fate as their master. While theological disputes went on in the context of the synagogues, Caiaphas and his family seem to have acted against the movement only when Christian activities threatened to lead to unrest. He and his colleagues presumably let their disapproval of the new sect be known, and may have lent support to men like Paul who tried to stop the spread of the new way within Diaspora synagogues, but there were no attempts either to kill any of the twelve or to stamp out the new movement.

The attitude of Annas's family contrasts sharply with that of Agrippa I, whose brief reign lasted from 41 to 44 C.E. Characteristically for a grandson of Herod the Great, Agrippa dealt with the new movement swiftly and violently. He executed James Zebedee "with the sword" (Acts 12:2), a punishment that suggests Agrippa held him responsible for civil disorder.[32] And Peter was arrested at Passover, perhaps because he was stirring up apocalyptic expectations and, like James, threatened the stability of the city. Despite attempts by some scholars to find high priestly involvement behind the scenes, there is no indication that Agrippa acted on anything but his own initiative. Given Luke's interest in highlighting high priestly hostilities, he would surely have mentioned any high-priestly participation, had it been there in his tradition.[33] As a result of Agrippa's measures, the remaining disciples seem to have fled from the city, and leadership

of the church passed to James, the brother of Jesus. Perhaps the high priestly leaders at the time approved of what happened, but Herod's actions were noticeably
more aggressive than those of Caiaphas and Annas had ever been.

One final piece of evidence needs consideration, because it is often used to
substantiate ongoing hostilities between the house of Annas and the early Christians. In 62 C.E. James (the brother of Jesus) was put to death by Annas's son (and
Caiaphas's brother-in-law) Ananus. Taking advantage of the fact that the province
was temporarily without a Roman governor, Ananus had James and certain other
unnamed men executed. A group of prominent Jerusalemites complained to both
the new governor Albinus and Agrippa II, who deposed Ananus and replaced him
with Jesus son of Damnaeus (*Antiq* 20.199–203).

Was James executed because of his Christian beliefs? Had the house of Annas
borne a grudge against early Christianity for three decades, waiting only for a
suitable opportunity to strike against the new movement? And do the actions of
the "prominent Jerusalemites" show that James (and indeed his followers) were
widely respected in the city (in contrast to the impious high priest)? All of these
assumptions have been read into the story, but a recent article by J. S. McLaren
shows that none can be substantiated. Josephus set the episode within a series of
narratives describing rivalries between various high-priestly factions. Although
James is identified as "the brother of the so-called Christ" (who was referred to
in *Antiq* 18.63–64), there is no mention of his Christianity or any indication
that he was put to death for his Christian beliefs. And the "prominent
Jerusalemites" seem less interested in the fate of James and those who were executed with him, than in outmaneuvering their rival, Ananus. The story, then,
"should be read . . . as an example of on-going rivalry among certain Jews vying
for prominence" in Jerusalem in the early 60s.[34] James had obviously achieved
some standing in the city (his Christianity was clearly no bar to this) and was
caught up in the high-priestly rivalries that characterized Jerusalem in the years
prior to the revolt.

There is, then, no support for the commonly held view that the house of
Annas conducted a vendetta against early Christianity. Christians for their part
may have had understandable reasons to feel hostile towards the house of Annas
because of its role in Jesus' execution, but there is no evidence that their feelings
were reciprocated. The new movement, from Caiaphas's point of view, would
have been an irritation, a potential source of trouble that made his task of officiating as high priest—keeping a watchful eye on the temple and maintaining
order in the city—a little more difficult than it had been. He would not, however, have had to deal with Christians for long; very soon Caiaphas was dismissed
from office.

9

Later Years

Caiaphas was deposed only a few months after Pontius Pilate—two events that may well have been connected with one another. In this chapter, we shall look at the circumstances surrounding Caiaphas's dismissal, establish a connection between his downfall and that of Pilate, and explore Caiaphas's later life. We need to start first, though, with the deposition of Pilate.

Pilate Is Recalled to Rome

The events that led to Pilate's deposition started in the region of Samaria. Late in 36 C.E., an unnamed prophet set himself up as the Samaritan messiah (or *Taheb*), promising that he would restore true worship to the ruined sanctuary on the sacred mountain of Gerizim. Large numbers of people flocked to him, taking up arms and assembling at the village of Tirathana in readiness to follow their messiah up the sacred mountain. Not surprisingly, Pilate was alarmed by all this activity and blocked their route with a detachment of cavalry and heavily armed infantry. In the ensuing battle, many prisoners were taken, and the ringleaders and most influential men were put to death.

This, however, was not to be the end of the matter. The Samaritan leaders went to the legate of Syria, Vitellius, and complained about Pilate's heavy-handed treatment of their compatriots. Vitellius wisely decided to refer the matter to the Emperor Tiberius in Rome. There is no indication that he thought that Pilate was at fault; he may simply have wanted both sides to have a hearing at the highest level so that there could be no repercussions. Vitellius sent orders to dismiss Pilate by the hand of his friend Marcellus, who was to take charge of Judea during Pilate's absence.[1] Despite the adverse winter conditions, Pilate had little choice but to make his way back to Rome as quickly as possible in the hope of putting his case before Tiberius before his opponents brought their charges. He reached the city, however, to find that the old emperor had died on March 16, 37, and that Tiberius's twenty-five-year-old adopted son Gaius Caligula was emperor instead. This information dates Pilate's departure from Judea quite clearly to late 36 at the earliest, and perhaps more likely January 37.[2]

The Syrian Legate Visits Jerusalem

What happened next is difficult to reconstruct, as Josephus's account is rather confused. According to *Antiq* 18.90–95, Vitellius went to Jerusalem at Passover, granted the people certain tax concessions, allowed the high-priestly vestments to revert to Jewish custody, and deposed Caiaphas, replacing him with his brother-in-law, Jonathan. Some time later, on his way to sort out a problem created by the Nabatean King Aretas, Vitellius visited Jerusalem a second time, along with Herod Antipas and his friends, while a "traditional festival" was underway (*Antiq* 18.122–25). At this second visit, the legate deposed Jonathan, replacing him with his brother Theophilus, received news of Tiberius's death, and administered from the people an oath of loyalty to Gaius. The order to intervene in Nabatea having died with Tiberius, Vitellius had no further mandate in the region and returned with his army to Antioch.

Josephus's report raises two problems. The first revolves around the date of the second visit. According to Josephus's chronology, this second visit cannot have been earlier than the feast of Pentecost, celebrated that year in early June. Yet it is inconceivable that it took almost three months for news of the emperor's death to reach a man as important as the Syrian legate! A more likely reconstruction is that this second visit occurred at Passover, which that year fell on 19/20 April.[3] In this case, the legate would have heard the news a month after Tiberius's death. As the sailing season had now opened, an interval of roughly a month seems about right. But what then are we to make of Vitellius's first visit, which Josephus specifically locates at Passover? The accounts can be reconciled most easily by adopting E. M. Smallwood's suggestion that Josephus was simply mistaken in locating the first visit at Passover. This first visit, she suggests, occurred soon after Pilate's dismissal, perhaps in January 37, and was followed, three months later, by a second visit that coincided with the Passover.[4]

The second problem revolves around the events that took place at each of these visits. In the course of a much earlier account of the high-priestly vestments, Josephus provides us with yet another story of Vitellius's visit to Jerusalem. In this version, the people asked the legate to allow them to keep the sacred high-priestly robes under their own authority. Vitellius obligingly wrote to Tiberius, who granted their request (*Antiq* 15.405). The difference is that in this earlier story Vitellius agrees only *to write* to Tiberius, and the delivery of the robes has to take place at a later date, while in 18.90–95 Vitellius apparently has no need to write to Tiberius and grants the request himself on the spot. The simplest solution, yet again, is that proposed by E. M. Smallwood. She suggests that the request to keep the vestments in Jewish care was made at Vitellius's first visit in January 37. Vitellius wrote to Tiberius and received his reply by early April 37. Breaking his journey to Nabatea, he visited Jerusalem a second time so that he might personally supervise the transferal of the vestments.[5] The legate might have deliberately timed his visit to coincide with Passover; in the interregnum caused by Pilate's departure, it allowed him to keep an eye on the city during the festival, and at the same time the transferal of the vestments could have been presented as a show of Roman goodwill and magnanimity.

Having made some sense of Josephus's narrative, we are now in a position to look in more detail at Vitellius's first visit to Jerusalem and Caiaphas's deposition.

Caiaphas Is Removed from Office

With Pilate's removal, Vitellius would have needed to keep a particularly watchful eye on Judea, and be ready to lend assistance whenever possible to Marcellus. It is understandable, then, that he made it his business to visit the province as soon as possible after Pilate's departure. In the course of this first visit, he abolished taxes on the sale of agricultural produce and agreed to write to the emperor requesting that the high-priestly vestments be transferred back into Jewish custody. Josephus concludes his account as follows: "After he had bestowed these benefits upon the nation, he removed from his sacred office the high priest, Joseph surnamed Caiaphas, and appointed in his stead Jonathan, son of Ananus the high priest. Then he set out on the journey back to Antioch" (*Antiq* 18.95). The question is, of course, why? Given the rather precarious situation in which Judea found itself at that particular time, why did Vitellius think that it was in Rome's best interests to depose the high priest? As happens so often, Josephus gives no reasons for Caiaphas's dismissal, but three possibilities come to mind.

1. Caiaphas lost his position because of his close association with Pilate and a general unpopularity with the people. This is the view of the majority of historians, yet it is actually rather difficult to substantiate.[6] We saw earlier that there is no reason to assume that any particularly close association *did* develop between Pilate and Caiaphas. The two men must have been able to work together tolerably well, each knew the expectations and boundaries of the other, and perhaps a working understanding developed between them. But there is no reason to assume that Pilate's downfall *necessarily* led to that of Caiaphas.[7] Nor does *Antiq* 18.95 suggest that Caiaphas was in any way unpopular with the people: in fact, the text specifically seems to make a distinction between the "benefits" brought by Vitellius and his deposition of Caiaphas.[8] Finally, if Caiaphas and his family were dangerously unpopular with the people, we might expect Vitellius to have

given the post to someone from another house, perhaps that of Boethus. Yet the next appointee was Caiaphas's brother-in-law, Jonathan son of Annas, a man who was quite probably acting already as captain of the temple and Caiaphas's right-hand man.[9] There is, then, nothing to support the commonly held belief that Caiaphas's deposition was due to unpopularity, and we must look for another explanation.

2. In 1996 A. Vicent Cernuda proposed the novel theory that Caiaphas lost his position because he converted to Christianity. Paul's conversion, he claims, had a profound effect on Caiaphas, and when the apostle visited Jerusalem three years later (Gal 1:18–23), the high priest was secretly baptized. Word, however, got out, and Caiaphas was forced to escape the negative backlash in Jerusalem by accompanying Peter to Rome. As an aristocratic priest, Josephus was scandalized by what he saw as Caiaphas's desertion of his duties and resolved to say nothing about the embarrassing incident in his work. Caiaphas's "dismissal" by Vitellius, then, is nothing more than Josephan fabrication, designed to cover up the high priest's ignominious departure.[10]

Imaginative though this theory is, it clearly rests on far too many dubious hypotheses to be persuasive. If the theory is accurate, the almost complete silence of early Christianity regarding Caiaphas's "conversion" is puzzling. Vicent Cernuda is aware of this difficulty, but explains it by suggesting that many Christians found the conversion of Jesus' chief opponent shocking and resolved to say as little about it as possible.[11] But this is hardly convincing. If the high priest who condemned Jesus had really been baptized, surely Christians would have quickly overlooked his part in Jesus' death and rejoiced instead in the conversion of such a prominent figure. Furthermore, Vicent Cernuda assumes that Paul, the Gospel writers, Josephus, Philo, and presumably other Jerusalemites all knew the embarrassing secret, yet all conspired to keep silent. But, if so many people knew about Caiaphas's conversion, it seems incredible that no traces of it remain in any early Christian tradition![12] The suggestion that Caiaphas lost his position due to his conversion to Christianity, then, lacks plausibility.

3. For a more likely solution we need to look at the historical situation of Judea in 37 C.E.. The province was without its appointed governor and was managed instead by Vitellius's friend Marcellus, a man who had been sent out from Antioch without much notice and presumably had little understanding of Jewish affairs. It is quite possible that prominent Jews such as Caiaphas made the most of the temporary power vacuum. At the very least, they must have felt a greater sense of freedom in conducting their affairs now that Pilate was absent. Yet it is also tempting to imagine that they took advantage of the lack of strong Roman rule by asserting themselves and attempting to gain concessions both for themselves and the people. The Judean aristocracy may have considered itself to be in a rather strong position: the complaints of their Samaritan neighbors had been taken seriously and were being heard at the highest level; who knew what advantages they themselves might be able to obtain?

The idea of a surge in aristocratic assertiveness fits in well with the probable events during Vitellius's first visit. Josephus claims that, in return for the marvelous welcome shown to him by the Jerusalemites, Vitellius remitted taxes on the sale of agricultural produce (*Antiq* 18.90). Yet Rome relied on taxation to pay for its armies in the East, and it would be a very strange Roman legate who, met by a friendly crowd, remitted certain taxes of his own initiative. The situation is made all the more suspicious since this brief exchange fits almost perfectly with Josephus's desire to show the high regard the Jewish nation had for good Roman governors and the beneficence and magnanimity bestowed on Jews throughout their history by high-ranking Roman officials. More probably, the request for a remission of agricultural taxes came from the Jewish leaders. They might have suggested to Vitellius that, given the uncertain times in which they lived, a cut in taxes might enhance Roman popularity and help to keep the peace. Anxious to maintain the stability of the province, Vitellius agreed to the concession.[13]

A similar sequence of events probably lies behind the agreement to allow the high-priestly vestments to revert to Jewish custody. It is clear that the initiative here did not lie with Vitellius but with Jews. In *Antiq* 15.405, it is the Jerusalem throng or crowd (the *plēthos*) who ask to have the sacred robe in their care; in *Antiq* 18.90, Vitellius "*agreed* that the vestments of the High Priest and all his ornaments should be kept in the Temple in custody of the priests." Again, the likelihood is that the request came from the highest temple personnel, quite possibly the high priest himself. Since this first visit did not coincide with a festival, Caiaphas would have had more freedom to meet with the legate and to persuade him to relinquish Roman control over the vestments. Once again, Vitellius agreed and promised to bring the matter to Tiberius's attention as soon as possible.

Caiaphas and his high-priestly advisers may have felt rather pleased with themselves: they had made the most of Pilate's absence and gained both tax reductions and the expectation that the high-priestly vestments would be returned. There was, however, an unexpected condition. If Caiaphas had already asserted himself and made demands on the legate, allowing the high priest to keep the sacred vestments in his own control could only increase his standing in the eyes of his community—and thus his potential danger to Rome. Perhaps, then, Vitellius decided that the best compromise was to recommend to Tiberius that the vestments be returned but that Caiaphas be removed from office. Caiaphas's deposition, then, may have been not because of his unpopularity or his becoming a crypto-Christian, but because he took advantage of a power vacuum in Judea, grew too assertive, and became too powerful for his own good.

Caiaphas's Later Years

Soon after his succession, the Emperor Gaius Caligula sent out another Roman knight, Marullus, as prefect of Judea.[14] What became of Pilate is unknown—a fact that led to the Christian speculation encountered on pp. 9–10. The reality, though, was probably much more prosaic. After eleven years in Judea, Gaius thought it was time to offer him a new commission.

What became of Caiaphas is equally obscure. Presumably he continued with the duties of an ordinary priest in the temple and at times engaged in public affairs. One public duty may have occurred shortly after his deposition. On his second visit to Jerusalem, the Syrian legate Vitellius was on his way to the Nabatean capital, Petra, with two legions and a number of auxiliary troops. His route took him through Judea, but no sooner had his army drawn close to the border than he was met by "the Jews of the highest standing" who asked him not to march through their land because the images attached to the standards contravened the law against graven images. Caiaphas and other members of his family may have been behind this delegation; they might perhaps have reminded Vitellius of the incident with Pilate a decade earlier and pressed upon him the importance of the matter. Anxious to keep the peace, Vitellius bowed to Jewish sensitivities and sent his army around Judea while he continued on to Jerusalem with only a small body of men (*Antiq* 18.120–22).[15]

Three years later, in 40 C.E., Judean affairs appeared to be on the brink of catastrophe. The Emperor Gaius ordered a statue of himself to be set up in the Jerusalem temple by the Syrian legate, Petronius. Although the accounts of this incident in Josephus and Philo are rather different, it seems that the Jerusalem aristocrats, the "leading men," met with Petronius and tried to find a solution.[16] Although the matter was finally resolved by Gaius's assassination in 41 C.E., no other incident in the first century prior to the revolt against Rome galvanized the Judean people into action and threatened the stability of the province to the same extent. If Caiaphas was still alive, he surely would have been one of the negotiators, particularly since it was the sanctity of the temple that was at stake, and he was now relieved from his high-priestly duties.

How long did Caiaphas live after his deposition? Josephus's narrative is strangely silent regarding his later activities. We know that Caiaphas was succeeded by his brother-in-law Jonathan, who officiated only once, at the Passover of 37, before also being deposed.[17] In the early 40s, Agrippa I proposed to restore the high priesthood to Jonathan, "conceding that he was more worthy of the honor" than the present incumbent, Simon Cantheras (*Antiq* 19.313–16). Jonathan, however, declined and suggested that his brother Matthias take the position instead. Jonathan went on to have an influential position in Judean affairs: he annoyed the procurator Felix by frequently admonishing him to improve his administration, and he was finally killed by a group of Jewish assassins known as the sicarii.[18] Why did Jonathan decline the high priesthood when Agrippa offered it to him? Is it significant that we hear nothing further of Annas?[19] Had the old priest died by now, and did Jonathan prefer to take his position as head of the family, exercising power from behind the scenes as his father had done? And what of Caiaphas? It seems odd that a man who held the high priesthood for so long should disappear just as Josephus's record becomes fuller. Did a rift develop between him and the rest of the house? Did he retire into private life? Or, perhaps more probably, did he die soon after his deposition? We will, of course, never know. Caiaphas's death, like his birth, remains shrouded in mystery.

The "Historical" Caiaphas

We have now come to the end of our historical survey of Caiaphas. As I cautioned at the beginning, our picture has been sketchy; there are large gaps, and much of the reconstruction is hypothetical. The study of any historical character is difficult—words, actions, and intentions are always open to a variety of interpretations. But difficulties are compounded greatly when we are dealing with characters from ancient history. It is hard enough trying to reconstruct the historical Jesus when we have at least some of the words attributed to him; in the case of Caiaphas, we have nothing that derives directly from him, and much of what we have in the Gospels is hostile toward him (as we shall see in part 2).

The Caiaphas who has emerged from this study is aristocratic and wealthy, but his membership of a high-priestly family would undoubtedly have given him much more status and authority in the eyes of ordinary Judeans than is often recognized. He owed his occupancy of the high priesthood to two events: first, his marriage into the house of Annas, a family that was to have an important role in Judean affairs throughout the first century; second, Gratus's high-handed decision to appoint high priests on an annual basis. Had Ishmael, Eleazar, or Simon occupied the high-priestly office substantially longer than a year each, Caiaphas might never have been promoted.

I have attempted to show that the most important concern to Caiaphas and his high-priestly colleagues was the Jerusalem temple: the central institution of Judaism, the place where Israel's God had been worshiped since the days of Solomon, and the focus of Israel's myths and hopes. Caiaphas's experiences during Herod I's reign and the events following the king's death were an all too worrying reminder of the vulnerability of the nation and the brutality of which Rome was capable. Were Caiaphas and his Sadducean colleagues collaborators? We might well ask what other choice they had. The aristocratic priests knew that Rome was there to stay and that the only way they could maintain the temple cult unhindered was to acquiesce to the presence of the hated Gentiles on Judean soil. It was a compromise, and undoubtedly not one that all Jews were prepared to accept.

It was primarily in connection with the temple that Caiaphas opposed Jesus. If Jesus had confined his ministry to Galilee or chosen to visit Jerusalem at any time other than the Passover, the high priest might have let things pass. But when Jesus arrived in the crowded city with an excited following, not only prophesying the temple's destruction, but performing symbolic deeds in the holy building itself, Caiaphas had to take action. The smooth running of the festival had to be protected at all costs; the thought of Roman intervention—with, at best, pollution of the holy place and, at worst, destruction of some or all of the temple—was too terrible to imagine. Jesus threatened everything that Caiaphas held most dear; the high priest would have regarded him as a troublemaker, a false prophet, and deceiver of the people, and would have had no scruples in handing him over to Pilate. Yet there is no reason to suppose that violence or hostility toward alternative viewpoints characterized either Caiaphas or the house of Annas. Contrary to the presentation of Acts, Caiaphas and his colleagues seem to have been content to allow Jesus' followers to exist in Jerusalem with minimal disturbance, taking action only when apocalyptic excitement threatened to disrupt the city.

The first few decades of direct Roman rule were a difficult time for all Judeans. Everyone had to come to some acceptance of the new political order, to work out how best to safeguard Jewish ancestral traditions and to maintain a delicate compromise between the expectations of Rome and obligations to God. Caiaphas held office for eighteen or nineteen years, by far the longest of the nineteen high priests in first-century Jerusalem, rivaled only by the nine-year tenure of Annas. He and other aristocrats deserve recognition for the difficulty of their position, commendation for their undoubtedly effective diplomacy and abilities as negotiators, and credit that they managed both to protect the temple and to maintain peace—a peace that would evaporate less than three decades later.

In part 2 I shall turn to the presentation of Caiaphas within the four canonical Gospels and see how the high priest is used as a literary character in each one.

PART 2
CAIAPHAS IN EARLY CHRISTIAN REFLECTION

10

The Gospels in Context

The earliest Christians knew only the bare outline of the events of Jesus' last hours.[1] Yet, as they eagerly preached the good news of his resurrection, it was inevitable that accounts of his death should begin to circulate. Those who heard the Christian proclamation would have wanted to know the circumstances of his death, the identities of the people involved, and how such shameful events could possibly have been God's will.

One of the most difficult things for Jesus' followers to understand must have been his rejection by the religious leaders of his day: for the Jewish messiah to be crucified by Rome was embarrassing enough, but for him to be handed over to Rome by representatives of his own nation was utterly inexplicable. If Jesus was the messiah, why had the high priest and other Jewish rulers not recognized him? Had they acted simply out of ignorance?[2] But, if so, how could such ignorant men be God's anointed leaders? And what were the implications of the continued rejection of Jesus by Israel's religious guides? All these questions needed answers and would have concerned Christian scribes as they mined their Scriptures and tried to make sense of the astonishing events that had taken place.

At first, stories circulated orally, gathering details and scriptural allusions as they were passed from one group of Christians to another. What these early traditions made of Caiaphas and his colleagues is impossible now to know.[3] Our earliest surviving record of the clash between Caiaphas and Jesus is to be found in the Gospel of Mark, which dates roughly to 70 C.E., followed within a decade or two by the Gospels of Matthew, Luke, and John. The next four chapters will explore the different ways in which each evangelist presents the high priest and his confrontation with Jesus.

Before we turn to an analysis of the texts, however, we need to watch one more historical event unfold. By the late first century, the Roman province of Judea had ceased to exist, and the two great movements that would one day become "Christianity" and "Judaism" had begun to move away from one another, locked in conflict and bitter antagonism. Like all good pastors, the Gospel writers were aware of their social and religious context and shaped their message to speak to the situation of their hearers. It is crucial, then, that we understand something of this historical situation. To this we must now turn.

The War with Rome—and Its Aftermath

By the late summer of 66 C.E., Judea was plunged into a bloody and disastrous war. The seeds of revolution had been germinating for the last two decades: the premature death in 44 C.E. of Agrippa I, on whom so many hopes had rested; the extension of Roman rule into Galilee; the severe famine of 46–48 C.E.; the appointment as procurator from 52 to 60 of Antonius Felix, a man who, in the words of Tacitus, "practiced every kind of cruelty and lust, wielding the power of a king with all the instincts of a slave";[4] and Agrippa II's frequent changes of high priest from 62 onwards, actions that only encouraged rivalry among high-priestly families and their supporters and created political chaos in Jerusalem.[5] By the mid 60s, the situation was highly volatile and unstable; it needed only a spark to set the whole thing alight. That spark came in 66: Jewish-Gentile relations broke down in Caesarea at the same time that the corrupt and incompetent procurator Gessius Florus tried to seize money from the temple treasury. The people's resentment could no longer be contained and—despite the efforts of Jewish leaders to calm the situation—violent clashes with Roman soldiers ensued. Quickly the revolt escalated beyond anyone's control; a high-priestly aristocrat by the name of Eliezar persuaded the priests to stop the daily sacrifice on behalf of the emperor, and Judea was plunged into a conflict that was both civil war and open revolt against Rome.

The chief priests and aristocrats desperately tried to maintain their tenuous control of society by organizing resistance to Rome, but their efforts were to be short-lived. The nation was too divided, and rival factions were too distrustful of one another to be able to offer any kind of real resistance to the Roman legions. Within a few months Galilee had fallen, and Judea quickly followed suit. It would have been relatively easy for the Roman general Vespasian to take Jerusalem too, but affairs of state intervened. In 68 C.E., Nero was assassinated; in the unstable year that followed, Vespasian was proclaimed emperor by his armies in the East. As soon as possible, he left for Rome, leaving his capable son Titus to manage the war in Judea. Vespasian's bid for the imperial purple was successful; what the newly established Flavian dynasty needed now was the glory and honor of a successful foreign campaign. And so it was that early in 70 C.E. Titus began the siege of Jerusalem.

The horrific conditions of the besieged city are described in some detail by Josephus (who was by now safely in the Roman camp, gathering information from deserters). With a dramatic pathos worthy of Thucydides, Josephus describes the wars between rival factions and the famine and bloodshed that beset the city. He tells in some detail the story of a mother driven by hunger to eat her own child, and the shock and outrage that the event inspired even in a city numbed to atrocities.[6] Yet an even greater calamity was about to beset the Jewish people, something so unimaginably terrible that it would be felt by Jews throughout the empire and beyond for many centuries to come.

As the Roman siege engines burst into Jerusalem, Titus marched up to the temple and set it on fire. Throughout the war the priests had maintained their daily sacrifices and were reluctant even now to leave their posts; but as the flames engulfed the magnificent building, they were forced to flee. The temple burned to the ground, bringing the war—and the Jewish cult—to a dramatic end.

The dust had hardly settled on the ruined temple before the Flavians set about proclaiming their victory throughout the empire. In Rome, Vespasian and his sons Titus and Domitian enjoyed a magnificent triumph, marching through the streets with seven hundred captured Judeans and spoils from the Jerusalem temple. A series of coins was specially commissioned: inscribed with the words *Iudaea Capta* (Judea captured), they featured a picture of a weeping woman (representing the Jewish people) sitting at the feet of a victorious Roman legionary. To add to Jewish humiliation, the tax that had once gone to the Jerusalem temple was redirected and now went to pay for the rebuilding of the temple of Jupiter Capitolinus in Rome.[7] And, if things were not bad enough, a wave of anti-Jewish feeling spread throughout the empire in the wake of the Roman victory.

In the aftermath of the war, large parts of Judea were reduced to rubble. Thousands of people were sold into slavery, the province was entrusted to governors of senatorial rank, and the relatively autonomous local rule that the land had known for sixty years was brought to an end.[8] In the power vacuum that was left, it was the Pharisees who gradually assumed religious (and where possible, political) leadership of the nation. Gathering at Javneh (or Jamnia, a town near the Mediterranean on the south coast of Israel), the Pharisaic rabbis began to pick up the pieces of their religious identity and to define what it meant to be part of the community of Israel. While the temple stood, there had been scope for many different interpretations of Judaism; what united them all was the Jerusalem cult. Now, with the temple in ruins, there was a need for much greater uniformity of belief and practice and for clearer boundaries between who was a Jew and who was not.[9]

Rabbinic authority was limited initially to Palestine, but Jewish synagogue leaders in the Diaspora would have engaged in similar processes of defining boundaries. The Jewish tax, with the accompanying debates over who was obliged to pay, would have brought issues of Jewish identity to the fore, and less tolerant attitudes would have forced many Jews to keep a low profile within their own communities. For Jews everywhere, this was a period of quiet introspection, a time to reflect upon what it meant to be Jewish, to ponder the reasons for the destruction of the temple, and, most of all, to hope—to long for the time when God would allow his temple to be rebuilt and its cult restored. This would not have appeared at all improbable: when the Babylonians destroyed Solomon's temple in 587 B.C.E., it had been rebuilt within seventy years. When the Syrian Antiochus Epiphanes had defiled the temple in 167 B.C.E., it had been cleansed three years later. In the aftermath of the war, petitions for the restoration of the temple were included in Jewish daily prayers, and the synagogue liturgy was arranged as an interim substitute for temple worship.[10] Most Jews, then, would have expected the temple to be rebuilt; the task ahead of them was to ensure the survival of the community of Israel until that happened.

It may have been precisely over the matter of the temple that some of the most serious disputes broke out between Christians and their fellow Jews.[11] Christians were the only Jews for whom the loss of the temple was unproblematic. Their own leader had prophesied its destruction, and as we have already seen, they had already begun to see their own community as God's eschatological temple. Inspired by the universalistic prophecies of the postexilic prophets, Christians had been accepting Gentiles into their "temple" community for several decades and, at least in those Christian groups outside Palestine, had not required Gentile converts to keep the Jewish law. Now that the temple was gone, the Christian "temple" community quite effortlessly took its place, waiting, perhaps with growing expectancy, for Christ's return and the inauguration of the messianic age. As far as Christians were concerned, they represented the "true Israel," those among whom God's promises were coming to fruition. Furthermore, they could use the fall of the temple to their own advantage: the catastrophe, they could argue, was nothing other than divine judgment on their fellow Jews for their rejection of Jesus.

Other Jews, of course, saw things differently. While the Jerusalem temple stood and Christians continued to take part in Jewish worship, there would have been relatively little conflict. Now that the temple was gone, however, Christian claims would have angered their contemporaries. Linked with the increasingly high Christology developing around Jesus, and the mission to Gentiles, many Jews would have concluded that Christians were willfully denying the central institutions of Israel. At a time when Jews felt increasingly isolated and threatened, such deviation could not be tolerated. Local synagogue leaders would have been quite certain that they themselves represented "true Israel"; and, whatever God's reason for allowing the destruction of the temple, it certainly had nothing to do with the death of Jesus of Nazareth.

Gradually a rift developed between Christians and other Jews. The precise reasons for the "parting of the ways" lie in a complex blend of theological and social factors, and the split was faster and more intense in some places than others. Within some Jewish communities debate would have been fierce, and Christians would have been excluded from the synagogue quickly and found themselves increasingly ostracized from social and commercial dealings with other Jews. For these Christians, the task was to define their new identity over against Judaism. In other places, hostilities were less fierce, and Christians might have continued attending the synagogue for several decades, if not centuries.[12]

It is against this uneasy and often turbulent background that the canonical Gospels were composed. Each one was written as a document of faith for its own time; each one reflects (in varying degrees) years of polemical exchange between Christian communities and their Jewish neighbors; and each one reflects its own particular social context. Together, they reflect a period of Jewish-Christian relations characterized by hurt, anger, and resentment. This background, as we shall see, has had a profound effect upon the way in which each evangelist presents the Jewish high priest, Joseph Caiaphas.

11

Caiaphas in Mark

The Gospel of Mark was written around 70 C.E., directly after the Jewish war with Rome and the destruction of the temple.[1] The brooding sense of suffering and anxiety that overshadows the work suggests that the author wrote for Christians who had recently been persecuted for their faith. He writes to strengthen these people in their commitment to Christ, to show that their sufferings were all foreseen by Jesus, and to encourage them to persevere. Many of his readers seem to have seen the destruction of the temple as a sign heralding Jesus' return. Mark warns them that this is not the case; they must be patient and endure a little longer, but he assures them that Jesus' triumphal return will not be long.

The Gospel has traditionally been linked with Rome, though somewhere closer to Palestine—perhaps Syria or even Galilee—is equally possible.[2] Church tradition maintains that the author was a companion of Peter, but there is no clear evidence for this in the text.[3] What we can say, though, is that the author appears to have been an Aramaic speaker (although he writes in Greek, it is not his first language) and a respected leader within the early church. He was also, at least originally, a Jewish Christian: this is suggested by his ready use of Old Testament proof texts (1:2–3), his awareness of Jewish customs (7:1–13), and his interest in the temple (11:11, 15–18; 13:1–2). I said he was "originally" a Jewish Christian because there are clues within the text which suggest that he is writing for a community that now includes many Gentile Christians, and that he and his church have begun to think of themselves as distinct from their Jewish neighbors.[4] For Mark, the split has occurred, but there is still residual conflict: he warns his readers that they "will be beaten in synagogues" (13:9), and his preoccupation with the Jerusalem temple and the fate of the Jewish leadership shows that his Jewish origins are never far from his mind.

At first glance, Mark's Gospel might appear rather naive and simplistic. He has no miraculous birth stories or tales of cosmic preexistence, but chooses to start his account on the banks of the Jordan with Jesus' baptism by John. Sixteen chapters later, there are no resurrection appearances, no great commissioning, and no ascension; the narrative stops abruptly, and the reader is left at the empty tomb with the terrified women to make of it what she will. This simplicity, however, is an illusion. On closer inspection the Gospel has great literary depth and theological sophistication, something that comes across most clearly in Mark's presentation of Jesus' death.

Everything in Mark's Gospel is linked to Jesus' death, and it is in the "passion narrative" (that is, chapters 14–16) that many of the earlier themes of the Gospel find their culmination.[5] Three of these will be particularly important for our present study. First is the theme of Jesus' identity. Throughout the Gospel, Mark has stressed that Jesus is the Christ, the Son of God, yet Jesus' audiences (and even the disciples) have been slow to grasp this. The reason is that, for Mark, Jesus' identity can really be understood only by his death: Jesus was indeed the Christ, but a Christ who would die on a cross; the Son of Man who would suffer and then be vindicated by God—all of which, Mark stresses, was foretold by the prophets. A second important theme is conflict. In the passion narrative the earlier conflicts of the narrative reach their culmination, and Jesus comes face to face with representatives of both Israel and Rome. Resulting from this is our third theme: rejection. Jesus will be rejected not only by the leaders of his own nation but also by his closest followers (14:27, 50, 51–52, 66–72) and even, apparently, God himself (15:34). The Markan Jesus goes to the cross almost entirely alone: it is a bleak, stark portrayal, but also one that serves as a model for Mark's own persecuted community, some of whom may themselves be called upon to "take up their own cross" (8:34–38) and walk in the way of their Master. It is an invitation and a challenge: following Jesus will not be easy; there will be trials and tribulations, loneliness and despair, but those who endure to the end will be rewarded with eternal life in the kingdom of God.

It is in the passion narrative, too, that Mark explores the motivations of Caiaphas and the chief priests and the implications of their actions. The confrontation between Jesus and Caiaphas forms one of the central scenes of the whole Gospel. We shall see that Mark, writing forty years after the events, and drawing on years of Christian speculation, develops the scene into one of momentous proportions. Through their rejection of Jesus, Caiaphas and his colleagues unwittingly seal their own fate.

Mark and the Disappearance of Caiaphas

Caiaphas takes center stage only once in Mark's Gospel—in the Jewish trial narrative of 14:53–65. A curious feature of this narrative, however, is that throughout his relatively lengthy account, the evangelist never once gives the *name* of the high priest. In verse 53, Jesus is led simply to "the high priest"; the exchange in verses 60–62 occurs between Jesus and "the high priest"; and in verse 63 the (still unnamed) high priest tears his garments.[6] What makes Mark's silence here particularly noteworthy is the fact that his passion narrative is full of people's names, people who mean little to us now but who were presumably well known to his readers: Simon the leper; Barabbas; Simon's sons, Alexander and Rufus; and Mary's sons, James the Younger and Joses. His reluctance to name the high priest, then, is striking and in all probability deliberate. But what lies behind Mark's curious silence? Four solutions have been proposed.

1. The simplest solution is that Mark did not know the high priest's name.[7] This is possible, but unlikely. The basic passion narrative would have been well-known to Mark's readers. It is clear by the way in which he simply mentions Pilate in 15:1, without any reference to his official position, that the evangelist expects his readers to be fully conversant with the dramatis personae of his story. And, significantly, all of the other Gospel writers quite independently link Caiaphas to the story, a fact which strongly suggests that Caiaphas's name was an integral part of Christian tradition from the very beginning.[8] That Mark was unaware of the name of the high priest, then, is improbable.

2. A second solution has been put forward by Rudolf Pesch, who argues that the fact that the high priest is not named suggests that Mark is incorporating a very early passion account here, one which was written while Caiaphas was still high priest. Pesch's point is that in the same way that a British person could refer to events in 2002 as "the Queen's jubilee" without having to specify *which* queen (since she is still the reigning monarch), the people who put together the earliest passion narrative had no need to specify *which* high priest, since Caiaphas was still in post. This means that the narrative was written prior to Caiaphas's deposition in 37 C.E.[9]

This is an ingenious solution, but there are two problems with it. First, as we have seen, Caiaphas and Pilate were deposed within a few months of one another. Unless we are to assume that the passion account was penned in the short time between Pilate's deposition (probably in January 37) and Caiaphas's replacement (probably Passover 37), it is difficult to see why Pilate is named but Caiaphas is not. Surely if Pesch were correct, we would expect Pilate also to be referred to as "the governor" or (more accurately) "the prefect." The second difficulty is that Mark probably wrote his Gospel in the early 70s, years after Caiaphas had been deposed. Recent studies have shown the evangelist to be an extremely skill-

ful narrator with great literary flair and sensitivity. Even if he were using an earlier narrative that did not name Caiaphas, it was surely not beyond his capabili-
ties to supply the name of the high priest (as Matthew did when he took over his
Markan source). Pesch's early passion narrative hypothesis, then, does not explain
Mark's silence.

3. Another explanation comes from Gerd Theissen, an explanation that in
many respects is a refinement of that of Pesch. Theissen suggests that Mark made
use of an early passion story composed in Palestine, quite possibly in the 40s C.E.[10]
Both this early passion source and Mark's redaction of it concealed the name of
the high priest because the early Christian community had firsthand experience
of the wrath of both Caiaphas and his influential in-laws, the house of Annas. As
Theissen notes, "Traditions circulating in their sphere of influence were well
advised not to mention their names in a negative context."[11]

Theissen's solution stands or falls by the assumption that Mark thought it was
too risky to mention Caiaphas by name. We have seen in chapter 8, however, that
the hypothesis of an enduring antagonism between early Christianity and the
house of Annas may well owe more to Lukan theology than to historical fact. Yet,
even if the Christian community *was* afraid of the house of Annas, Theissen's
solution is really plausible only if we assume that Mark was writing prior to the
revolt and in a context where the house of Annas had some influence, that is, in
Judea. The thesis is less likely if, as the majority of scholars maintain, Mark wrote
outside Judea, and even less likely if, as many suppose, Mark wrote after the fall
of Jerusalem.[12] By now, the clan of Annas had perished and none of its members
were in any position to harm the early Christian community. Why not now
record the high priest's name?

4. A fourth solution was proposed by Raymond Brown. He suggests that
Mark's omission of the high priest's name reflects the *Gentile* origin and destina-
tion of the Gospel.[13] Superficially, this seems to make sense: the name Caiaphas
would have meant little to Mark's Gentile readers, and so the evangelist chose to
mention him only by his official function. And yet, despite the fact that Mark
seems to be writing for a largely Gentile audience, we shall see that he exhibits a
great interest in both the Jewish leaders and the temple, a fact that suggests the
relationship between Christians and Jews is still important for the author. Given
this interest, it seems unlikely that Mark omitted Caiaphas's name simply because
his audience was Gentile.

Each of the last three solutions takes a basically historical approach to the
problem: Mark's silence is due either to the historical situation of those who
penned the underlying passion narrative or to the historical setting of Mark's
readers. None of them, however, is convincing. In the rest of this chapter, I shall
suggest a different solution, one that takes a more literary-historical approach. In
order to reach this solution, we need first to compare the Jewish and Roman trial
scenes, then look at the Jewish leaders outside the trial narratives, and finally turn
to the Jewish trial narrative itself.

The Jewish/Roman Trial Scenes

In Mark's Gospel, Jesus has two trials: one before the Jewish religious authorities and one before the Roman prefect, Pontius Pilate. One of the many strange aspects of these two trials is that there is no causal connection between them.[14] Although he briefly describes a second meeting of the Jewish council the following morning (15:1), Mark at no point explains *why* Jesus has to be handed over to Rome. And if, as most modern readers assume, Pilate was simply ratifying the sentence passed by the Jewish court, why does he proceed as though he were opening up the case anew? Of course, on one level, the two trials perfectly illustrate Jesus' third passion prediction, that "the Son of Man will be handed over to the chief priests and the scribes, and they will condemn him to death; then they will hand him over to the Gentiles; they will mock him, and spit upon him, and flog him, and kill him" (10:33–34). Perhaps Mark thought nothing more needed to be said; events are turning out exactly as Jesus had predicted. Or perhaps Mark simply expected his readers to know the legalities of the case. At all events, it is clear that Mark was less interested in outlining the legal niceties of Jesus' condemnation than in presenting us with two trial scenes, one Jewish, one Roman.

More curious still is the clear parallelism between the two trials, as the following three points will indicate:[15]

1. In both, the central character—whether it is the high priest or Pilate—asks Jesus two questions. In the Jewish trial, Jesus is first asked a general question concerning the temple, in response to which he remains silent (14:61). Then the high priest asks him a specific question regarding his identity: "Are you the Messiah, the Son of the Blessed One?" Jesus replies: "I am" (*ego eimi*, 14:62). In the Roman trial, the two questions are reversed: Pilate goes straight to the matter of Jesus' identity: "Are you the King of the Jews?" Jesus replies (slightly more cautiously), "You say so" (*su legeis*, 15:2). Then, in response to Pilate's question regarding the more general charges of the chief priests, Jesus once again makes no answer. Pilate's words in verse 4, "Have you no answer?" (*ouk apokrine oude;*) are an exact echo of those of the high priest in the earlier scene (14:60). In both trials, then, Jesus remains silent when questioned about more general matters but replies in the affirmative when challenged regarding his identity.

2. Both accounts contrast Jesus with another: in the Jewish trial his courageous response to the high priest is interwoven with Peter's cowardly evasions when challenged first by a lowly maid and then by some bystanders (14:66–72). And in the Roman trial narrative, Jesus' innocent condemnation frames Barabbas's guilty pardon.

3. Finally, both accounts include a consultation (the high priest and other members of the council; Pilate and the people), culminate in a verdict ("All of them condemned him as deserving death," 14:64; "Crucify him!" 15:13), and conclude with a scene of mockery and derision appropriate to each trial (Jesus is mocked as a prophet in 14:65; as a king in 15:16–20).

Mark, then, presents us with two parallel trial scenes. In terms of both the flow of the narrative and their individual structures, they are equally prominent, suggesting that Mark (and his readers) were equally interested in how Jesus fared in a Jewish court and in a Roman court. Quite possibly this was prompted by their own recent experiences at the hands of both synagogue leaders and local Roman officials.

And yet, for all their parallelism, there is a striking difference between Jesus' central adversaries. Caiaphas, as we have already seen, is referred to only by his *office*. Pilate, on the other hand, is referred to only by his *name*, which Mark repeats eight times in the course of only fifteen verses. (When Matthew rewrites this Markan scene, one of the changes he makes is to introduce the Roman as "Pilate the governor" (*hēgemōn*, 27:2) and to substitute "the governor" for at least four of Mark's references to Pilate's name.[16])

Why does Mark avoid referring to Pilate by his office? The most obvious answer is that he wants to minimize official Roman involvement. Jesus is tried not by a representative of Rome—a governor—but by Pilate, one particular man at one particular time. Mark leaves it open as to whether another Roman might have come to a different conclusion. This ties in well with the evangelist's attempts to place as much blame as possible for the death of Jesus on the Jewish leaders: it is they who hand Jesus over to Pilate, act as the counsel for the prosecution against Jesus, and stir up the people to demand the release of Barabbas. In the end, Pilate sends Jesus to the cross not because of the demands of Roman law, but because of the demands of the Jewish crowd (15:15). Pilate is not exonerated in Mark's Gospel—he plays his part in Jesus' condemnation—but it is clear that the real villains of the piece, as far as Mark was concerned, were the Jewish leaders.[17]

Does this, then, help us to see why Mark does not name Caiaphas? Does the evangelist refer to him as "high priest" in an attempt to broaden Jewish responsibility for Jesus' death?[18] In order to test this hypothesis, we need to turn now to Mark's presentation of Jewish leaders in the rest of the Gospel.

Jewish Leaders outside the Trial Narrative

Mark's plot, as we have seen, moves through conflict. Already in chapter 2 Jesus is locked in controversy with scribes and Pharisees, who as early as 3:6 have teamed up with the Herodians in a bid to kill him. Later, in chapter 3, "scribes . . . from Jerusalem" are added to the ranks of Jesus' adversaries (3:22–27), and as the narrative progresses, even Jesus' family (3:19b–21, 31–35) and townspeople (6:1–6) reject him. As Jesus makes his way to Jerusalem, the threat of conflict intensifies with Jesus' threefold passion predictions (8:31, 9:31, 10:33), only to reach its climax as Jesus enters the holy city and bears the full brunt of the Jewish leaders' hostility. After the incident in the temple, the chief priests, scribes, and elders question his authority (11:27–33), Pharisees and Herodians challenge him over taxes (12:13–17), and Sadducees try to entrap him with questions about the resurrection (12:18–27). The murderous intentions of the chief priests have been plain from 11:18, but with 14:1 their plans to arrest Jesus "by stealth" and to kill him begin to take shape. Even after they have apparently won and Jesus hangs on the cross, the chief priests (along with the scribes) cannot resist mocking him, taunting him to come down and save himself (15:31–32).

Mark's presentation of the Jerusalem-based Jewish leadership has been shaped by two overarching themes. First, the evangelist gives clear reasons for the chief priests' opposition to Jesus. Following tradition, he suggests that their rejection of the Messiah was all foreordained in the Scriptures; but he also adds another reason: the leaders did away with Jesus out of *envy* (15:10). It is easy to be dismissive of Mark's appeal to "envy" here, but recent research has stressed the immense cultural importance of envy in an ancient world where men were engaged in a constant struggle for fame, glory, and honor. Mark's presentation of Jesus as Christ, Son of God, and Lord, along with his insistence on Jesus' popularity everywhere he goes, fills the high priests with envy, as they see their own position as the leaders of Israel jeopardized. In their distress they seek to do away with Jesus, to shame him in the most humiliating way of all, through his death. This is a very clever literary device. On one level, it explains the actions of the Jewish leaders and Jesus' shameful death, but, on another level, by presenting Jesus as the *object* of high-priestly envy, Mark can exalt his hero still further.[19]

The second theme contains a terrible irony. Jesus' treatment at the hands of the chief priests has been prepared for in some detail by his first passion prediction:

> [T]he Son of Man must undergo suffering, and be rejected by the elders, the chief priests, and the scribes, and be killed, and after three days rise again. (8:31)

The trial, then, will represent Jesus' *rejection* by the Jewish authorities of his day. But that will not be the end of the matter by any means. In his parable of 12:1–12, set soon after his arrival in the city, Jesus tells the story of a man who planted a vineyard and let it out to tenants. As the parable proceeds, it is clear that the tenants represent the Jewish authorities. Throughout their tenancy they have treated God's servants, the prophets, shamefully, and now they take it upon themselves to kill the owner's "beloved son," in the vain hope that the inheritance will come to them. "What then will the owner of the vineyard do?" Jesus asks. "He will come and destroy the tenants and give the vineyard to others" (12:9). The parable ends with Psalm 118:22–33: even though the son will be rejected, he will nevertheless be vindicated.

Reading Jesus' first passion prediction alongside this parable, the reader is already prepared to see in the Jewish trial the religious authorities' rejection of Jesus. But this rejection will swiftly herald not only Jesus' vindication but also their own rejection by God.[20] Through their actions, the Jewish leaders will themselves be utterly destroyed. The prophecy of 12:9 begins to take effect almost immediately. As Jesus breathes his last on the cross, the temple veil is rent asunder by God, as God leaves the sanctuary and abandons the Jewish leaders to their fate.[21] For Mark's original readers, of course, the fulfillment was even clearer: the temple stood in ruins, its cult was now obsolete, and the old religious order was at an end.

Jewish Trial Narrative (14:53–65)

We need to turn now to the text of the trial and follow the dramatic course of events. Jesus is led to the high priest, where "all the chief priests, the elders, and the scribes were assembled" (14:53). Several times throughout the narrative, Mark repeats these various groups (14:55, 64; 15:1), and twice he refers to the assembly as "the council" (*to synedrion*, 14:55, 15:1). What he is doing here is bringing together all the representatives of the Jewish leadership and, like a modern film director, creating a dramatic courtroom scene, the final showdown between the forces of good and the forces of evil.

Until the advent of literary studies, scholars tended to be preoccupied with the legality of the Jewish trial. Bookshelves of monographs and learned articles investigated the intricacies of first-century jurisprudence and compared Mark's trial with the detailed legal practices set out in the Mishnah.[22] With admirable ingenuity it was suggested that the Mishnaic regulations were not in place in the first century, or that they represented an "idealized account" of how the later rabbis thought a Jewish court *ought* to conduct itself, or that perhaps Jesus was tried according to Sadducean rather than Pharisaic/rabbinic regulations. There may be some truth in some—or all—of these suggestions. But if we look at the literary context of Mark's account, it is clear that these suggestions are all simply missing the point.

Mark *intends* his trial scene to be a travesty of justice, a kangaroo court.[23] The scene is intentionally shocking to anyone with an inkling of justice. The evangelist has told us quite clearly that the sole aim of this court is to do away with Jesus (14:1); the first thing the judges do is to seek testimony against the prisoner (14:55); and when Jesus is condemned, it is members of the council who spit on Jesus and ridicule him (14:65).[24] Perhaps Mark knew that Jewish courts did not meet at night—if so, this is precisely why he sets his courtroom drama at night (he could, after all, have expanded on the meeting the following morning in 15:1). Perhaps Mark knew that capital cases began with reasons for acquittal— if so, that is why he opens his scene with the council seeking "testimony against Jesus to put him to death" (14:55). Perhaps Mark knew that Jewish courts did not allow a person to be convicted on the basis of his own testimony—if so, this is precisely why Jesus is condemned on nothing more than his own confession.

Mark's account is deliberately a parody of justice, a gathering of evil men. Only in this way can he explain Jesus' condemnation at the hands of the leaders of Israel, and only in this highly momentous scene can he prepare for God's rejection of these same leaders.

The Charges against Jesus

As we have already seen, the trial itself turns on two issues: (1) the charge that Jesus spoke against the temple and (2) the question of Jesus' identity. The link between the two issues may well have been provided by the messianic prophecy of 2 Samuel 7:13–14. As we shall see, both highlight Jesus' messianic status and both speak to the situation of Mark's own community, underscoring the fact that for Mark theological reflection and present concerns were much more important in this scene than what we might refer to as "historical facts." We need to look at these charges in turn.

1. *The temple charge.* According to Mark, many bore false witness against Jesus, but their testimony did not agree. Then some of the false witnesses stood up and declared: "We heard him say, 'I will destroy this temple that is made with hands, and in three days I will build another, not made with hands.'" The charge is an interesting one; it is clear from earlier in Mark's Gospel that Jesus *has* been speaking and acting against the temple. The day after his entry into Jerusalem, Jesus performed a symbolic action in the temple that, at least in Mark's presentation, symbolized its destruction. A day or so later, in response to the disciples' astonishment at the size of the temple stones, Jesus prophesies, "Not one stone will be left here upon another; all will be thrown down" (13:2). [25] Jesus, then, has clearly been saying subversive things about the temple, but his words here are new. They are, of course, presented by *false* witnesses, but Mark adds that even here the witnesses could not agree. So what are we to make of this saying? Is it true or is it false?

Perhaps the answer is that it is both true and false. It would be clear to Mark's readers that Jesus' reference to "three days" is a veiled allusion to his resurrection, and that the "other temple, not made with hands" is the Christian church. In one sense this prophecy has come true: the temple "made with hands" has been destroyed and has been replaced, as far as Mark's readers are concerned, with the community of the resurrected Jesus. But if any took the prophecy to mean that the destruction of the temple heralded Jesus' triumphant return, they were wrong. Jesus never said that he would destroy the temple himself; the dramatic events of 70 C.E. were not the prelude to his glorious return. Perhaps this is why Mark insists on the falsity of the allegation. Certainly in response to the high priest's demand that he answer his accusers, Jesus refuses to endorse the words and, as noted earlier, remains silent. [26]

2. *Jesus' identity.* In the course of the trial narrative, Mark's abilities as a dramatist are clear. The focus of the scene gradually narrows from the "whole council," to the charges of "many," then "some," and finally the question of the high priest. The two principal actors—the high priest and Jesus—confront one another across a silent, expectant courtroom, as the high priest asks Jesus the most crucial question of all: Are you the Messiah, the Son of the Blessed One? (14:61). On one level, we cannot help but be stunned by the hypocrisy of the man—after all he has done to engineer the death of Jesus, he is worried about saying God's name and substitutes instead the circumlocution "Blessed One"! More impor-

tantly, though, in a Gospel where Jesus' closest followers do not understand who he is until after the resurrection, it is deeply ironic that it is the hostile high priest who has grasped Mark's two central titles for Jesus: Christ and Son of God.

In response to the high priest's insightful question, Jesus replies with an unequivocal "I am." His simple affirmation of his identity contrasts with Peter's blustering denials immediately after this scene (14:66–72) and perhaps provides a model for Christians who find themselves hauled in front of hostile Jewish courts. But Jesus has not finished. He continues to answer the high priest, in words which echo the hopes of the earliest Christians: "And 'you will see the Son of Man seated at the right hand of the Power,' and 'coming with the clouds of heaven.'"[27] Despite his present humiliation, Jesus will be vindicated. Throughout the Gospel, Mark has presented Jesus as a true prophet, whose predictions come true. In the very next scene his earlier prediction of Peter's betrayal will be fulfilled (14:29–31), assuring Mark's readers that this prophecy of Jesus' second coming will also come true in the very near future. If the fall of the temple is not itself the sign that Jesus is about to return, Jesus' second coming is, nevertheless, still imminent.[28]

Words of comfort to Mark's readers, however, are regarded as sacrilege by the high priest, who rends his garments and accuses Jesus of blasphemy. Again we have an echo here of the trials of Christians in Mark's own day. It is they who are charged with blasphemy by Jewish courts for their claims about Jesus. In the trial of Jesus they see their own trials. Mark, as a sensitive pastor, shows his readers that all they have suffered had already been endured by Jesus himself.[29]

The Sentence

Finally, the high priest asks the rest of the council for their decision. Without hesitation Mark reports that "[a]ll of them condemned him as deserving death" (v. 64).[30] Again, the scene is full of irony. This is the first time in the Gospel that Jesus has made his identity known, but no sooner has he declared himself than he is rejected by the Jewish leaders. There is no room here for any mistakes, no one could say afterwards that they were not sure who Jesus was or who he claimed to be. Jesus has openly accepted the titles of Christ and Son of the Blessed One, and the Jewish leaders have, in the full knowledge of what they are doing, rejected their messiah. By condemning Jesus to death, the high priest and the Jewish leaders start the chain of events that will lead to their own destruction. They have accused Jesus of wanting to destroy the temple, but it is the leaders of Israel who destroy their own temple through their rejection of their Messiah, a rejection that will bring down God's judgment on them. The next person in the Gospel to recognize Jesus' identity is, significantly, a Gentile (15:39).[31]

Summary

The high priest in Mark's Gospel is a rather colorless character, a type, a representative of all high priests, all Jewish leaders who have rejected the claims of early Christianity. This is why Mark does not name him. It is not because the evangelist does not remember his name, or because he is drawing on a very early tradition put together when Caiaphas was still high priest, or even because the Jewish trial is largely a Markan creation. It is because the trial takes on an almost mythical quality. Mark's readers would have understood this: they saw in the Jewish trial not a persnickety exercise in the historical reconstruction of Jesus' own trial, but a grand momentous drama in which, through their rejection of God's Messiah, the Jewish leaders bring down destruction on themselves.

Read with the benefit of hindsight, Mark's Jewish trial is indeed, as Burton Mack has put it, "a very vicious fiction."[32] Yet this is perhaps not entirely fair to Mark. It is important to remember that the early Christians were still minority groups at this period, working out their identity vis à vis Judaism. If Mark's community no longer thought of themselves as Jewish, the break was not long in the past, and the Gospel still bears the imprint of the bitterness and hurt that characterized its break with the parent faith. Unfortunately, though, by refusing to name Caiaphas and broadening responsibility for Jesus' rejection to the entire Jewish leadership, Mark began a process whereby Caiaphas's name was lost and Jesus' death was ascribed not to individuals but to the "the Jews" as a whole.

We shall now turn to two presentations of Caiaphas that are dependent on Mark—those of Luke and Matthew. It is important to remember that by the time these evangelists wrote (in the late first century), Mark's Gospel was not yet "Scripture." It was clearly an important document and was passed from church to church, read out (presumably in worship) and copied, but both later evangelists were writing for very different situations and felt quite happy to adapt the earlier work so that it spoke to the needs of their own communities. We shall turn first to Luke, who, though less hostile toward the Jewish leaders than Mark, similarly uses the motif of an unnamed high priest to signal the break between "Judaism" and "Christianity"—though he will employ this device not in the trial of Jesus, but in that of Stephen.

12

Caiaphas in Luke–Acts

Luke was unique among the Gospel writers in that he added a second volume to his work: the Acts of the Apostles. The two books together present a "history of salvation," a chronicle of the spread of God's promises from the Jewish world to Rome, the capital of the Roman Empire. Like Mark, the evangelist shows a particular interest in Gentile converts to Christianity; yet, unlike his source, the author is deeply concerned about the *Jewish heritage* of the new way. He has a high regard for Jewish Scriptures and institutions and clearly sees the church as the fulfillment of Israel's past. This suggests that even if Luke were a Gentile (as most scholars suppose), he must have had close ties with the synagogue before his conversion to Christianity.[1] The provenance of the work is open to debate, but most would locate it in one of the urban centers of the eastern empire, a decade or two later than Mark.[2]

Luke's "history" starts in the Jerusalem temple. Angelic appearances, psalms, and biblical phrases transport the reader back to the world of the Jewish Scriptures. We are introduced to Jesus, who is raised in a pious Jewish family. His earthly mission is to Jews who, throughout most of the Gospel, flock to him by the thousand, astonished at his teaching and glorifying God because of it. Yet

Jesus' ministry brings division, particularly among the Pharisees and rulers of the nation, and there are hints that Israel will not ultimately accept him (4:16–30, 11:14–23, 14:24, 19:44). The narrative reaches a climax in the trial before Pilate, where not only the leaders but the people demand Jesus' death. Acts blames the Jewish people as a whole for what happened (2:22–23, 3:12–13, 4:10, 10:39, 13:27–28), but it also concedes that they acted in ignorance (3:17, 13:27), and the Gospel shows that as soon as they see what they have done, the people repent (23:48).

In the early chapters of Acts, many Jews continue to join the new movement. Luke presents the period of the early church as a golden age: the law-observant disciples are continually in the temple praising God; they are filled with the Spirit, have the gift of healing, share their possessions. The movement attracts vast numbers of converts, all of whom are offered forgiveness and salvation. It is abundantly clear that God has been faithful to Israel: all the promises and blessings contained in the Jewish Scriptures have come to pass in the life of the Jerusalem church.

It is not long, however, before opposition once more rears its head. At first, conflict is limited to the Jewish leaders (4:1–22, 5:17–40), whose hostility is out of step with the high regard felt toward the new movement by ordinary people (4:4, 5:17). But as the narrative progresses, the people themselves become increasingly hostile (6:9–12), until it is quite obvious that the Jerusalemites will reject the Christian message (8:1–3). Peter's conversion of the Roman centurion Cornelius in Caesarea (the Roman capital of the province) signals an important geographical shift in Luke's story. The gospel will no longer be taken exclusively to Jews but will be offered to Gentiles (an innovation prepared for already by Luke 2:29–32, 3:6, and 24:4). Agrippa's persecution (an act which "pleased the Jews," 12:3) provides the impetus for the movement of the church out of Jerusalem and into the Roman world.[3] The story will now center on Paul and his missionary activities, and the fulfillment of Jesus' command that the gospel must be taken "to the ends of the earth" (1:8). From this point onward, "the Jews" tend to be hostile toward Christianity. Paul continues to take the message to them first in every new city and does sometimes have a degree of success (28:23–24), but the theme that dominates the closing chapters of Acts is Paul's triple declaration that if Jews are not prepared to listen, the Christian message must be taken to Gentiles.[4]

Luke's attitude toward Jews has often been misunderstood: it is not so much that he is rejecting Judaism as that he is claiming that the *true heirs to the promises are Christians*. Christians alone can claim an unbroken continuity with Israel's past; in that sense, the Christian church is the true Israel, the true heirs of God's promises in the Old Testament. Luke's two volumes are full of scriptural quotations and allusions that prove everything in the history of the church came about in accordance with God's will. The narrative itself imitates the style of the Greek Bible (the Septuagint), particularly the opening chapters of the Gospel, suggesting that the evangelist thought of his work as "biblical history," a continuation of the Jewish Scriptures—the last act in which Gentiles come to share in the promises bestowed on Israel.

Such an interpretation would, of course, have brought Luke into conflict with his Jewish contemporaries, who were already by this time beginning to regard Christians with some disdain. It is unlikely, however, that Luke expected many Jews to read his work: his primary audience would have been Gentile Christian converts to the new way, people who, perhaps like Luke himself, had been on the fringes of the synagogues and knew their Jewish Scriptures. Luke provides such people with a foundational myth, a story that assured his readers that God had kept God's promises to Israel and which guaranteed that the spread of the movement into the Gentile world was truly God's will.

Caiaphas plays a significant role (either by his presence or absence) in three important sections of Luke's story: (1) the setting of Jesus' ministry; (2) Luke's trial narrative, and (3) the early chapters of Acts. We shall look at each of these in turn, noting how Luke's presentation of Caiaphas has been guided by his own particular interests. We shall see that, despite significant differences between Mark and Luke, Luke's use of an anonymous high priest, especially in Acts, has been inspired by his Markan source.

The Setting of Jesus' Ministry: Annas and Caiaphas Are Introduced (3:1–2)

After recounting the story of Jesus' birth and early childhood, Luke begins a new section, focusing on the preaching of John the Baptist and leading into the ministry of Jesus. He opens with a series of rulers, the effect of which is to tie events in the history of salvation with events on the wider world stage.[5] Things began, he claims, in the fifteenth year of Tiberius Caesar (29 C.E., a date with a fair degree of plausibility about it). Pontius Pilate was governor of Judea, while Herod was tetrarch of Galilee, his brother Philip tetrarch of Ituraea and Trachonitis, and Lysanias tetrarch of Abilene. All this information is perfectly accurate and ties in with what we know from other sources. Indeed, unlike many writers of his day, who tended to refer to Herod and Philip rather loosely as "kings," Luke reproduced their titles accurately, a detail that lends an air of reliability to his narrative.

The next phrase, however, is more problematic: "*during the high priesthood* (singular) *of Annas and Caiaphas.*" This verse has struck many commentators as confused or inaccurate. Does Luke imagine that the two men shared the high priesthood? Or does the singular noun suggest that the evangelist originally wrote only "Annas" and that a later editor added "and Caiaphas" to bring the Gospel into line with Matthew, John, or historical fact (a suggestion that, however attractive, finds no support in any extant manuscript)?[6] The same confusion exists in Acts 4:6, which similarly reads: "Annas the high priest (singular), Caiaphas, John [Jonathan], and Alexander, and all who were of the high-priestly family." What are we to make of Luke's odd terminology? Are we to assume that in both cases he was simply confused?

Perhaps modern scholars have been rather overpedantic here. The names of both men presumably came down to Luke from his tradition; both played a part in Jesus' death, and the evangelist was clearly keen to include them both in his narrative. These traditions may well have referred to each man as "high priest"— Annas out of respect for his previous position and prestige within the community, Caiaphas because he was the acting high priest at the time.[7] Referring to two men as high priest, however, would have caused theological difficulties. Luke knew perfectly well that there was only one high priest, one mediator between God and humanity, and that the reference to the high priest had to be singular. This perhaps led to the awkward construction that we find in both Luke 3:2 and Acts 4:6, a construction that may not have sounded so odd to Luke and his readers as it does to modern scholars.[8]

At all events, though, it is clear from Luke's following narrative that he has little real interest in either Annas or Caiaphas as historical individuals. Neither man will play a role in Jesus' Jewish trial, and in the opening chapters of Acts they will be presented as rather stereotypical opponents of the new movement. Luke seems to have included them at this point because he wants to ground his story not just in wider political history, but quite specifically in the history of Israel. His story opens "during the high priesthood of Annas and Caiaphas," at a time when traditional priestly leaders ruled God's people, but it will end in Acts with the rejection of these leaders in favor of the Spirit-led apostles, the new leaders of the new Israel. Before turning to Acts, however, we must turn to Luke's passion narrative and investigate his rather curious omission of the high priest in his account of Jesus' Jewish trial.

Luke's Trial Narrative

Luke departs from his Markan source to a much greater extent in his passion narrative than anywhere else in the Gospel.[9] One of his most striking alterations is in his arrangement of the trial narrative, where he has transformed Mark's two parallel trials (one Jewish, one Roman) into a single trial narrative with four distinct parts:[10]

1. Jesus' interrogation by the Jewish leaders (22:66–71)
2. Preliminary interrogation by Pilate (23:1–5)
3. Interrogation in front of Herod (23:6–12)
4. Gathering of Pilate, Jewish leaders, and people for the verdict (23:13–25).

In the following analysis we shall look in some detail at the first scene (the one that corresponds most closely to Mark's Jewish trial) and then, more briefly, consider the continuation of the trial in the three subsequent scenes. First, though, we need to consider the motives of Jesus' opponents for wanting him dead.

The Decision to Kill Jesus

In Mark, the Jewish leaders wanted to do away with Jesus because of his actions in the temple (11:18), actions that implied God's coming eschatological judgment on both the temple and the Jewish leaders. Luke, however, has a much more positive estimate of the Jerusalem temple.[11] The Gospel begins there (1:8–23, 2:22–39), and throughout his ministry Jesus never speaks or acts against it. Of course, by the time Luke was writing, the temple had been burned to the ground, and the evangelist does have Jesus prophesy its destruction (13:34–35, 21:5–9), but Jesus never *threatens* the temple or its worship. The incident in the temple is pared down drastically, and the brief remaining narrative shows Jesus opposed only to the merchants (19:45–46). On the cross, Jesus is not mocked as a temple destroyer, and he dies communing with his Father in the temple.[12] Even after Jesus' death, the disciples are "continually in the temple blessing God" (24:53), and the temple retains its validity throughout the whole of Acts. Luke knows that the temple is not indispensable (a point made quite eloquently by Stephen's speech, 7:2–53), but while it stands, it has a positive role as the house of God.

What leads to Jesus' death in Luke is not his prophetic sign of the temple's destruction, or any criticism of the institution, but rather the fact that *he makes the temple the center of his messianic activity*. As soon as he arrives in Jerusalem he goes to the temple (19:45) and teaches there every day (19:47), preaching to large crowds until his arrest (21:37–38). The link between Jesus' teaching and the hostility of his opponents is clear from 19:47–48: "Every day he was teaching in the temple. The chief priests, the scribes, and the leaders of the people kept looking for a way to kill him; but they did not find anything they could do, for all the people were spellbound by what they heard." In Luke's presentation, "Jesus has taken possession of the temple and taught in it as Israel's Messiah."[13] He has won the allegiance of the people but threatened the legitimacy of the religious leaders, who challenge his authority to speak and act as the lord of the temple (20:1–8). What is at stake for Luke is Jesus' messianic authority, and this single theme will dominate his Jewish interrogation.

The Jewish Interrogation (22:66–71)

Luke's Jewish trial scene is significantly different from that of his Markan source. The councillors do not meet clandestinely at night but assemble the morning after Jesus' arrest. Gone is the temple charge (presumably because in this Gospel Jesus has not threatened the temple); gone too are the false witnesses and the charge of blasphemy.[14] Each of the three central characters— Jesus, the chief priests, and the high priest—is cast rather differently. Jesus is not silent in Luke's presentation but courageously speaks out to the assembled Jewish leaders, providing a model for his disciples in Acts, who often find themselves on trial. Jesus' opponents, the "chief priests and scribes," are presented in much more measured terms than in Mark: Jesus is mocked by guards, not by members of the Jewish council (22:63, Mark 14:65), and the whole scene has an air of respectability that was totally lacking in Mark.[15] Throughout the interrogation, this group speaks in chorus and acts in unison, a presentation that is rather cumbersome and almost pantomimic in places. The reason for this is that *the high priest plays no part whatsoever in the proceedings against Jesus*; lines spoken by the high priest in Mark, therefore, have to be reassigned to the chief-priestly chorus.

Luke's omission of the high priest is one of the most striking features of his account. The evangelist admits that one of the high priest's slaves was present in the arresting party (22:50) and that Jesus was brought initially to the high priest's palace (22:54), but the next morning he is led away by "the chief priests and scribes" to their council (*synedrion*). Luke seems to think of this "council" as a *place*, perhaps a council chamber where regular meetings were held.[16] If so, not only does the high priest take no part in the proceedings, but the action no longer takes place in his palace.[17] We shall explore the significance of this omission after analyzing the trial itself.

Are You the Christ, the Son of the Blessed?

Luke's Jewish trial narrative focuses entirely on Jesus' messianic authority. All that the evangelist has retained from Mark is the central question of Jesus' identity— "Are you the Messiah, the son of the Blessed One?"—though he will treat the two halves of the question separately.

First, the chief priests and scribes demand, "If you are the Messiah, tell us" (22:67). Jesus replies, "If I tell you, you will not believe; and if I question you, you will not answer." His words here echo the earlier exchange of 20:1–8, when the Jewish leaders challenged Jesus' authority and were left speechless; but they are also prophetic in that Jesus is about to tell his opponents of his heavenly enthronement, though they will not believe his words. Jesus continues, "But from now on the Son of Man will be seated at the right hand of the power of God" (22:69). In Mark's Gospel, these words looked forward to Christ's second coming "with the clouds of heaven"; Luke's "from now on," however, subtly transforms the whole phrase into a prophecy of Jesus' vindication and royal enthronement after his death and resurrection.[18]

In response, the councillors ask their second question: "Are you, then, the Son of God?" This, for Luke, is the most important title for Jesus; it was foretold in the birth stories (1:32–33, 2:11), recognized by Satan (4:3, 9), and confirmed by God (3:21–28, 9:35). Jesus replies, "You say that I am," perhaps pointing to the irony of the fact that while the Jewish leaders *say* that Jesus is the Son of God, they do not themselves believe it. The councillors take Jesus' words as proof of his guilt and, without further ado, prepare to take him to the Roman governor. Despite witnessing Jesus' messianic authority every day in the temple, the Jewish leaders are incapable of belief.

The Continuation of the Trial (23:1–25)

Jesus is immediately taken to Pilate, before whom he is accused by the Jewish authorities of "perverting our nation." The council members provide two specific examples—forbidding the payment of tribute and claiming to be the Messiah, a king—both of which the reader knows to be false. Pilate quickly satisfies himself that Jesus is no threat and declares him innocent. Seeking a way out of a troublesome case, he sends Jesus to Herod, who happens to be in Jerusalem (23:6–12). The Jewish tetrarch questions Jesus at length, hoping to see a sign, while the chief priests and scribes continue vigorously accusing him. Tiring of the silent prisoner, Herod treats Jesus contemptuously and sends him back to Pilate. Yet, despite his scorn, Herod serves as a second witness to his innocence (23:15); his earlier desire to kill Jesus (13:31) making his lack of action all the more striking.[19]

In the final, climactic scene, Pilate summons the "chief priests, the leaders, and the people" (23:13–25). The Roman governor attempts to give a verdict, announcing that he will chastise the prisoner and then release him. The people and their leaders, however, shout "Away with this fellow!" and demand instead the release of Barabbas, a man who, Luke notes, "had been put in prison for an insurrection that had taken place in the city, and for murder" (23:19). In this Gospel there is no Passover amnesty, a fact that makes the choice of the people all the more perverse and inexplicable.[20] Furthermore, the Jewish leaders do not need to stir up the people; the crowd rejects Jesus of its own volition, "demanding with loud shouts that he should be crucified" (23:23).

The key to understanding Jesus' rejection by the Jewish people here is Luke's presentation of Jesus as a *prophet*, the last of the great prophets of the Old Testament. Throughout the Gospel, Jesus is often compared to Moses, Elijah, and Elisha.[21] As a prophet, Jesus offers his people salvation; but it is also part of his prophetic destiny that he must suffer and die in Jerusalem (9:22, 17:25, 24:7, Acts 3:21, 17:3). Jesus himself lamented: "Jerusalem, Jerusalem, the city that kills the prophets and stones those who are sent to it!" (Luke 13:34). In this final scene of the trial, the Jewish people join with their leaders and, true to the spirit of their ancestors, who continually persecuted the prophets, reject Jesus.

The verdict to the whole trial comes in 23:24, where with great irony Pilate "gave his verdict that their demand should be granted." Despite the Roman governor's repeated attempts to acquit him, Jesus will go to his death as an innocent prophet and martyr. It is clear that, for Luke, injustice has triumphed in the governor's court.[22]

Luke's Jewish interrogation, then, is the first stage of a composite trial. Jesus is arrested by the Jewish leaders because of his messianic authority, an authority that fills the chief priests with alarm. As subsequent scenes unfold, however, Jesus is rejected as the Messiah and the Son of God, not only by the Jewish leaders, but by the whole nation. While Mark placed responsibility for Jesus' rejection on the *Jewish leaders*, Luke places responsibility much more broadly on the *chief priests, rulers, and the people.* In keeping with the nation's habit of doing away with God's prophets, Israel has rejected the most important prophet of all.

The Disappearance of the High Priest

But why has Luke erased all mention of the high priest?[23] Was it in order to broaden responsibility for Jesus' death from the high priest to the whole chief-priestly assembly?[24] Or was it so as not to detract from the central christological questions at the trial? Either of these explanations is perfectly possible. Yet, in view of the evangelist's dependence on Mark and the narrative development of Luke–Acts, another explanation seems more probable.

For Mark, as we have seen, the Jewish trial narrative is a climactic, momentous event, signaling God's rejection of the Jewish leaders and their temple. For Luke, however, the purpose and significance of the trial is quite different. The composite trial of 22:66–23:25 represents only Israel's rejection of its prophet-Messiah. God will not yet abandon his people, any more than in the past, when they persecuted earlier prophets. As we have seen, Jews continue to convert well into Acts, and Luke is keen to present the period of the early church as a time when God's promises to Jews were being fulfilled. The decisive point in Jewish-Christian relations comes for Luke not with Jesus' death, but with that of *Stephen.* Following Stephen's trial and execution (which, significantly, are modeled on those of Jesus in Mark), God will turn from Jews to Gentiles.[25]

In this rearrangement of his Markan material Luke's omission of the high priest makes sense. He will delay the entrance of the supreme pontiff until the trials of the apostles in Acts 4–5, where he and his high-priestly family will act as a foil to ordinary Jews, who are repenting of their rejection of Jesus and turning to the new movement in droves. But it will be in the trial of Stephen and the subsequent high-priestly persecution of Christianity that Luke's high priest will take on the role carved out for him by Mark. It will be here that the high priest will reject the early Christian movement and, following this rejection, the traditional leaders of Judaism will show themselves to be no longer capable of guiding God's people—a people that will now be composed of both Jews and Gentiles.

The Early Chapters of Acts

The book of Acts charts the development of the church from the Jewish to the Gentile world. Two elements are important here: (1) the people who make up the new movement and (2) their leaders. The figure of the "high priest" plays a role in defining both of these.

1. In Luke's presentation, Jesus makes his people two offers of salvation. Like Moses in Stephen's speech (7:20–44), he makes two appearances: the first in weakness, the second in power. The Gospel describes his first visitation and rejection by the people, who in their ignorance fail to grasp his identity. In the book of Acts, the resurrected Jesus reigns in power at the right hand of God (7:56); his message is brought to the people by the Spirit-filled apostles to the accompa-

niment of signs and wonders (2:43, 3:1–10, 5:12). They invite the Jerusalemites to repent of their earlier rejection of Jesus and offer them salvation and a place in God's kingdom. "This time, however, the cost of refusal is separation from Israel's people."[26]

At first, the apostles meet with a great deal of success. The company of believers expands at an exponential rate (2:41–42, 47; 4:4; 5:14–16; 6:7), and it is clear that God's promises to Abraham are fulfilled in the life of the Jerusalem church. The only blots on the landscape are the high-priestly rulers, who alone appear to oppose the new movement (4:1–3, 5–21; 5:17–40). Gradually, however, opposition spreads: members of Stephen's Greek-speaking synagogue dispute with him (6:9–14); the church suffers its first wave of persecution at the hands of Paul (8:1, 3; 9:1–2); and, by the middle of Acts, "the Jews" as a whole are pleased by Agrippa's execution of James (12:3). By now, it is clear that members of the new movement will be drawn predominantly from the Greco-Roman world. The Jewish people, for Luke, have been offered two chances of salvation and have refused them both. Although he still welcomes Jews into the church, the "new Israel" will be composed predominantly not of Jews but of Gentiles.

2. But who are the leaders of the "new Israel"? It is clear that for Luke the appropriate leaders of the new movement are the apostles. He wastes no time at the beginning of Acts in telling us that Judas was replaced by Matthias, a man who had accompanied Jesus throughout his ministry (1:15–26). Together, these twelve men represent the twelve tribes of Israel, a powerful signal to Luke's readers that the church is the new, restored Israel. Filled with the Spirit and possessing a boldness that amazes even their opponents, these twelve men are the natural leaders of the new movement.

This apostolic leadership, however, is challenged almost from the start by representatives of "old Israel," the traditional high-priestly leaders who twice summon the apostles before their council (4:1–21, 5:17–40). These leaders make a grand entry into Luke's narrative; in the very first trial scene they are introduced separately and by name, a technique that reminds the reader of the privileged place they occupied at the beginning of the story (Luke 3:2): "Annas the high priest, Caiaphas, John [Jonathan], and Alexander, and all who were of the high-priestly family" (Acts 4:6). Luke clearly wants his readers to take note of their presence and to contrast their leadership with that of the apostles.

As the two trials progress, an ever-widening gulf opens up between the traditional high-priestly leaders (who are incapable of discerning the will of God) and the apostles (who are filled with God's Spirit).[27] The increasingly desperate attempts of the high-priestly leaders to silence the apostles result only in an increase of the apostles' power and authority (4:21–5:16). And as they find themselves constantly thwarted, the high-priestly leaders are presented in an ever poorer light: they are filled with jealousy (5:17), afraid of the people they are supposed to govern (5:26), and become enraged and want to kill the disciples (5:33). Faced with God's apostles, not only the high priest but "the council and the whole body of the elders of Israel" (5:21) are entirely powerless. As L. T. Johnson puts it: "Whatever political machinations are still available to the Sanhedrin, religious authority over Israel . . . has passed to the apostles."[28]

Matters come to a head in the trial of Stephen (6:8–8:1). We saw in the chapter on Caiaphas and the earliest Christians that Luke seems to have grafted references to the "high priest" (7:1) and "the council" (6:12, 15) onto a tradition that told of Stephen's lynching at the hands of his own Greek-speaking synagogue.[29] More importantly, though, many of the details that Luke omitted from Mark's Jewish trial of Jesus find a home here: the false witnesses (6:13), the temple charge (6:13–14), and the accusation of blasphemy (6:11). Luke, then, seems to have deliberately modeled Stephen's trial on that of Jesus in Mark. The reason for this is not hard to find: just as Mark's Jewish trial signaled God's repudiation of Israel's leaders, so Luke's trial of Stephen shows quite decisively that the old Jewish leaders are no longer the trustees of God's promises. The future of Israel will lie instead with Gentile Christianity and its apostolic leadership. The truth of this is apparent both from Stephen's speech (which assures the reader that God is not tied down to a land or a nation or a temple, but that he transcends all ethnic boundaries) and from Stephen's final vision of the glorified Jesus (7:56).[30] Luke's nameless "high priest" in 7:1, then, performs exactly the same narrative role as Mark's unnamed "high priest." Whether Luke imagined the pontiff to be Annas (the only person specifically referred to as "high priest" in Luke 3:2 and Acts 4:6) or Caiaphas is immaterial.[31] The high priest is the figurehead and symbolic leader of "old Israel," which now, for Luke, finds itself opposed to God.

Stephen's trial ends without a verdict. Perhaps for Luke no verdict was necessary: the truth of Stephen's words would manifest itself in the spread of Christianity as it moved beyond the jurisdiction of Israel's misguided high-priestly leaders into the Greco-Roman world.

Summary

Luke has little interest in Caiaphas. He is named twice, presumably because his name was known to Luke from tradition. Yet, like Mark, the evangelist is more interested in the symbolic function of the high priest than the historical incumbent. In fact, a reader of Luke–Acts could quite easily assume that the high priest referred to in Acts was not Caiaphas but his father-in-law Annas.

Luke omits any reference to a high priest in the Jewish interrogation of Jesus because he will leave high priestly opposition to a later stage in his story. This comes in Acts where, drawing on Mark, he uses a hostile and nameless high priest to signal the break between the new movement and Judaism—a movement led by God contrasted with a movement led by people. Following the high priest's involvement in the early chapters of Acts, it becomes increasingly clear that the majority of Jews will not accept Christianity and that the mission must be directed instead to Gentiles. For Luke, this new mission is perfectly in accord with God's will, Christians are the heirs to God's promises, and Christianity is the proper response to God's revelation, not just in Jesus, but throughout Israel's history.

We shall turn now to the Jewish-Christian Gospel of Matthew. Although the author, like Luke, drew on Mark's Gospel, he will develop the exchange between Jesus and Caiaphas in a quite different manner.

13

Caiaphas in Matthew

Matthew's Gospel was written about the same time as Luke's, though for a quite different readership. The author followed his Markan source closely in terms of content and the order of material but, like Luke, was not afraid to interpret Mark for his own community, making a number of alterations and additions that gave his work greater relevance for his readers. Tradition associates the Gospel with Syria (perhaps Antioch), though a number of modern scholars would put it closer to Palestine, perhaps in a city of Upper Galilee or Syro-Phoenicia.[1]

What is particularly striking about the Gospel is its *Jewishness*: it is structured around five blocks of teaching (reminiscent of the five books of the Torah); it abounds in Old Testament quotations; assumes the validity of the Jewish law; and presents Jesus in typically Jewish terms as the Messiah, Son of David, and the new Moses. All this suggests that the Gospel was written for a Jewish-Christian community. And yet it is also clear that members of Matthew's church were no longer welcome in their local Jewish synagogue. The evangelist writes disparagingly of "your synagogue" or "their synagogue," and references to the synagogue are never positive. There is even evidence that members of the community have been persecuted by the local synagogue, and the Gospel still

120

bears the scars of the hurt and hostility that has characterized relations between the two groups in the recent past.[2]

The breakdown of relations between Matthew's church and the synagogue explains why the Gospel is so hostile toward non-Christian Jews. Matthew simply cannot understand why his opponents have not accepted Jesus as their messiah: either they are incapable of understanding their own Scriptures, or they are willfully disobedient. His anger is directed most forcibly towards Israel's leaders, particularly the "scribes and Pharisees" (who probably represent synagogue leaders of Matthew's own day)—they are nothing but hypocrites, blind guides, and murderers (chapter 23). Yet ordinary Jews also come in for criticism: early on in the Gospel they are well disposed towards Jesus, but as time goes on, their failure to accept Jesus means that they will be judged (23:34–39), and their privileged place in God's plans for the salvation of humanity will be offered instead to Gentiles (8:11–12; 21:41, 43).[3] For Matthew, it is his own community, "the church" (16:18, 18:17), that constitutes the "new Israel"; his Gospel reassures them that God's promises in the Scriptures are truly coming to pass in their midst.

As this chapter unfolds, we shall see that Matthew's Jewish background has had a profound influence on his presentation not only of the Jewish leadership but—most importantly for our purposes—of the Jewish high priest, Caiaphas. Matthew, no less than Mark, sees the Jewish rejection of Jesus as a sign that Jews will themselves be rejected (in fact, as we shall see, he broadens Mark's Jewish leaders to the people as a whole). But where Mark used a nameless "high priest" to represent the doomed Jewish leadership and the end of the Jewish temple and its cult, Matthew uses Caiaphas to say something about *Jesus*. In order to explore this further, we shall look first at Matthew's presentation of priestly rulers in general, then turn to two passages where Caiaphas is specifically named: the prologue to the passion narrative (26:1–5) and the Jewish trial (26:57–68).

Matthew's Chief Priests

Compared with Mark, Matthew's chief priests are engaged in greater controversy with Jesus and presented in an even more negative light. As the narrative progresses, their portrayal degenerates until they are cast in an almost satanic role. In the course of the next few paragraphs we shall chart this downward spiral.[4]

The chief priests first appear, perhaps rather surprisingly, in Matthew's birth narrative (2:1–6). Here they play a secondary role to the villainous King Herod, who will not tolerate another "king of the Jews." The priestly leaders confirm that the Christ is to be born in Bethlehem but, like the rest of the Jerusalemites, share Herod's anxiety and do nothing to save the child from the king's plots. This time, of course, Jesus evades the evil intrigues of his opponents, but the story prepares for the grand conflict at the end of the Gospel, where once again "all Jerusalem" will join with their priestly leaders in rejecting their messiah.

Throughout Jesus' Galilean ministry, he engages in controversy with Pharisees and scribes. As soon as he enters Jerusalem, however, it is once again the chief priests (this time joined by the "elders of the people") who form the principal opposition. [5] The first clash occurs almost immediately: Jesus rides into Jerusalem and goes straight up to the "temple of God" where he creates a disturbance (21:12–16). While Mark used this incident to foretell the destruction of the temple, Matthew gives it a quite different meaning.[6] The scene is prefaced by the question of the crowds, "Who is this?" (21:10), and is followed by Jesus' healing in the temple and being proclaimed "Son of David" (21:14–15). The temple has always been portrayed positively in Matthew, and now serves as the place where the Son of David is revealed. Jesus enters the temple as the Messiah, and establishes his authority over the sacred place (12:6).[7] Not surprisingly, the chief priests are indignant: the temple is the site of *their* power, and they are not about to make room for a Galilean upstart (21:15). In the course of the following scenes, they challenge Jesus' authority (21:23–27) and, along with Pharisees and Herodians, try to catch him out. Yet they are no match for the Galilean teacher; each time they are outmaneuvered by him until they are finally reduced to silence (22:46).

The chief priests, however, are not deterred. When argument and debate fails to overcome Jesus, they resort to more underhanded methods (26:3–5). Like Herod earlier in the story, they will stop at nothing to maintain their own power and status. Their trial of Jesus is, like that in Mark, nothing but a travesty of justice; but Matthew manages to paint his villains as even more treacherous and base. In this Gospel, "the chief priests and the whole council *were looking for false testimony against Jesus* so that they might put him to death" (26:59). False witnesses, of course, testified against Jesus in Mark (14:15), but the earlier evangelist gave no hint that the Jewish leaders actively sought them out. Matthew's Jewish leaders know that the only way they can prevail against Jesus is to resort to underhanded means, though even this fails to provide them with grounds for a conviction (26:60). At the end of the trial, by omitting any reference to the abusive behavior of the guards, Matthew highlights Jesus' mistreatment at the hands of his Jewish judges—men who stoop so low as to mock a condemned man and to make particular fun of his messianic claims (26:67).

In the following scenes, Matthew's chief priests slip into ever deeper depravity. In the cold light of day, Judas returns to the chief priests, confesses his sin, and thereby becomes a witness to Jesus' innocence (27:4).[8] The "chief priests and the elders," however, are indifferent: "What is that to us? See to it yourself," they say (27:4). With great irony, Matthew shows them worrying about the legality of putting blood money back in the temple, completely oblivious to the enormity of their crimes. Before Pilate, the chief priests and elders act as Jesus' accusers, inciting the crowd to cry not only for Barabbas's release, but also for Jesus' crucifixion. Matthew has modified his Markan source so that the trial no longer centers around Jesus as "king of the Jews," but as "Messiah," and it is clearly as the Messiah or Christ that Jesus is rejected. Running throughout the tightly structured drama of chapter 27 is the haunting question of responsibility. Each character in turn attempts to pass responsibility for the death of Jesus onto someone else: Judas brings back the blood money, and Pilate washes his hands. Now, whipped up by their leaders, responsibility falls on those who accept it: the Jewish people. Using a traditional Israelite formula indicating responsibility for a death in the eyes of God, they cry out with one voice: "His blood be on us and on our children!" (27:25).[9]

We next meet the Jewish leaders at the cross. Like the evil men of Psalm 22:6–8, they mock God's righteous one. Yet there is something still more sinister about their taunts. Matthew expands his Markan source to read: "He saved others; he cannot save himself. He is the King of Israel; let him come down from the cross now, and we will believe in him. He trusts in God; let God deliver him now, if he wants to; for he said, 'I am God's Son'" (Matt 27:42–43). The explicit use of the title "Son of God" and the threefold questioning are reminiscent of Satan's threefold temptation of Jesus in the wilderness, particularly the second temptation, in which Satan tries to persuade Jesus to throw himself from the pinnacle of the temple, trusting that God would keep him safe. Like Satan, the chief priests (along with the passersby and the robbers crucified with Jesus) try to stand in the way of the fulfillment of God's plan. The whole scene is, of course, highly ironic: just as Jesus could have met the demands of Satan earlier in the narrative, so he could save himself now. The chief priests cannot understand that Jesus will save his people by relinquishing his power and dying on the cross.

Even after Jesus' death, the chief priests still plot against him. They go to Pilate and, telling him of Jesus' prophecy that he would rise from the dead, ask to set a guard on the tomb (27:63–66).[10] After the resurrection, some of the guards go into the city and tell the chief priests all that has taken place. The chief priests take counsel and, resorting to bribery once again, persuade the soldiers to say that Jesus' disciples came by night and stole the body while they slept, justifying the deception by claiming that they are protecting the soldiers from getting into trouble with Pilate (though the reader has to wonder what a Roman governor would make of guards who slept on duty!). The chief priests have taken every precaution possible to prevent the resurrection, but ultimately all their efforts are ineffectual; human beings cannot oppose the will of God. The chief priests would rather bribe soldiers than accept the resurrection; their only defense against God is fraud. Within the narrative, the lies and deceit of the chief priests become ever more desperate and futile.

Matthew's Jewish leaders have not only failed to recognize Jesus themselves, but have also persuaded the people to reject him. There is nothing for them now but to await the judgment foreseen by Jesus (23:38; 24:3–25:46). Matthew's readers, of course, would see the terrible fulfillment of this judgment in the destruction of Jerusalem: Rachel has once again wept for her children (2:18, citing Jer 31:15), but this time there will be no restoration. For Matthew, the rejection of the Messiah by the Jewish people signals the beginning of the "new Israel," the church.

Matthew's Jewish leaders, then, are cold, heartless, manipulative, and callous;

they are opposed to God and not fit to guide the people. This harsh appraisal is undoubtedly colored by the evangelist's experiences of Jewish leaders of his own day—some of his own hostility has almost certainly been projected back into the time of Jesus. But the leaders are also a foil for Jesus' majesty: in the midst of all the Jewish hostility, Jesus' messianic identity has shone through Matthew's account; even his enemies have become unconscious witnesses to his identity and power. These features will be apparent, above all, in the two passages directly involving Caiaphas, to which we now turn.

Matthew and the Reappearance of Caiaphas (26:1–5)

Mark opened his Passion Narrative with a brief note that the chief priests and scribes "were seeking how to arrest (Jesus) by stealth and kill him" (14:1–2). Matthew, however, is much more dramatic: he begins with two short scenes, both of which help to set the tone of what is to come.[11]

The narrative opens not with the plots of the chief priests, but with Jesus, who for a fourth time predicts his death: "You know that after two days the Passover is coming, and the Son of Man will be handed over to be crucified" (26:2). This is a clever literary device that reminds the reader that the prime mover in Jesus' passion is not the Jewish leaders, but God.[12] The passion prediction underscores Jesus' majesty and prophetic foreknowledge; he is not a victim of the machinations of the Jewish authorities but goes to his death because it is part of God's plan. The second scene presents a formal meeting of the "chief priests and the elders of the people" who gather to decide when and how to arrest Jesus (26:3–5).[13] The juxtaposition of these two episodes gives the impression that they are happening at the same time, and the contrast between them could hardly be stronger. Jesus' calm demeanor contrasts sharply with the furtive plotting of the Jewish leaders. They were incapable of defeating him through argument and debate (chapters 21–23) and now resort to force and malice. They think they are in charge of the situation but have no idea what they are up against; their dark intrigue can only emphasize their blindness. If Jesus is the hero, it is clear who are the villains of the piece.

In a further departure from Mark, Matthew not only adds a specific reference to the high priest here but also names him. The Jewish leaders gathered, he says, in the palace of the high priest, "who was called Caiaphas" (26:3).[14] The effect of this is to set up a parallelism between the two scenes: Jesus, the hero, surrounded by his disciples, contrasted with the high priest, the archvillain, surrounded by Jewish leaders. But why has Matthew chosen to add Caiaphas's name? Although the evangelist likes to refer to his characters by name, he does not usually add names that were not in his Markan source.[15] Why, then, the reference to Caiaphas? Was it simply because the high priest's identity was so well established within the Jewish-Christian traditions to which he was heir?[16] Or was it, perhaps more likely, *to emphasize the contrast between the two men, Jesus and Caiaphas?* This contrast, we shall see, will be developed still further in the Jewish trial scene, which continues to name the high priest as Caiaphas.

The Jewish Trial (26:57–68)

Matthew follows his Markan source closely throughout this scene: we have the same formal nighttime gathering of priestly leaders and representatives of the people, and the same charges. One noticeable difference, however, is that, through a number of subtle alterations, Matthew's "chief priests, scribes, and elders" retreat from center stage so that they form little more than a hostile backdrop to the main events. This narrative device allows the reader's attention to focus on the two key actors: Jesus and Caiaphas.[17]

The contrast between the two men is developed almost at once with the temple charge. Matthew's account here is so different from his Markan source that it will be as well to quote both:

> Some stood up and gave false testimony against him, saying, "We heard him say, 'I will destroy this temple that is made with hands, and in three days I will build another, not made with hands.'" But even on this point their testimony did not agree. (Mark 14:57–59)

> At last two came forward and said, "This fellow said, 'I am able to destroy the temple of God and to build it in three days.'" (Matt 26:60–61)

Matthew has made two important changes to his source here. First, while Mark stresses that the temple charge was *false*, Matthew's narrative strongly suggests that his version of the charge is *true*. He has already told us that the chief priests' hunt for false witnesses resulted in nothing (26:60), and the temple charge is brought by the two witnesses required by Jewish law.[18] What they say, then, is significant and valid. Second, the words of the accusation are different. No longer does Jesus say "I will destroy" (so Mark 14:58), but "*I am able* to destroy." Matthew's readers, of course, knew that the temple was now in ruins and that it had symbolically been "rebuilt" within the Christian church, yet there is a difference in emphasis here. The Jesus who entered Jerusalem and revealed himself in the temple in 21:12–17 now once again emphasizes his *power over the temple and its cult*. There is no Markan contrast between the old temple ("made with hands") and the new temple of the church ("not made with hands"); for Matthew, the temple is *rebuilt*, not *replaced*. The temple of the Christian community is the direct successor to the "temple of God" in Jerusalem, and Jesus has authority over both.[19]

Hearing the temple charge, the high priest rises to his feet. Paring down Mark's account, Matthew presents a dramatic confrontation between Caiaphas and Jesus.[20] If anyone has "power over the temple," it is the high priest, the cultic head of the nation. The temple is the focus of *his* power and authority. "Have you no answer?" the high priest demands. "What is it that they testify against you?" Jesus, however, meets Caiaphas's questions with silence, prompting the high priest to ask the crucial question: "I put you under oath before the living God, tell us if you are the Messiah, the Son of God." As in Mark's narrative, the high priest has, ironically and unintentionally, revealed Jesus' identity. In response, Jesus answers,

"You have said so," and continues, "But I tell you, from now on you will see the Son of Man seated at the right hand of Power and coming on the clouds of heaven."[21] Despite present appearances, Jesus really is the Christ, the Son of God, and will return in the future in glory as the judge of the world.

Jesus' response, though, enrages the high priest, who tears his robes at what he considers Jesus' blasphemous words. A curious feature of Matthew's account is that he has changed Mark's word for "robes" here. Rather than *chitōn* (which generally refers to a tunic or undergarment), Matthew has substituted *himation* (a cloak or, in the plural as here, clothes).[22] Coming at such a crucial stage in the narrative, it is difficult not to suspect that there is some significance in Matthew's change of wording here. The explanation may lie in the Greek version of Leviticus 21:10, a verse that comes among a number of rules and regulations for both priests and nonpriests: "The priest who is exalted above his fellows, on whose head the anointing oil has been poured [i.e., the high priest] and who has been consecrated to wear the vestments (*ta himatia*), shall not dishevel his hair, *nor tear his vestments* (*ta himatia*)."

At the very least, Matthew shows the high priest deliberately breaking the law. But he may intend an even deeper meaning. The evangelist may imagine that Caiaphas is wearing not simply his own clothes, but the *high-priestly* vestments.[23] Perhaps he understands the rending of the high priest's vestments as a foreshadowing of the fact that the role of the earthly high priest would come to an abrupt end with the destruction of the temple, an event that for Matthew is a direct result of Jewish rejection of Jesus (27:25). Oblivious to all of this, of course, the high priest asks his fellow councillors for their judgment, a judgment that they all give as "death" (26:66). From now on, Caiaphas/the high priest plays no further role, and simply merges into the ill-defined mass of "chief priests" who act as the hostile, even satanic, opponents of Jesus.

Through a number of subtle changes, then, Matthew's trial scene heightens the contrast between Caiaphas and Jesus. Caiaphas thinks he has power over the temple, but his position as high-priestly mediator between God and Israel is about to end, just as the physical temple in Jerusalem is soon to be reduced to rubble and ashes. For Matthew, it is Jesus who truly has power over the temple—not just the Jerusalem temple (while it still stood) but, more importantly, power over the temple of Christian believers.

Jesus the High Priest

There is a sense in which, for Matthew, Christ has usurped Caiaphas's high-priestly role. The idea that the messiah would exercise priestly functions was not alien to first-century Jews, but Matthew's understanding of Jesus' priestly character is not linked to his concept of *messiahship* (which is exclusively kingly and expressed through such titles as "Son of David" and "Son of God"), but to his concept of believers as the *new temple*.[24] The evangelist imagines the temple of believers as a place where God is uniquely present (1:23, see also 18:20, 28:20) and as a priestly community in which individual members are called to be perfect, like the priests who served in the old temple (5:48, Exod 19:6). Within this "temple," Jesus performs the two fundamental roles of the high priest. First, he saves his people from their sins (Matthew even makes this the meaning of his name in 1:21, although the name actually means "God is help").[25] Second, through his death on the cross, Jesus symbolically destroys the old sanctuary (27:51) and opens up a new way for all people to come to God.[26]

Once Jewish Christians saw themselves as an eschatological temple, it was perhaps inevitable that Jesus should be cast in the role of a heavenly high priest. While this development could quite easily have occurred while the temple still stood, it may well have gained momentum after its destruction, particularly among communities such as Matthew's, which had continued to hold its cult in high esteem. The clearest Christian description of Jesus as high priest is found in Hebrews, which was probably written by a Jewish Christian about the same time as Matthew. This document presents Jesus as the perfect high priest, the fulfillment of all priesthood, and the true mediator between God and humanity.[27] Romans 5:2 and Ephesians 2:18 perhaps employ priestly metaphors too when they speak of believers gaining access to God through Christ; Peter refers to all Christians as God's chosen race, "a royal priesthood" (a sentiment shared by Rev 1:6); and the vision of Revelation 1:12–18 depicts Jesus in priestly garb.[28] Later, in the early second century, Polycarp, the bishop of Smyrna, referred to Jesus as "the eternal priest" in his letter to the Philippians (12:2); and by the fourth century Eusebius, the bishop of Caesarea, claimed that the three offices of Christ were foreshadowed in Aaron, Joshua, and the anointed prophets (*Hist. eccl.* 1.3). For at least some Christians, then, if their own community was the temple, Jesus was the high priest.[29]

Did Matthew—unlike Mark, who saw an end to the high priesthood in general—see an enduring high priesthood in Jesus, which he contrasted with the worldly high priesthood of Jesus' accuser, Caiaphas? Would Matthew's Jewish-Christian readers have seen an implicit contrast between Jesus, the eternal high priest, and Caiaphas, the earthly high priest? And while Matthew's synagogue opponents longed for the rebuilding of the temple and the reestablishment of its cult, did his own community claim that they were the successor to the Jerusalem temple, and that the functions of the high priest were more than covered by the person of Jesus Christ?

Summary

While Mark's nameless high priest represents all Jewish leaders who reject Jesus, Matthew identifies Caiaphas by name and deliberately contrasts him with Jesus, both in the opening to the passion narrative (26:1–5) and in the Jewish trial (26:57–68). (It is presumably because of this heightened sense of contrast that some of the best-known artistic representations of Jesus before Caiaphas have taken their inspiration from Matthew's Gospel.)[30]

Caiaphas has a dual function in Matthew. In one respect, all the scheming, manipulative Jewish leaders act as a foil for Jesus, whose identity as Son of God,

Messiah, and Son of Man shines out from every page. The furtive plotting of Caiaphas and his high-priestly colleagues contrasts with Jesus' calm serenity and messianic authority. And yet, more specifically, the contrast between the two men shows that there is a sense in which, for Matthew, if his own community is the "new Israel" and the "new temple," Jesus is the "new high priest." Functions previously exercised by the high priest—atonement for sin, divine mediation, and acting as the figurehead of the temple—are all now performed by Jesus. We shall turn now to a Gospel in which this conception of Jesus as the high priest is even more pronounced—the Gospel of John.

14

Caiaphas in John

Even a cursory reading of John's Gospel reveals a narrative world strikingly different from that of any of the other Gospels. The author expresses his distinctive theology through heavy symbolism, dramatic irony, and a strongly dualistic outlook. The work reaches a height of sophistication and subtlety unmatched anywhere in the Synoptic Gospels and also reaches new depths in its record of the hostility and bitterness between believers and synagogue leaders in the late first century.[1]

The most striking feature of John's Gospel is its presentation of Jesus. He is the divine Word, the agent of God in creation, who descends to an alien and often hostile world for a short time before ascending once again to his heavenly home. Sure of his role and unity with the Father, he discusses his status with opponents and speaks openly of his mission, which is to reveal the Father to those living in a world characterized by darkness, death, slavery, and sin. Paradoxically, Jesus' revelation reaches its height at the crucifixion: he makes his way to the cross perfectly in control of the situation, voluntarily sacrificing himself on behalf of others (10:7–8, 11, 14). This, for John, is the hour of Jesus' glorification, the time when he is "lifted up" and his glory and that of the Father are revealed. The cross is the means of salvation and, at the same time, the moment of God's judgment on all people (9:39, 12:31). For John, Jesus' death takes on not only a universal but a cosmic dimension: through Christ, God has overcome the world; all that is necessary for believers is faith.[2]

In many respects John's portrait of Jesus is thoroughly Jewish: Jesus is the messiah of Israel, the fulfillment of the Scriptures (5:39, 46; 10:35), the one predicted by Moses (1:45, 5:43–47). He is presented as divine Wisdom, the mediator between God and the world in both creation and redemption.[3] And yet, rather curiously, Jesus' opponents in this Gospel are not the Sadducees, scribes, and Herodians known to us from the Synoptics, but simply "the Jews" (or, less frequently, "the Pharisees")—as if Jesus were not a Jew himself! As the narrative progresses, "the Jews" take on an increasingly symbolic role as the representatives of darkness and unbelief. They do not believe Jesus (8:46), blindly rely on their own position as children of Abraham (8:39, 9:41), and seek worldly honor (12:43). John goes so far as to ascribe satanic origins to them; their father is the devil; like him, they are nothing but murderers and liars (8:43–47). There is no hope for them: they will die in their sin (8:24). In line with Johannine dualism, followers of Jesus and "the Jews" represent two opposing sides (9:28); it is up to individuals to choose between them.[4]

The explanation for John's hostility towards "the Jews" lies in the social setting of his community. It is clear from several references within the Gospel that the evangelist is writing for a group of Christians that has recently and traumatically been expelled from the Jewish synagogue and is perhaps still suffering some kind of persecution (9:22, 14:42, 16:2). John's readers have been forced to rethink their entire identity, to regard synagogue authorities as something "other" and hostile, and to consider what it means in this new situation to be followers of Christ. "The Jews," then, represent not Jesus' historical opponents, but the Pharisaic synagogue leaders of John's own day who reject not only Jesus but also his followers. This particular social setting explains the almost sectarian feel to the work, its interest in insiders/outsiders, and its concern that believers confess their allegiance openly. It also explains the constantly reassuring tone of the Gospel: John shows his readers that everything that has befallen them was predicted by Jesus, promises them Christ's continued protection, and assures them of eternal life (20:31).

For John, salvation is no longer through Jewish institutions, but through faith in Jesus and the revelation he brings. Relations with the synagogue have broken down, and the evangelist knows that new converts will be drawn from the Gentile world (10:16, 12:32). And yet, unlike Mark, he is unwilling completely to reject his Jewish heritage. Not only is Jesus the fulfillment of the Scriptures, but he is also the *replacement of Jewish feasts and institutions:* Jesus transforms the water of Jewish purification into good wine (2:1–11); he replaces the temple as the place of God's revelation (1:14, 2:19–22, 4:21–24); he contrasts the "bread" of his body (presumably the Eucharist) with the manna given by Moses in the wilderness (6:25–65); he claims priority and superiority over Abraham (8:58); and, most dramatically of all, he dies as the new paschal lamb (19:14). It is clearly important for John to show that Jewish institutions—far from being rendered futile or rejected—have been fulfilled and transcended by Christ. Although he will use completely different language and imagery, John, no less than Luke and Matthew, regards his community as the heirs to God's promises in the Scriptures, a new people defined not by ethnic descent, but by rebirth through the spirit.[5]

Caiaphas is a much more important character in John than in any other Gospel. He is named several times within the narrative (11:49; 18:13, 14, 24, 28); a striking fact given the Gospel's preference for referring to Jesus' opponents simply as "the Jews." He makes three appearances: (1) in a council meeting in chapter 11; (2) in the events after Jesus' arrest at the high priest's palace; and (3) implicitly at 19:11, in the trial before Pilate. We shall look at each of these in turn and see that John's particular interest is not so much in Caiaphas, but in his high-priestly office—an office that the evangelist, like Matthew, will deliberately contrast with Jesus.

A Council Meeting (11:47–53)

The first half of the Gospel is dominated by conflict between Jesus and "the Jews." The chief priests and Pharisees meet as early as 7:45–52 but are unable to apprehend Jesus. At this meeting, Nicodemus speaks up for Jesus, stressing the need to gather further evidence (7:51). Hostilities intensify in chapters 8–10, as charges and countercharges are flung back and forth between Jesus and his opponents. "The Jews" clearly want to kill Jesus (8:28, 40); they try to arrest him (10:39) and even try to stone him (8:59, 10:31), though without success. Finally, in chapter 11, they convene another meeting; this time there is no attempt to bring Jesus before them, and no one speaks up on his behalf. The scene itself forms a central section in John's Gospel, following directly Jesus' dramatic raising of Lazarus (11:1–46), and the author shows with characteristic irony that Jesus' gift of life to Lazarus will lead to his own death.

Similarities between this gathering and the preliminary meetings of the chief priests in the Synoptic Gospels (Mark 14:1–2, Luke 22:1–2, Matt 26:1–5) have often been noted.[6] There are, however, three significant differences: (1) the date of the meeting, (2) the motives of the Jewish leaders for doing away with Jesus, and (3) the content of the scene.

1. *Date.* In the Synoptics, the council meets when Jesus is already in Jerusalem, two days before the Passover (Mark 14:1–2). In John, however, the meeting takes place *several weeks before the Passover*. After the meeting, Jesus stays in a town called Ephraim for what seems to be some time (11:54), and in 11:55 people are only just beginning to think about going up for the feast.[7] In John's presentation, then, the authorities decide to kill Jesus long before he makes his final journey to Jerusalem, a feature that makes Jesus' decision to go to the city despite the clear dangers involved all the more courageous (11:55–57) and underlines the Johannine presentation of Jesus willingly laying down his life.

2. *Motive.* All three Synoptic Gospels record the Jewish leaders' anxiety over Jesus' popularity with the crowds, but each one adds a more specific reason for

their wanting Jesus' death. In Mark they are irate because Jesus has threatened the temple; in Luke and Matthew it is specifically Jesus' messianic teaching in the temple that worries them. John, however, has moved the temple incident to an earlier part of the Gospel (2:13–22) and so has severed the link between Jesus' actions and the decision to put him to death. The motive of the Jewish leaders in John is their concern at the popular enthusiasm caused by Jesus' miraculous signs, enthusiasm that they worry might lead to Roman intervention and disaster for the nation (11:47–48).

3. *Content.* While the Synoptic Gospels mention a preliminary meeting only briefly, John presents a short yet highly memorable scene in which, drawing on his considerable skills as a narrator and a master of irony, he will bring out the true significance of Jesus' death.

The meeting is convened by "the chief priests and the Pharisees" (11:47). In view of our earlier historical reconstruction, the presence of Pharisees here is probably best explained as John's attempt to implicate the Jewish leaders of his own day (the heirs of the Pharisees) in the plot against Jesus.[8] The councillors worry that Jesus is becoming too popular: "What are we to do?" they ask. "This man is performing many signs. If we let him go on like this, everyone will believe in him, and the Romans will come and destroy both our holy place and our nation" (11:47–48).[9] On the face of it, this is a not unreasonable worry. A leader with a large following could well cause Roman intervention, intervention that might lead to the loss of the temple and the nation.[10] (Perhaps John's audience also heard here an echo of the synagogue leaders of their own day, who, they thought, were more concerned with safeguarding their ancestral traditions than listening to the word of God.) And yet, on another level, the authorities' fear is deeply ironic. By the time John wrote, the Romans had indeed destroyed the temple and subjugated the Jewish people, and the reader knows that the calamity they seek to avoid will in fact befall them.

As the councillors debate, one man stands up to speak: Caiaphas. John notes that he was "high priest that year" (11:49). Some have taken this to mean that John imagined that the high priest was replaced annually; more probably, however, the sense is that Caiaphas was high priest that fateful year, the year of Jesus' death.[11] Caiaphas's manner is brusque and matter of fact; his opening words, "You know nothing at all," show his self-confidence and authority over other members of the council. "You do not understand," he continues, "that *it is better for you to have one man die for the people than to have the whole nation destroyed*" (11:50). Caiaphas has the last word in the discussion, his decision is final.

On one level, these are the shrewd words of political expediency, the sober weighing up of the situation, and the stark expression of realpolitik. The reader may suspect that Caiaphas's use of the phrase "better *for you*" suggests that what really matters to the high priest here is not simply the fate of the temple and the nation, but the maintenance of the status quo, his own supremacy, and that of his advisers. The pragmatic Jewish leader has no scruples in offering one man's life to safeguard his own position. Yet, on another level, Caiaphas's words are deeply ironic. John obviously subscribes to the popular belief that prophetic powers were associated with the office of high priest.[12] Although the high priest is unaware of it, he has unconsciously given expression to the words of God and outlined in the clearest terms both the sacrificial nature and the significance of Jesus' death.

The narrator picks up Caiaphas's words and explains that Jesus' death will benefit not just the nation (that is, Jews) but will also "gather into one the dispersed children of God" (that is, Gentiles) (11:52). Ironically, the gathering of the council and the death sentence it is about to pass make possible the ingathering of all the children of God. The reader might well recall Jesus' words in 2:19–21: "Destroy this temple, and in three days I will raise it up"—words in which, the narrator explains, "he was speaking of the temple of his body." The councillors worry about the physical temple in Jerusalem, but the Johannine Christians know that it will be replaced by the risen Jesus, the new temple to whom all nations will flock.[13]

Caiaphas within the narrative, however, has no idea of the universal significance the death of Jesus will have. The final verse returns to the plot: "So from that day on they planned to put him to death" (11:53).

In this scene, Caiaphas comes across as a hostile character, intent on self-preservation and callous in his disregard for human life. As high priest, he epitomizes Jewish opposition to Jesus and, like "the Jews" generally in this Gospel, allies himself with the satanic forces of darkness and sin. Yet it is also apparent that John has some residual regard for the office of high priest; in that role, even a hostile character can unconsciously speak the words of God. We shall see this same double attitude in the next scene involving Caiaphas—the events that take place at his own residence after Jesus' arrest.

At the High Priest's Palace (18:12–28a)

We are now at the beginning of John's passion narrative. Jesus' "hour" has come, and he begins his journey to the cross, where the "ruler of this world" (Satan) will be cast out (12:30–31). The confrontation with "the Jews" that has dominated the earlier part of the Gospel is now at an end; Jesus' opponents have had ample opportunity to accept his revelation, and all that remains now is for them to be judged by their response.

Jesus' arrest and Jewish custody are narrated in a series of tightly constructed scenes. Jesus is arrested in the garden and, in a presentation very different from that of the Synoptic Gospels, offers himself willingly to his captors, three times declaring himself to be the divine "I am" (a declaration that causes his captors to fall to the ground in astonishment, 18:1–11). Jesus is taken first of all to Annas, who, John informs us, was the father-in-law of Caiaphas, who was "high priest that year" (18:12–13). Caiaphas, he reminds us, had "advised the Jews that it was better to have one person die for the people" (18:14). Meanwhile, "the other disciple," who was "known to the high priest," helps Simon Peter to gain entry to the high priest's courtyard, where, confronted by a slave girl who kept the door,

Peter denies Jesus for the first time (18:15–18).[14] Moving inside the high priest's palace, Jesus is questioned by "the high priest" (18:19–23), after which Annas sends Jesus to "Caiaphas the high priest" (18:24). Of what occurred before Caiaphas, John tells us nothing. The action moves back to Peter, outside in the courtyard, whose last two denials neatly parallel Jesus' three affirmations of his identity in the garden. Next time we see Jesus he is being led away from Caiaphas's palace to the governor's headquarters, the praetorium (18:28). The night is now passed, and, with heavy symbolism, John remarks that it was early morning, the night is over, and a new dawn is about to begin.

John's account raises a number of difficulties, three of which will have a bearing on our understanding of Caiaphas in this scene. First, who is the disciple "known to the high priest," and what is his narrative significance? Second, why does John have no formal trial in front of a Jewish council? Third, what is the purpose of the preliminary hearing in 18:19–23, and what is "the high priest's" role within the narrative? We shall look at each of these in turn.

The Disciple "Known to the High Priest" (18:15–16)

In all three Synoptic Gospels, Peter simply enters the high priest's courtyard, which is presumably a public place where people could come and go freely (Mark 14:54, Matt 26:58, Luke 22:54–55). John, however, imagines that the courtyard was inside the palace and that entry was by means of a gate attended by a gatekeeper. He, therefore, alone of the evangelists needs to explain how Peter gained entry. The explanation he offers is that another disciple had also followed the arresting party and, being known to the high priest, had entered the courtyard along with Jesus. Knowing that Peter was outside, the disciple known to the high priest went outside to speak to the doorkeeper and brought Peter in.[15]

Our first question is: who is this other disciple? The traditional answer has been the Beloved Disciple, the ideal disciple who holds a privileged place in the second half of the Gospel.[16] In fact, a number of ancient manuscripts added the definite article here, making this reference parallel "the other disciple" of 20:3–10 (which does refer to the Beloved Disciple). Yet there are two difficulties with this identification. First, although the Beloved Disciple often appears in scenes with Peter, there is always some kind of rivalry between them in which the Beloved Disciple comes off slightly better. In this scene, though, there is no real contrast: certainly the "other disciple" does not deny Jesus, but nor does he stand by him or defend him. The "other disciple" is here solely to allow Peter to gain entry into the courtyard so that he can deny his master; after that he drops out completely. His role within the narrative, then, is a negative one. Second, and more importantly, this other disciple is not referred to as the disciple whom Jesus loved, but— in a quite different manner—as the disciple "known to the high priest." The word used here, *gnōstos*, suggests a close, even intimate acquaintance.[17] Given John's highly dualistic outlook, it is difficult to imagine that the disciple whom Jesus loved could also be an intimate of the high priest.

If this "other disciple" is not the Beloved Disciple, who is he? Two further possibilities are Nicodemus and Joseph of Arimathea; both were members of the council, both would have had access to the high priest's palace, and both would presumably have held some authority with the gatekeeper.[18] But, attractive as this theory is, 18:15 suggests that both Peter and the "other disciple" had followed Jesus from the garden, a detail which suggests that the "other disciple" is *one of the Twelve*.

In fact, an overview of what we know about this disciple makes his identity quite clear. He has accompanied Jesus and the arresting party to the high priest's palace and, because of his relationship with the high priest, has been able to enter the courtyard freely. Furthermore, although it is known that this man is a disciple (the slave girl asks Peter if he *also* is a disciple, 18:17), no one challenges him about his relationship with Jesus. In view of this, the likeliest identification for the "other disciple" is *Judas*. John has not specifically told us of an understanding between Judas and Caiaphas (unlike Matt 26:14–16, 27:3–5), but Judas's betrayal and presence at Jesus' arrest presupposes such an association.[19]

There is, however, one remaining question: why does John not simply refer to the "other disciple" as Judas? Why does he refer to him as the disciple "known to the high priest"? And why does he stress this connection (twice in two verses, vv. 15–16)? Perhaps the reason is that John has no further interest in Judas as one of Jesus' disciples. He has now crossed to the other side, he is a friend of the high priest and must be identified as such. Judas has already chosen his path; Satan has entered into him (13:2), and he finds a natural home with the leader of "the Jews."[20]

In John's presentation, then, Peter allows the "other disciple"/Judas to take the initiative and bring him through the door into the high priest's courtyard, a place where the forces of darkness and evil are at their height.[21] Despite the fire that flickers in its grate, Peter cannot withstand the darkness around him. In the presence of Jesus' adversaries, he denies his master and symbolically takes his place alongside Judas; the denier and the betrayer together. In this Gospel, Peter does not break down in tears after the cockcrow (18:27); like Judas, he simply succumbs to the hostile forces that engulf him and disappears from the narrative, leaving Jesus to face the interrogation of the high priest entirely alone.[22]

Jesus' Interrogation by "the High Priest" (18:19–23)

In a striking departure from the Synoptic scene, John records no formal gathering of a Jewish council; there are no assembled chief priests and scribes, no witnesses, no charges, no accusations, and no verdict. Instead, Jesus is first taken to Annas, who briefly questions him before sending him to Caiaphas. Of any proceedings that took place before Caiaphas, John is silent, resuming the story in verse 28, only to tell us that Caiaphas now passed Jesus to Pilate.

Why, in a Gospel that is often so antagonistic towards "the Jews" is there no formal Jewish trial? The simple answer is that, as we have seen, Jesus has been in constant dispute with "the Jews" and, in a sense, *the whole of John's Gospel has been Jesus' trial before the Jewish authorities*. In fact, many elements associated with

Mark's trial have already surfaced: the temple charge was dealt with in 2:19–22; the question as to whether Jesus was the Christ, the Son of God, and also the accusation of blasphemy were raised in 10:24–39; Jesus' vision of the open heavens was recounted in 1:51; and a council gathered in 11:47–53 and heard Caiaphas give his verdict (11:49–50).[23] By the time Jesus arrives at Caiaphas's palace, all discussion is at an end; he has revealed the Father, and the hostile "Jews" have not only rejected him but delivered their verdict. To recount another trial here would be superfluous. All that is necessary now is for the evangelist to remind the reader of the earlier verdict—something he does in 18:14—and to have Caiaphas hand Jesus over to Pilate and begin the chain of events that will lead to his death.[24]

But why does John bother with any kind of Jewish trial at this point? More specifically, what is the reason for *the interrogation before Annas*, a scene that at first sight appears to be a poor substitute for the Synoptic gathering of a grand council? The scene is clearly the evangelist's own construction: even if he inherited a tradition telling of a nighttime hearing before Annas, he has completely rewritten it so that it exhibits his own outlook and theology.[25] What, then, is its purpose? We shall see that the scene has two important purposes: first, it represents the climax to the rejection of Jesus by "the Jews"; second, John uses the exchange to say something about Jesus himself.

The scene is admirably set by E. Haenchen, who imagines "a room in the gloomy palace, perhaps illuminated by a fireplace and a few torches. The old High Priest is sitting on a chair. The prisoner stands before him. One or other of the officers is present."[26] The high priest begins by asking Jesus about his disciples and his teaching. Jesus answers with characteristic boldness in words which sum up his entire ministry: "I have spoken openly to the world; I have always taught in synagogues and in the temple, where all the Jews come together. I have said nothing in secret. Why do you ask me? Ask those who heard what I said to them; they know what I said" (18:20–21). Jesus is the revealer, the one sent by God to offer salvation to all people. Everything he has done has been done in public—only unbelievers are incapable of seeing this (7:4, 10:24). The high priest's officer, however, taking offense at Jesus' manner, slaps him on the face and asks if that is any way to talk to the high priest. Jesus, serene as ever, has the last word: "If I have spoken wrongly, testify to the wrong. But if I have spoken rightly, why do you strike me?" Confronted by Jesus' self-assurance and majestic demeanor, neither the high priest nor his servant have any answer to make.[27]

The high priest's officer performs a double function in this scene. On one level, his slap is symbolic of the refusal of "the Jews" to respond to Jesus' revelation. The officer, like everyone else associated with the high priest in John's narrative, sides with the dark and hostile forces of the unbelieving world. And yet, on another level, by evoking the law of Exodus 22:28, which forbade cursing a ruler of the people, the officer has drawn attention to Jesus' treatment of the supreme pontiff and invited the reader to draw a comparison between Jesus and the high priest.

But who precisely is the high priest in this scene? Superficially, this may seem like a rather odd question. According to the flow of the narrative, the high priest is clearly Annas; Jesus was taken to him in 18:13 and will not be taken to Caiaphas until 18:24. John refers to him as "high priest" as a sign of courtesy and respect.[28] And yet a good case could also be made for Caiaphas: he is the only person specifically referred to as high priest in the Gospel (11:49, 18:13, 24), and given his prominent role in the earlier meeting of 11:47–53, the reader might well expect him to take center stage once again here. Sensing this difficulty, a number of early manuscripts altered the order of the verses, bringing verse 24 (in which Jesus is transferred to Caiaphas) up to verse 13, an arrangement that clearly makes Caiaphas the high priest who interrogates Jesus.[29] And although the majority of modern commentators would identify the high priest here with Annas, an earlier generation was more inclined to see him as Caiaphas.[30]

Why has John allowed such ambiguity at this point? Is the confusion due to uneven editing of his sources, or was he simply confused?[31] More probably, in a Gospel which delights in word plays and double meanings, the uncertainty is deliberate. John introduced Annas in 18:13 as the father-in-law of Caiaphas; the two men are related by marriage, and the evangelist clearly wants us to see a close connection between them. They undoubtedly share a similar purpose and outlook, but what really binds them together is the high priesthood: one is a former high priest, the other is "high priest that year." The note that Jesus is taken to Annas (v. 13) is obscured both by the repetition of Caiaphas's prophecy (v. 14) and Peter's first denial (vv. 15–18). When Jesus stands before the high priest in verse 19, then, both Annas and Caiaphas are in the reader's mind. John seems to be deliberately ambiguous here so as to deflect attention away from either man and onto *the office of high priest*. What has happened, in effect, is that in John's presentation, the office of high priest has detached itself from either man and become independent.[32] This narrative strategy allows John to contrast Jesus not with Annas or Caiaphas (in whom, writing in the late first century, the evangelist presumably had little interest) but with the office of high priest.

The comparison is not a happy one for the high priest. Jesus speaks with dignity and majesty; his words echo the voice of God or Wisdom in the Old Testament and take on a permanent and universal dimension.[33] The high priest, however, begins his interrogation with some semblance of control but, as the narrative progresses, seems almost visibly to disappear.[34] Despite his power and eminence, he relies on his attendant to speak up for him and, in the end, has nothing to say. In verse 24 the high priest (now identified as Annas) sends Jesus to Caiaphas, who, despite being "high priest that year," does nothing but hand Jesus over to Pilate. Neither Annas nor Caiaphas is referred to again by name in the narrative. Whatever power the high priesthood once exerted is completely drained by its confrontation with Jesus. Its representatives are turned into nothing more than passive agents, merely handing Jesus over to Rome. Throughout this whole exchange, Jesus' authority and superiority over "the high priest" are abundantly clear.

The contrast, however, may go further than this. The role of high priest, as we have seen, was to act as mediator between God and Israel: he was considered the natural conduit for God's revelation, and the gift of prophecy was popularly linked to the office.[35] There is a sense in John's Gospel in which *Jesus himself acts as high priest*. Throughout the narrative, Jesus is the mediator between God and his people; he reveals the Father and is always present at the nation's festivals. The farewell discourses develop the idea of Jesus as the forerunner, the one who goes before believers (13:16, 14:2–3, 16:22) and continues his mediation in heaven (14:13–14; 16:23–24, 26–27).[36] More striking still is Jesus' prayer of chapter 17, situated immediately before his arrest and confrontation with "the high priest." This prayer has been known as the "high-priestly prayer" since the sixteenth century, though the fact that Jesus takes on a high-priestly role was noticed at least as early as Cyril of Alexandria in the fifth century. In the prayer Jesus brings his offering (himself) to the Father, consecrating himself and his followers (v. 19) and asking that those given him be sanctified and kept separate from the world (vv. 15–19).[37] Finally, it is difficult to read the reference to Jesus' "seamless tunic" in 19:23 as anything but a reference to the high-priestly robe that was similarly woven from one piece of cloth. As the Son of God dies on the cross, the seamless robe of the high priest is redundant and discarded; God's people are about to be reconstituted around Christ (19:25–27).[38] A view of Jesus as the "true" high priest would fit perfectly with John's interest in Jesus as the fulfillment of Jewish institutions and feasts; his salvific activity encompasses the role of high priest, thus rendering any high priest of "the Jews" utterly superfluous.[39]

Jesus' interrogation before the high priest, then, is of enormous theological significance. For John, the high priest is the symbolic figurehead of "the Jews"; his court is one of darkness that even the most intrepid of apostles cannot withstand. And yet, when confronted with Jesus, the light of the world, the high priest's power crumbles. He has no answers, no revelation of his own, no further prophetic utterances. Jesus' hearing in front of "the high priest" quickly becomes the trial of the high priest, who flatly refuses to acknowledge Jesus' revelation. It also contrasts Jesus and the high priest. Although the high priest begins firmly in charge, his central position is very quickly usurped by Jesus, who counters his questions with dignity and majesty. For John, the role and office of high priest has been transcended and superseded by Jesus.

The Trial in front of Pilate (18:28–19:16)

Caiaphas and Annas are presumably part of the group of chief priests and officers which brings Jesus before Pilate (18:35; 19:6, 15). Neither man, however, is mentioned any more by name; they have once again taken their place among the hostile "Jews." Only once does the narrative refer back to Jesus' earlier encounter with the high priest (19:11), and the purpose of the passage—as we shall see—is to contend that primary responsibility for the death of Jesus lies not with the representative of Rome but with the supreme representative of "the Jews."

John's Roman trial narrative exhibits a carefully formulated seven-scene structure dominated by two charges: first, that Jesus is the king of the Jews and, second, that he has "made himself [NRSV, "claimed to be"] the Son of God."[40] The opening verses set the scene. "The Jews" bring Jesus to Pilate but refuse to enter his headquarters, so that they would not become impure before the feast. Ironically, ritual purity concerns them more than handing over their Messiah! On a narrative level, their refusal to enter means that they remain outside while Jesus is taken inside, and Pilate must go between the two.

Pilate enters his headquarters and asks Jesus if he is the king of the Jews, admitting that Jesus has been handed over to him by Jesus' "own nation and the chief priests" and that the formulation of the charge is theirs (18:35). The governor quickly realizes that Jesus is no threat and brings Jesus out again to the Jewish chief priests and officers, offering to release him as part of a customary Passover amnesty. They, however, are unwilling to entertain such an idea and ask instead for Barabbas, who, John says, was a *lēstēs*, a robber or, perhaps, a revolutionary (18:38b–40). This rejection is intensified in the next scene when Pilate, after having Jesus scourged, brings the prisoner out in front of the chief priests and officers in mock-kingly regalia. "The Jews" have only one response: Crucify him, crucify him! (19:6).

When Pilate states for a second time that he finds no guilt in Jesus, "the Jews" change strategy and claim that Jesus has "made himself the Son of God" (19:7). The reader, of course, knows that this is utterly untrue: Jesus has not *made himself* the Son of God but has existed in a unique relationship with God since the beginning of time (1:1). Despite witnessing Jesus' revelation, "the Jews" in John's narrative are still ignorant of this. Pilate, however, takes notice of this charge and becomes afraid, perhaps suspecting that there is more to Jesus than meets the eye. When his questions regarding Jesus' origins meet with no response, he reminds the prisoner that he has power either to release him or to crucify him. Jesus, serene as ever, replies: "You would have no power over me unless it had been given to you from above; therefore *the one who handed me over to you is guilty of a greater sin*" (19:11).

Who is Jesus referring to here? The word translated "handed over" (*paradidōmi*) can also mean "betray," which might suggest that the Johannine Jesus has Judas in mind here. But although this word is often used of Judas (6:64, 71; 12:4; 13:2, 11, 21; 18:2, 5; 21:20), it is difficult to see why Jesus should launch into an attack on his betrayer at this point. More likely Jesus is referring quite literally to the one who handed him over to Pilate—Caiaphas, or by extension the high-priestly representative of "the Jews." Jesus will go to his death on a Roman cross, convicted by a Roman governor, but as far as John and his community were concerned, primary responsibility rests on the high-priestly leader who handed him over.[41]

Once again Pilate tries to release Jesus, and once again "the Jews" stall him, reminding him that "everyone who makes claims to be a king sets himself against the emperor" (19:12). At this, the narrative changes; Pilate brings Jesus out and makes his way toward the judgment seat. But who sits on the seat? The Greek is quite deliberately ambiguous here: on one level it is clearly Pilate who is about to pass judgment on the prisoner; yet on a symbolic level it is Jesus, the King of Israel and Son of God, who is about to judge the unbelieving world. "The Jews" shout once more for crucifixion and, in answer to Pilate's "Shall I crucify your King?" the chief priests alone answer: "We have no king but the emperor" (19:15). Their cry takes place in John at the moment when preparations for the festival celebrating God's deliverance of his people were about to begin (19:14) and forms a stark contrast to the words of the Passover haggadah which praised the kingly rule of God.[42] In front of Jesus, the heavenly judge, "the Jews" have exposed their unbelief; the chief priests have rejected not only their Messiah, but also God himself.

Summary

Caiaphas in John plays a dual role, similar to his role in Matthew. On one hand, he is the supreme representative of "the Jews," leaders of Judaism who reject Jesus and finally, in the governor's court, reject even God. He is unambiguously hostile toward Jesus, and his palace is a center of darkness, where even the strongest disciple succumbs to evil forces and betrays his master. The interrogation before the "high priest" is unnecessary as far as the narrative goes—Jesus has already been tried and sentenced in the first half of the Gospel. What the scene allows the evangelist to do, however, is to provide a climax to the rejection of Jesus by the supreme leader of "the Jews," the man John regards as most responsible for Jesus' death (19:11).

And yet, on the other hand, John's references to Caiaphas by name and official function attract our attention onto his role as "high priest," and the ambiguity in the interrogation scene over the identity of the high priest allows the reader to make connections and comparisons between Jesus and the high priest. The two men come together face to face and the reader sees that the power, authority, and religious significance of the high priest now rest with Jesus. For John, Jesus is not only the fulfillment of the law and the replacement of the temple and its feasts but also the new high priest, the one who mediates between God and God's people and who atones for sin.

15

Conclusion

We have now looked at Caiaphas as a literary character in each of the Gospels, and the four chapters together should make it plain why I refrained from using these works as historical sources for Caiaphas in part 1 of this book.

We began with Mark's Gospel and saw that, by refusing to name "the high priest," the earliest evangelist turned his trial of Jesus into a grand courtroom drama in which the Jewish leaders initiated their own judgment and condemnation. Mark deliberately omitted Caiaphas's name in order to broaden responsibility from one particular high priest to all high-priestly leaders of Israel, a feature that gives the Jewish leaders' rejection of Jesus a timeless, almost mythical, quality that spoke to the needs of a community which found itself increasingly distanced from Jewish leaders of its own day.

Next we turned to Luke, who initially appeared to have more interest in Caiaphas as a historical individual (Luke 3:2, Acts 4:6). On closer inspection, however, we found that this was not really the case. The evangelist omits not only Caiaphas's name but any reference whatsoever to a high priest in the Jewish proceedings against Jesus; when the high priest does make an appearance in Acts, he is merely cast in the role created for him by Mark. Like the earlier evangelist, Luke uses the literary device of a courtroom drama before an unnamed high priest to symbolize the woeful inadequacy of the leaders of "old Israel," their utter rejection of the Christian movement, and, indirectly, God's condemnation of them. With the benefit of a much longer two-volume narrative, and the theological necessity of presenting the Jerusalem early church as a golden age in which God's promises to Israel have been fulfilled, the decisive moment for Luke occurs not at the death of Jesus, but at that of Stephen. Luke is much more positive in his assessment of Jewish people and institutions than Mark, but the view of the high-priestly leaders of "old Israel" as vengeful, self-seeking, and misguided is common to both.

Turning to Matthew and John, we see a slightly different process at work. Both evangelists were deeply hostile towards the Jewish leaders of Jesus' day, a hostility presumably fueled by the hurtful experiences of their own communities at the hands of local synagogue leaders. Yet, perhaps because of their strong Jewish heritage, neither evangelist was able simply to dismiss the figure of the high priest. Matthew specifically names him as Caiaphas and, both in the preliminary meeting of the Jewish leaders and their trial of Jesus, heightens the contrast between the two antagonists—Jesus and Caiaphas. This presentation suggests that Matthew and his Jewish Christian community were beginning to explore connections and parallels between the role of the high priest and that of Christ. Like Mark and Luke, Matthew has no particular interest in Caiaphas himself; his interest is rather in the fact that Caiaphas is a human representative of the Jewish high priesthood, which, for Matthew and his readers, has been encompassed and transcended by Jesus.

These themes, present in Matthew only in embryonic form, are much clearer in John. The fourth evangelist departs from his usual practice of referring to Jesus' opponents as "the Jews" to name his archaccusers, Caiaphas and Annas, drawing attention to their high-priestly status. Through a deliberate ambiguity, Jesus is tried by "the high priest," and the reader is invited to contrast Jesus' majestic divinity with "the high priest," who, as the interrogation draws on, seems almost visibly to crumble away. For John, Jesus is not only greater than the high priest but now fulfils his mediating and atoning role. This fits perfectly with John's insistence that Jesus is the replacement of Jewish feasts and institutions: Jesus is not only the paschal lamb, but the "true" high priest, who offers himself for the sins of the world.

It is important to remember that what we have in the Gospels are reflections of intra-Jewish arguments. "Judaism" and "Christianity" are in the process of going their separate ways, but the two are not yet distinct. Each evangelist was profoundly influenced by his own socio-historical situation, the needs of his readers, and, perhaps most importantly, his own relationship with contemporary Jewish leaders. It is their very proximity to the Jewish synagogue, their recent traumatic history, and their minority status and fear that they may well be overwhelmed that lead to the highly negative characterizations of the high-priestly leaders in the Gospels. Their Jewish neighbors hope and pray for a rebuilt temple and a restored high priesthood; Christian communities neither want nor need either. They are themselves a new temple, "not made with hands," and if they have any need for a high priest, they have one in Jesus Christ. It is perhaps just as well that the hostile rebukes of their synagogue opponents have not survived!

None of the evangelists, then, has any real interest in Caiaphas as an individual. The discussions of Jesus' death and meaning in the Gospels have moved a long way from historical accuracy; they have been shaped just as much by a long history of heated discussions with Jewish neighbors as by historical traditions. The questions that occupied the evangelists and their communities were religious ones: Why had Israel's priestly leaders rejected Jesus? How could the church claim to be the "new Israel"? Who belonged to this new group, and who did not? The Gospels were written as documents of faith for their own times, providing answers for their own situations.

By the late first century, the temple priesthood had ceased to exist and was beginning to be nothing more than a fading memory. The heinousness of the actions of Caiaphas and his colleagues grew in the minds of Jesus' followers; they were clearly evil men, ignorant of their Scriptures and willfully opposed to God. How else could their rejection of Jesus be explained? They appear in the Gospels as caricatures: jealous of Jesus' success, intent on his murder, ready to bribe to achieve their ends, hopelessly unconcerned with justice, and prepared to go to any lengths to prevent the resurrection. More disastrously, though, Mark's decision not to name the high priest during Jesus' trial (and Luke's obliteration of any reference to the high priest at this point) led to a loss of focus on Caiaphas and to a transferal of "blame" for the death of Jesus onto, at best, a representative council of Jews and, at worst, the Jewish people generally. It is in their descriptions of Jesus' trial, however, that the Gospels are at their most polemical. The only way we can ever hope to understand the historical factors that led to Jesus' death is to put the Gospels to one side and, instead, reconstruct events around the one man who was central to the whole affair—Joseph Caiaphas, the high priest who handed Jesus over to Rome.

Appendix A: Significant Dates

37–4 B.C.E.	Reign of Herod the Great	
	ca. 20	Birth of Joseph Caiaphas
	ca. 4	Birth of Jesus of Nazareth
4 B.C.E.–6 C.E.	Herod's son Archelaus tetrarch of Judea	
4 B.C.E.–37 C.E.	Herod's son Antipas ethnarch of Galilee and Perea	
6–41 C.E.	First phase of direct Roman rule of Judea (by prefects)	
	6–15	Annas high priest
	18–37	Caiaphas high priest
	26–37	Pontius Pilate prefect of Judea
	ca. 33	Death of Jesus of Nazareth
	ca. 35	Conversion of Paul of Tarsus
41–44	Reign of Agrippa I (Herod's grandson)	

44–6w6	Second phase of direct Roman rule of Judea (by procurators)	
	ca. 50–64	Paul active around Mediterranean
66–74	Jewish Revolt	
	70	Fall of Jerusalem and destruction of the temple
	ca. 70	Mark's Gospel written
	ca. 80–100	Matthew, Luke–Acts, and John written
132–35	Revolt of Bar Kokhba	

Appendix B: High Priests of Judea

From the Reign of Herod I to the Destruction of the Temple (37 B.C.E.–70 C.E.)

Name	House	One who appointed	Dates
Appointed by Herods			
Ananel		Herod I	37–36, 34 B.C.E.
Aristobulus III	Hasmonean	Herod I	35
Jesus b. Phabes		Herod I	to ca. 22
Simon Boethus[1]	Boethus	Herod I	ca. 22–25
Matthias b. Theophilus		Herod I	5–4
Joseph b. Ellemus		Herod I	5
Joazar b. Boethus	Boethus	Herod I	4[2]
Eleazar b. Boethus	Boethus	Archelaus	from 4 B.C.E.
Jesus b. See	Boethus	Archelaus	until 6 C.E.
Appointed by Rome			
Ananus (Annas) b. Sethi	Annas	Quirinius, Syrian legate	6–15 C.E.
Ishmael b. Phiabi I		Gratus, prefect	ca. 15–16
Eleazar b. Ananus	Annas	Gratus, prefect	ca. 16–17
Simon b. Camith		Gratus, prefect	ca. 17–18
Joseph Caiaphas	Annas	Gratus, prefect	ca. 18–37
Jonathan b. Ananus	Annas	Vitellius, Syrian legate	37
Theophilus b. Ananus	Annas	Vitellius, Syrian legate	from 37

Name	House	One who appointed	Dates
Appointed by Herods			
Simon Cantheras[3]	Boethus	Agrippa I	from 41
Matthias b. Ananus	Annas	Agrippa I	
Elionaeus b. Cantheras	Boethus	Agrippa I	ca. 44
Joseph b. Kabi		Agrippa I ?	
Ananias b. Nedebaeus		Herod of Chalcis	47–49[4]
Ishmael b. Phiabi II		Agrippa II	49–62
Joseph Camei		Agrippa II	until 62
Ananus b. Ananus	Annas	Agrippa II	62
Jesus b. Damnaeus		Agrippa II	ca. 62–65
Jesus b. Gamaliel		Agrippa II	ca. 63–65
Matthias b. Theophilus	Annas	Agrippa II	65–67
Appointed by Zealots			
Phanni b. Samuel	Zealots		67–70

Note: Many of the above names have various spellings in Josephus and rabbinic literature. In the interests of consistency, I have followed the spellings of Josephus.

Appendix C: Was Caiaphas a Zadokite?

It is beyond question that Caiaphas belonged to a priestly family. What is less clear is whether he belonged to the distinctive high-priestly line of Zadok. This question is of considerable importance, since it goes to the very heart of Caiaphas's legitimacy as high priest and his status in the eyes of his contemporaries. Was he simply an ordinary priest who was promoted to the high priesthood? Was he in no way distinguished from the thousands of other priests in first-century Palestine, except for the fact that he was chosen by Rome? Or did he belong to an old high-priestly family, which guaranteed him a certain amount of honor and respect despite being appointed by Rome?

It is probably well to acknowledge at the outset that although a number of scholars have argued for a Zadokite lineage,[1] prevailing scholarly opinion has tended to deny that Caiaphas belonged to a high-priestly family.[2] The conventional view is that the Zadokites held the high priesthood only until the disturbances in the second century B.C.E. that led to the Maccabean revolt. The high priesthood was then claimed by the heirs of the Maccabees, the (non-Zadokite) Hasmoneans, who held the position until the reign of Herod I. Later high priests are generally regarded as insignificant, non-Zadokite priests, plucked from obscurity by Herod or the Roman governors and installed as puppet high priests, with no personal claim to any kind of authority in the eyes of the people. There is, however, very little evidence for this view. Only two pieces of first-century evidence are ever cited, and neither stands up to scrutiny.

1. The first is *Antiq* 20.247, which notes that Herod "assigned the office [of high priest] to some insignificant persons who were merely of priestly descent." Superficially, this does seem to suggest that the high priests appointed by Herod were ordinary priests as opposed to Zadokites. But a closer reading of this passage in its context and in the light of Josephus's own particular bias reveals a quite different picture.

The passage comes at the end of the *Antiquities*, at a point where Josephus pauses to review the entire history of the Jewish high priesthood. Josephus's own pro-Hasmonean sympathies come out quite clearly in this passage. He lavishes great praise on the Hasmonean high priests, suggesting that the high priesthood was raised to new heights under them (20.238–46). It is clear—both here and elsewhere in his work—that for Josephus the Hasmoneans, his own ancestors, had proved themselves worthy of the office of high priest. But Josephus has a problem: how is he to admit that his heroes were usurpers, that they ousted the legitimate holders of the position and installed themselves? What he does is extremely clever and quite simple—he simply erases any mention of the Zadokites. He traces the high priesthood from Aaron and shows that all the high priests down to the second century were descended from his two sons. Josephus acknowledges some disruption at this point but passes it off as merely the transfer from one Aaronite family to another. After Alcimus (the last Zadokite), he says the high priesthood was vacant for seven years, after which the Hasmoneans "resumed the tradition, appointing as high priest Jonathan" (20.238). There is not the slightest hint here that the non-Zadokite Hasmoneans have usurped the position.

Then we come to the passage with which we started. Herod, Josephus says, "abandoned the practice of appointing those of Hasmonean lineage as high priests . . . and assigned the office to some insignificant persons who were of merely priestly descent." The contrast here is not between *ordinary priests* and *Zadokites* (as scholars all too often suppose) but between *ordinary priests* and *Hasmoneans*. Herod's great crime is that he did not allow the Hasmoneans to continue to hold the high priesthood. The fact that he gave it to "men of merely priestly descent" tells us nothing—the earlier high priests were also of merely Aaronite lineage; the Zadokites have been taken out of the equation. So, all we can infer from 20.247 is that the new men were not Hasmoneans. The crafty historian tells us nothing about Zadokite descent.

2. The second piece of evidence comes from the time of the Jewish revolt and is used by a number of scholars to suggest that earlier high priests were not Zadokites.[3] Again, Josephus is our guide. He tells us that the Jewish Zealots in the besieged city took it upon themselves to appoint a high priest. The text is as follows:

In the end, to such abject prostration and terror were the people reduced and to such heights of madness rose these brigands, that they actually took upon themselves the election to the high priesthood. Abrogating the claims of those families from which in turn the high priests had always been drawn, they appointed to that office ignoble and low born individuals, in order to gain accomplices in their impious crimes; for persons who had undeservedly attained to the highest dignity were bound to obey those who had conferred it. Moreover, by various devices and libellous statements, they brought the official authorities into collision with each other, finding their own opportunity in the bickerings of those who should have kept them in check ; until, glutted with the wrongs which they had done to men, they transferred their insolence to the Deity and, with polluted feet invaded the sanctuary.

An insurrection of the populace was at length pending, instigated by Ananus, the senior of the chief priests, a man of profound sanity, who might possibly have saved the city, had he escaped the conspirators' hands. At this threat these wretches converted the temple of God into their fortress and refuge from any outbreak of popular violence, and made the Holy Place the headquarters of their tyranny. To these horrors was added a spice of mockery more galling than their actions. For, to test the abject submission of the populace and make trial of their own strength, they essayed to appoint the high priests by lot, although, as we have stated, the succession was hereditary. As pretext for this scheme they adduced ancient custom, asserting that in old days the high priesthood had been determined by lot; but in reality their action was the abrogation of established practice and a trick to make themselves supreme by getting these appointments into their own hands.

They accordingly summoned one of the high-priestly clans, called Eniachin, and cast lots for a high priest. By chance the lot fell to one who proved a signal illustration of their depravity; he was an individual named Phanni, son of Samuel, of the village of Aphthia, a man who not only was not descended from high priests, but was such a clown that he scarcely knew what the high priesthood meant. At any rate they dragged their reluctant victim out of the country and, dressing him up for his assumed part, as on the stage, put the sacred vestments upon him and instructed him how to act in keeping with the occasion. To them this monstrous impiety was a subject for jesting and sport, but the other priests, beholding from a distance this mockery of their law, could not restrain their tears and bemoaned the degradation of the sacred honours.[4]

War 4.147–57

Josephus is clearly outraged at the actions of the Zealots, and we need to pick our way through his account carefully. What annoyed Josephus so much was that the rebels ignored the claims of the families from which the high priest had usually been drawn (that is, Jewish aristocrats) and appointed instead an uneducated man of low birth. The Zealots, however, set great store on *the way in which the high priest was chosen*. In accordance with ancient custom, the high priest had to be chosen by lot, that is, by God. The names of all the high-priestly families had to be put forward, and if the lot fell on a humble stonemason, then so be it. What is surprising about this story is that Phanni's high-priestly (Zadokite) lineage plays such a minor role: the Zealots assume it, Josephus ignores it. What was significant about Phanni was not that he was a Zadokite chosen after a long line of non-Zadokites, but that he was a man chosen by lot/God after a long line of men chosen by the secular power. This story, then, does not support the view that all previous high priests were not Zadokites. In fact, it may well suggest quite the opposite: it is *assumed* that the high priests are Zadokites; the question is how they should be appointed.

Neither argument generally put forward to deny the Roman-appointed high priests Zadokite lineage, then, is compelling. But is there any evidence to suggest that they were Zadokites? To find some clues we need to go back to the beginning of Herod's reign.

Despite Josephus's antipathy to Herod's first high priest, a Babylonian by the name of Ananel, he does inadvertently let slip that he was of a "high priestly family" (*Antiq* 15.22, 39-40); presumably he was one of the Zadokite priests who did not return to Palestine after the Babylonian exile.[5] It is possible that another of Herod's appointments, Boethus, was also a Zadokite, perhaps a relative of Onias IV, who fled to Egypt during the disturbances under Antiochus Epiphanes.[6]

By bringing back Zadokites to the high priesthood, Herod could ingratiate himself with all those in Israel who had reservations about the illegal usurpation of the high priesthood by his opponents, the Hasmoneans. Of course, this was a risky undertaking—the last thing Herod needed was for the people to rally round a popular Zadokite high priest and threaten his already tenuous position. Perhaps this explains why he favored little known men from the Diaspora, why he kept the position firmly under his own control, and why he shared the position among a number of different branches of the Zadokite family. Herod's policies regarding the high priesthood, then, were not designed to diminish the office, but were attempts to safeguard his own position after reinstating Zadokites. He could attempt to overcome his questionable origins by presenting himself as a great Jewish king, restoring the Jewish cult after the Hasmonean usurpation and (in due course) rebuilding the temple.

But what of Herod's other appointments? If Ananel and the family of Boethus were Zadokites, can we infer anything about the others? Soon after his victory at the battle of Actium in 31 B.C.E., Herod's patron, Augustus, promoted himself as the restorer of the traditional Roman cult. He revived old rituals, rebuilt ruined temples, and filled vacant priesthoods. If Herod had already embarked on a similar policy of representing himself as the restorer of the old Zadokite high priesthood, it is likely that he would have continued such a policy with the appointment of other high priests—particularly when it fitted in so perfectly with the policy of Augustus. Herod went out of his way to flatter the emperor in every way he could—he built temples in his honor, he rebuilt cities, he set up statues, he founded games. What better way to flatter an emperor who laid stress on ancestral religious traditions than to be seen to be doing the same with respect to Judaism?

If this had been Herod's policy—as seems quite probable—it would almost certainly have been continued first by the Syrian legate and then by the Roman prefects, who would have been reluctant to replace a traditional family with one of their own choosing.[7] Annas, then, and presumably his son-in-law Caiaphas, would have simply belonged to different branches of the prestigious Zadokite high-priestly family.

Appendix D: The Location of Caiaphas's Palace

Where did Caiaphas live as high priest? This has been the subject of much speculation from the fourth century to the present day. In this appendix I shall review the ancient references and modern archaeological discoveries before evaluating the historical accuracy of the traditions.

Ancient References

Once pilgrims began to visit Jerusalem—slowly at first after Constantine's conversion, and then in droves throughout the Middle Ages—there was a great interest in the location of sacred sites and monuments. These intrepid men and women wanted to feel connected with the places associated with Jesus. The location of the crucifixion and resurrection were of central significance, but other sites quickly became important too. One of these was the location of Jesus' trial in front of the high priest. The Gospels situated this within Caiaphas's palace, and so the position of the palace took on a special Christian interest.

Our earliest traditions locate Caiaphas's palace to the south of the city on Mount Zion, not far from the Zion Gate.[1] In the first century, this would have formed the southernmost part of the Upper City, the area favored by the wealthier inhab-

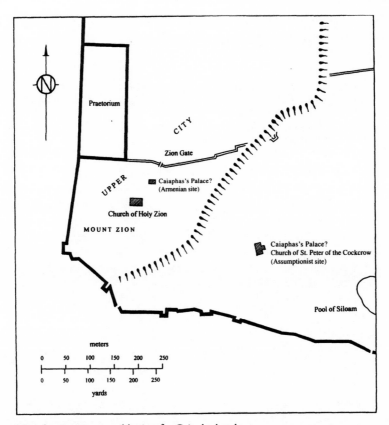

Map showing two possible sites for Caiaphas's palace.

itants of Jerusalem. The earliest recorded visitor was a pilgrim from Bordeaux who toured the Holy Land in about 333 C.E. Ascending Mount Zion, the pilgrim passed the Pool of Siloam and came across the ruins of Caiaphas's palace. Among the ruins was a "scourging pillar," said to contain the impression of Christ as he was scourged by Pilate. (The pilgrim, unfortunately, does not explain why a pillar associated with *Pilate* should be in the house of *Caiaphas!*) The ruined site was also known to Cyril, bishop of Jerusalem in the mid-fourth century, and used to great effect in his preaching. The ruined house of Caiaphas, he maintained, was more than simply a witness to the events of the Gospel: "its present desolation manifests the power of him who once was judged in it" (*Catech.* 13.38).

The site, however, did not remain ruined for long. At some point in the late fourth century, the scourging pillar was removed. The exuberant Egeria, a nun "from the other end of the earth," mentioned that it was becoming quite a tourist attraction, and Jerome, writing in 404, said that it now held up the porch of the church of Holy Zion (built on the Cenacle, the traditional location of the Last

Supper). The ruined palace itself was covered in the mid-fifth century by a church dedicated to Peter. These traditions are brought together by Theodosius in his *Topography*, written about 530:

> From Holy Zion to the House of Caiaphas which is now the Church of St Peter, it is about fifty paces. From the House of Caiaphas to the Praetorium of Pilate is about one hundred paces, the church of St Sophia is there . . . . The column which was in the House of Caiaphas, at which the Lord Christ was scourged, is now in Holy Zion.[2]

This is our first precise description that usefully locates the palace relative to other landmarks. According to Theodosius, then, Caiaphas's palace was fifty paces from the church of Holy Zion and one hundred from Pilate's praetorium (Herod's palace on the western side of the Upper City). Although Theodosius's directions are not entirely clear, it seems likely that we should be walking fifty paces to the north or west of the Church of Holy Zion to reach the palace of Caiaphas (and a further one hundred paces north or west to reach Pilate's praetorium).

Caiaphas's palace also makes an appearance on the Madaba Map. Found in 1884, thirty kilometers south of Amman in Turkey, this sixth-century mosaic map originally formed part of the floor of a large cathedral. It depicts the entire Holy Land, with Jerusalem at the center, shown larger and in more detail than the other cities. The artist looked east over the city—represented as an elongated oval—and

Part of the Madaba mosaic map showing Jerusalem. Caiaphas's palace is in the lower right-hand corner. (Photograph courtesy of D. J. Reimer.)

drew in certain landmarks in two dimensions. It is the oldest known pictorial map of Jerusalem and, despite its schematic execution, is one of our main sources for the topography of the city in Byzantine times. The map shows Caiaphas's palace on Mount Zion. Although it is not clear enough to pinpoint the exact location, the map clearly agrees in general terms with the earlier traditions.

Modern Archaeological Discoveries

At present, there are two contenders for the site of Caiaphas's palace: they are generally known as the "Assumptionist" and the "Armenian" sites, taking their names from the monastic orders associated with them.

The Assumptionist site is located on the eastern slope of Mount Zion. Excavations were carried out by French (Assumptionist) archaeologists on the site in 1888/89, 1911, and 1914. The second excavation revealed a fifth-century church. Two bronze seals bearing the imprint of a cock suggested that the church should be associated with Peter, and so it is commonly referred to as the church of "St. Peter of the Cockcrow." The question is, was this "the Church of St Peter" that was built above Caiaphas's palace? Below the church, excavators found a large grotto that, though perhaps originally a tomb, may have later functioned as a prison. This subterranean apartment was supported by seven pillars; the eighth was missing and could perhaps have been the one against which prisoners were scourged (remember the scourging pillar seen by the Bordeaux pilgrim, Egeria, and Jerome). In the same area, excavators found a fairly complete collection of Jewish weights and measures and an inscription containing the word *corban* (which means "offering"). The excavators believed that they had unearthed an official religious establishment in which prisoners could be held, measures guaranteed, and temple offerings stored. The site was, in short, none other than the palace of Caiaphas.[3]

Despite their best efforts, the Assumptionist claims have not found much favor. The following objections are often raised. 1. Another French archaeologist, L. H. Vincent, argued that the archaeological record did not support their overconfident thesis.[4] 2. Given the high purity requirements of a high priest, it would be extremely unlikely that his palace would be built anywhere near a former tomb. 3. The Assumptionist site is difficult to square with Theodosius's evidence. The distance from the Assumptionist site to the church of Holy Zion (the Cenacle) is over two hundred meters, not fifty paces as Theodosius calculated! Much closer is the second contender, the Armenian site, located only fifty meters to the north of the Church of Holy Zion.

This second site has been an Armenian monastery since the fifteenth century, but excavations have revealed a much older church beneath it. Could this, then, be the Church of St Peter referred to by Theodosius? The courtyard of the monastery was excavated by Israeli archaeologists in 1971/72 on behalf of the Armenian patriarchate and the Department of Antiquities and Museums. Excavations revealed a number of luxurious homes from the Herodian era. The houses were large, occupying two or even three stories, contained water installations (cisterns, baths, and pools) and mosaic floors. One particularly remarkable house is decorated with fine frescoes containing birds. There can be no doubt that these were houses occupied by some of Jerusalem's wealthiest inhabitants.[5]

Again, the excavators appear fairly confident that they have indeed found the house of Caiaphas. The site fits in tolerably well with Theodosius's evidence, and the majority of modern scholars acknowledge that if either site is genuinely Caiaphas's palace, the Armenian one is to be preferred. But this site is not without its difficulties. 1. The houses are clearly those of the Jerusalem elite, but there is nothing specifically to link any of them with a high priest. In fact, the presence of the bird fresco may well argue against identifying this particular house with a high-priestly family. As so often, there is no one clear interpretation of this feature. The excavators took the bird motifs as evidence of the laxity in upholding the second commandment among the wealthy, while another Israeli archaeologist, N. Avigad, took it as evidence that this particular house did not belong to a Jewish household![6] 2. The ancient tradition may itself be suspect. How likely is it that the Upper Room (the site of the Church of Holy Zion) was only fifty paces away from Caiaphas's palace? Would the disciples have met in such a place the night of Jesus' arrest? And, even more surprisingly, would they have sheltered here "for fear of the Jews" afterwards (John 20:19, Acts 2:13)? We must turn now to a consideration of the trustworthiness of the ancient tradition.

Historical Accuracy of the Traditions

People in ancient societies had long memories. Most would have lived in the same city all their lives, and traditions could easily have been transmitted orally across several generations. We might expect the first Christians to have kept alive not only a recollection of the events but also of the places associated with Jesus' last hours. The fact that our first reference to the location of Caiaphas's palace occurs two and a half centuries after the end of the high priesthood would not, ordinarily, be particularly problematic. Yet the history of Jerusalem throws a question mark over such easy assumptions.

In the century following Jesus' death, the city was decimated by two revolts and the people were scattered. First came the revolt of 66, prior to which, according to tradition, the small Christian community fled from Jerusalem and took refuge in Pella beyond the Jordan.[7] In the course of the revolt, the city was ravaged by four years of civil war, rioting, and looting. Many houses were burned, including the house of the high priest Ananias (Josephus, *War*, 2.426, 429). What the Jewish rebels left standing, the Romans destroyed at the end of their siege in 70 C.E.: according to Josephus, Jerusalem was so completely razed "that those who visited it could not believe it had ever been inhabited" (*War* 7.3). Roman legions again trampled the city in response to Bar Kokhba's uprising of 132–35 C.E. At the orders of the Emperor Hadrian, much of the old city was flattened, and a new pagan city, Aelia Capitolina, rose from the ruins. Jews were driven out from the city, and the practice of Judaism was banned for a time. Wide-scale destruction, the movement of people, and the transformation of Jerusalem into a Roman colony would have marked a significant break with all that had gone before. Even if anyone remembered the precise location of Caiaphas's house, it would have been difficult—if not impossible—to find.

Did Christians manage to preserve and transmit topographic details under these difficult conditions? Did they return to Jerusalem after the first revolt and reacquaint themselves with the places that had formed the backdrop to Jesus' earthly life? Did their Jewish neighbors help them to fill in the details? It is not impossible, but one thing counts strongly against these traditions. The early Christians expected the imminent return of Jesus. Their eyes were set to the future, not the past. The task in hand was to preach the gospel, not to venerate sites that were soon to be swept away. Only with the conversion of Constantine in the early fourth century, the building of the emperor's great basilicas, and the subsequent influx of pilgrims into the Holy City did locations become important. If no one in the fourth century remembered the site, we can be sure that one would quickly have been invented. The fact that even such central sites as Golgotha and Jesus' tomb are contested should warn us against placing too much reliance on traditions relating to Caiaphas's palace.

Probably all we can say with any certainty is that Caiaphas's palace was located somewhere in the Upper City, the area covered today by the Armenian and Jewish quarter and extending as far south as Mount Zion. The Armenian site has more to recommend it, but as we have seen, the whole tradition upon which it rests is itself suspect. It seems best to conclude that the precise location is unknown.[8]

Notes

The Tomb

1. Sources are cited in abbreviated form in these notes. Fuller details of each work can be found in the bibliography.

   Information regarding the Caiaphas tomb can be found in the three articles by Z. Greenhut and the three by R. Reich in the bibliography; also J. Zias, "Human." All these scholars suggest the tomb did belong to Caiaphas. For an alternative view, see W. Horbury, "'Caiaphas'"; E. Puech, "A-t-on redécouvert"; and A. Vicent Cernuda, "Conversión," 37, who also expresses reservations. On Jewish burial customs generally, see R. Hachlili and A. Killebrew, "Funerary"; L.Y. Rahmani, "Ossuaries" and *Catalogue*.

2. See Z. Greenhut, "'Caiaphas'" (*Atiqot* 21), 71, for a list of coin finds in Jewish tombs in Jerusalem until 1990. Also R. Hachlili and A. Killebrew, "Coin-on-Eye."

3. For the view that ossuaries and secondary burial in general were inspired by Greco-Roman practices, see L. Levine, *Judaism*, 63–67. For an alternative view, see note 10 below.

4. On the names of first-century Jews, see M. Williams, "Palestinian," and T. Ilan, "Notes."

5. See J. Naveh, "Nameless."

6. The bones in this ossuary, like all the bones in the tomb, were in such a poor state of preservation that it was impossible to take DNA samples, to piece

together a medical history, or even to take measurements. This is a common problem in Israel's damp hill country.

7. For this use of *bar* see R. Reich, "Ossuary" (*Jerusalem Perspective*), 16.

8. For further discussion, see D. Barag and D. Flusser, "Ossuary."

9. For Annas's tomb, see *War* 5.506.

10. This is suggested by W. Horbury, "'Caiaphas,'" 35. In the Jewish Scriptures, the place of the dead was known as "Sheol." Horbury notes that in the Septuagint (the Greek translation of these Scriptures) and Jewish funerary inscriptions from Egypt and elsewhere, Sheol is always equated with the Greek Hades—even though the latter has connotations of afterlife that are missing from Sheol.

 Some scholars have doubted that this is the tomb of Caiaphas because of the ossuary itself. It is still assumed by some that the use of ossuaries was a Pharisaic development, spurred on by the growing belief in an individual resurrection. (See in particular L. Y. Rahmani, *Catalogue*, Appendix A, 53–55; also "Ossuaries.") In support of this view, ossuaries do seem to have come into use once this belief in resurrection had developed. But, as was suggested earlier in the text, secondary burial is better seen as a response to Hellenistic practices than to Pharisaic teaching. This explains better why ossuaries ceased to be used after 70 C.E., even though Pharisaic power was increasing. It also gets around the difficulty of why ossuaries, which are supposedly linked to a belief in *individual* resurrection, tend to be crammed full with the remains of several people! The use of ossuaries probably tells us more about the Hellenism of first-century Jewish society than about the influence of Pharisaic teaching.

11. Tos.Yebamoth 1.10. See further discussion of this and other possible rabbinic references on 164 n. 3 below.

12. This is the conclusion of W. Horbury, "'Caiaphas.'"

13. On ossuary inscriptions generally, see L. Y. Rahmani, *Catalogue*, 11–12.

14. See F. Blass and A. Debrunner, *Grammar*, section 37, 20.

Perceptions of Caiaphas

1. A. France, "Le Procurateur de Judée" (1892); M. Bulgakov, *The Master and Margarita* (the English translation in the bibliography dates to 1967; the original Russian was written, though not published, in the Stalinist era).

2. On the historical Pilate, see my *Pontius.* On later, legendary Pilates see A. Wroe, *Pilate,* and H. I. MacAdam, "Quid?" We also have material remains from Pilate, dissolving the two thousand years that separate our time from his. During his stay in Judea he struck three different types of bronze coins. So numerous were these that they can still be picked up relatively cheaply from specialist dealers. And in 1961 a Latin inscription came to light in Pilate's former headquarters, Caesarea on Sea. The inscription had once belonged to a building dedicated to the Emperor Tiberius. Pilate had built it as a mark of loyalty, to show his respect to his imperial lord and master. The public inscription proudly declared: "Pontius Pilate . . . prefect of Judaea . . . dedicated it." The original building has long since disappeared, but Pilate's plaque can still be seen in the Archaeological Museum in Istanbul.

3. For the view that the fall of Jerusalem was the punishment on Jews for the death of Christ, see Origen, *Homily on Jeremiah* 15.15 and *Against Celsus* 34. On the process by which Jesus' death was attributed not to individuals but to "the Jews," see G. Sloyan, *Crucifixion*, 72–97, and J. T. Carroll and J. B. Green, *Death*, 182–204.

4. Origen's discussion of Caiaphas can be found in his *Commentary on the Gospel of John* 28.98–191 (the quotation is from 28.106, trans. R. Heine). In 28.107, he

spends some time proving that the Gospels denounced Caiaphas's wickedness. The fourth-century *Apostolic Constitutions* similarly concludes that not everyone who prophesies is holy and refers to Caiaphas as "the falsely named High Priest," 8.2.5.

5. Jerome, *Liber Interpretationis Hebraicorum nominum*. None of these meanings can be substantiated from any Hebrew or Aramaic root. It is clear that Jerome is simply deriving them from what he knows of Caiaphas's role in the New Testament. For other (more likely) derivations of Caiaphas's name, see 164 n. 3 below.

This unflattering image continued into the apocryphal gospels. The curious, legendary *Narrative of Joseph of Arimathea* imagines that Caiaphas was the uncle of Judas Iscariot and that the plan to kill Jesus originated with Caiaphas's daughter, a priestess in the sanctuary. For a translation of part of the legend, see J. K. Elliot, *Apocryphal New Testament*, 217–22.

6. *Apostolic Constitutions* 8.2. The work was probably compiled around 380 C.E. in Syria, though it undoubtedly contains much earlier material. See D. A. Fiensy, *Prayers*, 19.

7. For a translation of this letter see J. K. Elliot, *Apocryphal New Testament*, 224–25. H. Lietzmann et al., *Griechisch-christlichen Inschriften*, 41 n. 2. Caiaphas fared rather better than his father-in-law Annas, who was sewed into a fresh bull's hide and, as it dried, was squeezed to death. For similar traditions, see P. W. Van der Horst, "Jews," 200 n. 8, and G. F. Abbott, "Report."

8. Discussions of this document (which, with the addition of an extra section describing Christ's descent to hell, is sometimes known as the *Gospel of Nicodemus*) can be found in G. W. H. Lampe, "Acta," and F. Scheidweiler in W. Schneemelcher, *Apocrypha*, 501–5; for the text and introduction, see J. K. Elliot, *Apocryphal New Testament*, 164–204.

9. For text and introduction, see J. K. Elliot, *Apocryphal New Testament*, 100–107. The view that Caiaphas became a believer was also shared by the author of the Sahidic fragment of the Assumption of the Virgin, though this document refers to him not by name but as "the High Priest." See J. K. Elliot, *Apocryphal New Testament*, 700–701. For a modern variant on this view, see 86.

10. On the English mystery plays see P. Happe, *English*; M. Hussey, *Chester*; and R. Beadle and P. King, eds., *York*. For a discussion of the iconography of French mystery plays, see G. Frank, "Popular."

11. *Divine Comedy* I: Inferno, canto 23.

12. F. Dostoevsky, *The Brothers Karamazov* (1880), book 5, chapter 5. In his notebooks for the novel, however, Dostoevsky was rather more positive, acknowledging that Christ would forgive Caiaphas because the high priest loved his people (presumably a reflection on John 11:50). For the passage, see F. Dostoevsky, *Notebooks*, ed. E. Wasiolek, 102. A third reference to the high priest can be found in *A Raw Youth*, 269.

13. The quotations are from pp. xviii and 89. See also A. Borland, *Personalities*, who regards Caiaphas as "that not uncommon phenomenon—a man of low character in a high place" (47).

14. This is particularly striking in Norman Jewison's *Jesus Christ Superstar* (1973), in which the deliberations of the council contrast with the people's hosannas as Jesus enters Jerusalem. In Franco Zeffirelli's *Jesus of Nazareth* (1977), Caiaphas is presented as a weary, aloof man in black robes who almost single-handedly persuades the council that Jesus must die.

15. On Caiaphas, see D. Flusser, "Bury" and "Caiaphas"; B. Chilton, "Caiaphas"; P. Gaechter, "Hatred." On the temple priesthood more generally, see B. Chilton, "Annas"; J. Jeremias, *Jerusalem*; M. Goodman, *Ruling*; C. A. Evans, "Jesus"; R.

A. Horsley, "High Priests"; K. C. Hanson and D. E. Oakman, *Palestine*; T. Rajak, *Josephus*, 22–24; and H. Maccoby, *Revolution*, 98–99. M. Stern, "Aspects" is less negative, though he emphasizes the struggle for prestige between prominent families and suggests that the people began to look to the Pharisees as spiritual leaders (600–612).

More positive presentations can, however, be found in E. M. Smallwood, "High Priests"; E. P. Sanders, *Judaism*, 317–40; J. S. McLaren, *Power*; and J. P. Meier, *Marginal* 3:389–487. It will become apparent in the following chapters that my portrait of Caiaphas has more in common with this latter group of writers.

16. For varying interpretations of Judas's actions, see K. Paffenroth, *Judas*.
17. P. Gaechter, for example, can write of "Sadducean irreligiousness" ("Hatred," 13). See also H. Maccoby, *Revolution*, 98–99.
18. All disputants in the great Jewish controversies and schisms have claimed to be the true heirs of the Pharisees—leaders of the Reform movement, Orthodox Jews, Conservative Jews, and even some proponents of the Jewish feminist movement. On modern scholarly assessments of the Pharisees, see D. R. Schwartz, *Studies*, 66–70; T. Ilan, *Integrating*, 11–15; and E. P. Sanders, *Judaism*, 399–402.
19. P. Winter also makes this point, citing S. Rosenblatt, "The Crucifixion of Jesus" as an example of a Jewish scholar who held the high priests responsible for Jesus' death (*Trial*, 59). A more recent illustration is D. Flusser, who stresses Caiaphas's Sadducean connections and suggests that the death of Jesus was a Sadducean affair. The Pharisees, he maintains, strongly disapproved of handing over a Jew to a foreign authority and had nothing to do with Jesus' death ("Caiaphas" and "Bury").
20. J. D. Crossan, for example, imagines Jesus as a brilliant but illiterate peasant preaching a radical message of social inclusion, egalitarianism, and unmediated contact with God, a message that set him on a direct collision course with the unjust, oppressive priestly regime in the Jerusalem temple. The picture has, of course, immense contemporary appeal; yet, for that very reason, we should be wary of accepting it as historically accurate. Many people in the modern world may have lost faith in "organized religion," but we should be wary of assuming that it was the same in the first century. Crossan's view is expressed in his *Historical Jesus* and (in abbreviated form) in *Revolutionary Biography*. For critiques of Crossan's view, see below, 175 n. 9.

1. Sources

1. General introductions to Josephus include T. Rajak, *Josephus*; S. N. Mason, *Josephus*; L. H. Feldman, "Josephus"; and P. Bilde, *Flavius*; see also my "Currents." For a less positive assessment of both Josephus's person and his abilities as a writer, see S. J. D. Cohen, *Josephus*.
2. Josephus used a source (mentioned in *Antiq* 20.224–51 and *Against Apion* 1.36) that listed incumbents of the high priesthood.
3. Introductions to the Dead Sea Scrolls can be found in G. Vermes, *Complete Dead Sea Scrolls*, and J. VanderKam, *Dead Sea Scrolls*. Texts and introductory notes to pseudepigraphical literature can be found in the J. H. Charlesworth, ed., *The Old Testament Pseudepigrapha* (2 vols.); see also the studies on individual works by G. W. E. Nicklesburg and J. Tromp in the bibliography.
4. General introductions to rabbinic literature include J. Neusner, *The Mishnah*, Introduction, pp. xiii–lxii; P. A. Alexander, "Rabbinic"; and D. Goodblatt, "Babylonian." See also S. J. D. Cohen, *Josephus*, 253–60.

5. Introductions to the archaeology of Jerusalem can be found in Y. Yadin, ed., *Jerusalem;* H. Geva, ed., *Ancient;* and J. J. Rousseau and R. Arav, *Jesus.*

6. General introductions to the Gospels and Acts include S. L. Harris, *Understanding*, 351–446, and R. E. Brown, *Introduction*, 97–405. Much more literature can be found in the chapters relating to each Gospel.

2. Caiaphas the Young Priest

1. For such reconstructions see R. Reich, "Ossuary" (*Atiqot*), 74–76; R. Brody in D. R. Schwartz, *Agrippa I*, 190–95; and A. Vicent Cernuda, "Conversión," 49–51.

2. Josephus's family owned lands near Jerusalem before the war (*Life* 422). The wealth of other high priestly families was legendary: Boethus (b.Gittin 56a, b.Yebamoth 61a) and Phiabi (b.Yoma 35b). This kind of wealth could only have been acquired through property. See J. Jeremias, *Jerusalem*, 99, and D. A. Fiensy, "Composition," 218.

3. This tradition is preserved in tos.Yebamoth 1.10 (which also suggests that the high priestly branch of this family was descended from a levirite marriage). See also y.Yebamoth 1.6, 3.1 and discussion in J. Jeremias, *Jerusalem*, 93–94. The precise location of Beth Meqoshesh is uncertain; see M. Stern, *Aspects*, 584. For the suggestion that it was close to Jerusalem, see D. Flusser, "Bury," 23.

   It has sometimes been suggested that another rabbinic text refers to Caiaphas's son. Mishnah Parah 3.5 refers to a high priest named "Eliehonaeus the son of ha-Qoph" (variant ha-Qayyaph, or Caiaphas). Given the rarity of the name Elionaeus, this must be the same high priest that Josephus refers to in *Antiq* 19.342 as "Elionaeus son of Cantheras." But why does the Mishnah refer to him as the son of ha-Qoph/Qayyaph, while Josephus designates him "son of Cantheras"? There are two possibilities here: (1) that they are variants on the same name, and (2) that one source is mistaken. R. Brody suggested that they were both etymologically linked to a word for "basket" or "carrying" (Qayyaph being related to the Semitic, Cantheras to the Latin). In this case, both would belong to the same family, and Elionaeus could be the son of Joseph Caiaphas. See R. Brody, "Caiaphas"; D. Flusser, "Caiaphas," 81; A. Vicent Cernuda, "Conversión," 38–52; and M. Stern, who mentions this as a "conjecture" (*Aspects*, 606–8). D. R. Schwartz suggests that Elionaeus was Caiaphas's brother (*Agrippa I*, 185–89). While it is perfectly possible that names might change over time, the difficulty with this theory is that it assumes that two very different names were both being used at roughly the same time for members of the same family (i.e., Caiaphas and his son). For this reason it is more likely that one of our sources is mistaken. But which one? Elionaeus served as high priest in 44 C.E., when Josephus was about seven years old, and he may well have lived for some time in Jerusalem after his deposition. It is likely, then, that Josephus would have known both his name and family connections. The Mishnah, however, was written down much later, roughly 200 C.E., and it is much more likely that the name is incorrect here. In fact, the same passage erroneously refers to "Hanamel the Egyptian" rather than "Ananel the Babylonian" (*Antiq* 15.22). In this case, it seems unlikely that Elionaeus was either Caiaphas's son or brother. For a fuller discussion of m.Parah, see W. Horbury, "'Caiaphas,'" 42–43.

4. Josephus, *Life* 2. The twenty-four divisions are listed in 1 Chr 24:7. Chronicles claims that the twenty-four divisions were made during the rule of King David, but they were probably a much later innovation (see C. Werman, "Sons," 625).

5. For fuller discussion of Caiaphas's Zadokite heritage, see Appendix C. On

Zadok, see D. W. Rooke, *Zadok's*, 63–69, who argues, along with many other commentators, that Zadok was originally a Jebusite priest.

6. For biblical references to these genealogies, see Exod 28:1, Lev 16:32, 1 Kgs 13:2, Ezra 2:61–63 (= Num 7:63–65). Josephus also stresses the importance of these records in *Against Apion* 1.29–36.

7. Despite two rabbinic references to schools (y.Ketuboth 8.11.32c and b.Baba Bathra 21a) there is no evidence from the first century to support the existence of such institutions. See D. Goodblatt, "Judaean," 13–15. On study at home, see Deut 11:19.

   Two references in the Mishnah suggest that not all high priests were able to read the book of Daniel the night before the Day of Atonement (m.Yoma 1.6, m.Horayoth 3.8). Apart from the last high priest—Phanni b. Samuel—who was, according to Josephus, an illiterate stone mason, I find it hard to imagine that any of the others were illiterate. The references cited above are perhaps examples of later rabbinic writers pouring scorn on earlier high priests.

8. Discussions of the Sadducees can be found in J. Le Moyne, *Sadducéens*; G. Stemberger, *Jewish*; G. G. Porton, "Sadducees"; E. P. Sanders, *Judaism*, 317–40; and J. P. Meier, *Marginal*, 3.389–487.

   No ancient text specifically states that Caiaphas was a Sadducee, and not all aristocratic priests were Sadducees, as *Life* 197 clearly indicates. We do know, however, that Caiaphas's brother-in-law Ananus was a Sadducee (*Antiq* 20.199), and Acts 4:1 and 5:17 link both Caiaphas and his father-in-law Annas with the Sadducean party. It is, therefore, a reasonable supposition. There was some element of choice in which sect to join—Josephus, for example, claims to have decided to gain personal experience of all the various Jewish sects at about the age of sixteen (*Life* 9)—but most people would have naturally aligned themselves with whichever party their family adhered to.

9. See m.Yadaim 4.6, 7; m.Parah 3.7 (and tos.Parah 3.8); m.Niddah 4.2 (and tos.Niddah 5.2, 3); tos.Hagigah 3.35. Some disputes are over civil law—see m.Yadaim 3.7, Makkoth 1.6 and 'Erubin 6.1. Y.Baba Bathra 8.1, 16a records a dispute in which Sadducees uphold a daughter's inheritance rights. In later rabbinic texts, the Sadducees become stereotypical opponents of the sages, and it is difficult to know to what extent they reflect real first-century Sadducean teaching.

   Certain rabbinic passages suggest that Sadducean women followed Pharisaic regulations on matters of menstruation (m.Niddah 4.2, t.Niddah 5.2, b.Niddah 33b). This (along with Josephus's exaggerated claim that Sadducees had to submit to Pharisaic interpretations, otherwise the masses would not tolerate them, *Antiq* 18.17) is probably rabbinic/Pharisaic propaganda rather than a reflection of historical reality in the first century. See E. P. Sanders, *Judaism*, 10–12, 447; J. P. Meier, *Marginal*, 3:389–487; L. Grabbe, *Introduction*, 40; J. Neusner, *Politics*, chap. 4.

10. This is suggested by J. P. Meier, *Marginal*, 3:400–401.

11. G. Stemberger, *Jewish*, 95.

12. On the widespread use of Greek in Jerusalem, see L. Levine, *Judaism*, 76–80.

13. Josephus says that the knowledge of foreign languages was not highly valued by his people. It is possible, however, that this was an attempt to excuse his own marked accent! On the study of rhetoric in Jerusalem, see M. Hengel, *Pre-Christian*, 38 n. 276.

14. On the extension of Roman rule through the Near East, see F. G. B.Millar, *Roman*.

15. Josephus, *War* 1.407.

16. The disturbances after Herod's death are described in some detail in *War* 2.39–78

and *Antiq* 17.250–98. The description of events in Sepphoris is taken from Josephus; archaeological excavations, however, have presented no evidence of a violent conflagration in the city in 4 B.C.E. While Varus undoubtedly marched his troops through Galilee, it may be that Josephus's description of the total destruction of Sepphoris is exaggerated.

17. Josephus, *War* 2.70.

18. *Agricola* 30. These words are put into the mouth of the British chieftain Calgacus by Tacitus, whose broken relationship with the Roman Senate led him to make such observations.

19. For the census, see Josephus, *War* 2.118, *Antiq* 18.4. Josephus claims that an anti-Roman movement was formed at this time—a "philosophy" or "school," composed of people with a "passion for liberty that is almost unconquerable" (*Antiq* 18.9, 23). Although we have no evidence for a formal "Zealot party" prior to 66 C.E., Josephus's works make it clear that a strong anti-Roman feeling continued among at least some sections of the population. For the view that God is the author of history and acceptance of foreign rule, see, for example, Isa 41:2, 44:28, 45:1–4, 13; Jer 29:4–9, Prov 8:1–36; and Wis 6:1–11. Messianic hopes would have been inspired by texts such as Isa 11, Num 24, and the book of Daniel. The third group of responses outlined here are the sentiments of the Jerusalem-based pietist circles responsible for the *Psalms of Solomon* and the *Testament* (or *Assumption*) *of Moses*. On the *Psalms*, see R. B. Wright in J. H. Charlesworth, ed., *Pseudepigrapha* 2:639–70. The text of the *Testament of Moses* probably reached its final form shortly after Herod's death; see J. Priest in J. H. Charlesworth, ed., *Pseudepigrapha* 1.919–34.

   Josephus claims that a Jewish delegation asked for "autonomy" "under Caesar" at the time of Pompey (*Antiq* 14.29–60) and again after the death of Herod (*War* 2.80–92, *Antiq* 17.299–314). Whether these men lived to regret their request we do not know.

20. Although the temple is described in m.Middoth, the best description comes from Josephus, who was, of course, an eyewitness, *War* 5.184–227. Useful modern descriptions can be found in J. Patrich, "Structure"; E. P. Sanders, *Judaism*, 54–72; and R. Bauckham, "Josephus."

21. Acts 5:34, 22:3 for Gamaliel. Luke 2:46, Matt 2:23, 26:55, Mark 14:49, John 18:20 for Jesus.

22. This requirement is found in Exod 30:13–16. Half a shekel is equivalent to two drachmas—a couple of days' pay for a laborer. For the convoys see *Letter of Aristeas* 83; Josephus, *War* 3.52; Philo, *Embassy to Gaius* 37, 281, 311–16; and Cicero, *Pro Flacco* 26.67.

23. Philo, *Embassy to Gaius*, 154–58, 309–18.

24. Levites belonged to the tribe of Levi; priests also belonged to the tribe of Levi but had to be descended from Aaron.

25. Jews had offered sacrifices on behalf of the ruling power as far back as Persian and Hellenistic times (see Ezra 6:10, 1 Esd 7:31, 1 Macc 7:33, 2 Macc 3:32; Philo, *Embassy to Gaius* 232). Under Rome, occupied people were supposed to offer sacrifices *to* the emperor and Roman people, but since this would have offended Jewish monotheistic sensitivities, Jews were granted a special concession that allowed them to offer sacrifices *on behalf of* the emperor and the Roman people; see *War* 2.197, *Against Apion* 2.77.

26. *Aristeas* 95, the author's claim that everything was done in silence is probably an exaggeration; C. T. R. Hayward suggests that the author was acutely aware of the fact that the service was a replica of heaven on earth and so thought silence fitted the presence of God (*Jewish*, 11). This description of the temple service is based on E. P. Sanders, *Judaism*, 77–102.

27. Exod 25:9, 40; 26:30.
28. *Jub.* 30:14, 31:15, also 1 Kgs 22:19, Dan 7:11.
29. Elements within the temple were given cosmic interpretation: the seven branched candelabra, for example, was thought to represent heavenly bodies—the sun, moon, and five planets; while the twelve loaves of the bread of presence represented the zodiac (*War* 5.217–18). Worship was continual (the name for the twice-daily offering of lambs is *tamid*, which means continual or perpetual, and the lights of the temple were never extinguished). See the discussion in C. Meyers, "Temple," and M. Barker, *Gate*. For a number of texts from the second century B.C.E. to the first century C.E. that describe the temple and its ritual, see C. T. R. Hayward, *Jewish*.
30. *Aristeas* 99.
31. We do not know the precise age at which a man became a priest; J. Jeremias (following rabbinic tradition) suggests 20 (*Jerusalem*, 158). Ordination rituals are described in Exod 29 and Lev 8.
32. The priests' robes are described by Josephus in *Antiq* 3.152–58. Since Josephus was a priest himself, his description is likely to be accurate here.
33. J. Jeremias estimated that there were about 18,000 priests and Levites in Palestine at this time (*Jerusalem*, 198–206); E. P. Sanders puts it at 20,000 (*Judaism*, 78). See Josephus, *Against Apion* 2.108.
34. This practice is reflected in Luke when John the Baptist's father, Zechariah, of the division of Abijah, took his turn in the temple (Luke 1:1–9).

3. Public and Private Life

1. See J. S. McLaren, *Power*, 217–18.
2. The existence of this institution is doubted by a number of scholars. See, for example, M. Goodman, *Ruling*, 113–18; E. P. Sanders, *Judaism*, 472–90; D. Goodblatt, *Monarchic*; and L. I. Levine, *Judaism*, 90. The word *Sanhedrin* comes from the Greek *synedrion*, which means "sitting down with" and was regularly used in the Greco-Roman world to refer to an ad hoc advisory council summoned by a ruler. Josephus seems to understand things this way when he speaks of "a sanhedrin" in a loose and nontechnical sense. Such advisory councils were often convened by Roman or Hellenistic rulers in order to take counsel on pressing matters. It is now generally recognized that the picture of the Great Sanhedrin given in the Mishnah—of seventy-one scholars debating issues of Jewish law—is a later, idealized creation of the rabbinic schools. For the view that an institution known as the Sanhedrin *did* exist in the first century, see R. E. Brown, *Death* 1:339–57.

   Josephus refers to a council chamber in the covered public plaza near the temple known as the Xystos (*War* 5.144). This is often identified as the "Chamber of Hewn Stone" (*liskath-hagazith*) referred to in m.Sanhedrin 11.2. Perhaps larger assemblies were held here.
3. *Embassy to Gaius* 278. For similar sentiments, see Josephus, *Against Apion* 2.194, *War* 1.3, and *Life* 2–4.
4. Lists of high priests are preserved in Neh 12:10–11 and Josephus, *Antiq* 11.302, 347. On the high priest in Persian times, see D. W. Rooke, *Zadok's*.
5. The offices of king and high priest were divided twice. First was in the time of the Hasmonean Queen Salome Alexandra (76–67 B.C.E.). As a woman, she was not eligible for the high priesthood, and so her son Hyrcanus II occupied the post. In the final years of Hasmonean rule, the Romans again divided the two posts, allowing Aristobulus II to act as king (67–63 B.C.E.) and Hyrcanus II to act as high priest.

6. See Appendix C below for further discussion of this.

7. Josephus refers to Annas, Jonathan, and Ananias as "high priest" long after they had relinquished the position (*War* 2.243, 441; *Antiq* 18.34, 95, 20.205; *Life* 193). See also m.Horayoth 3.1–2, 4. Some Jews may well have refused to recognize the deposition of high priests and continued to call them by their honorific titles; see R. E. Brown, *Gospel*, 820. On Luke 3:2, Acts 4:6, and John 18:15, 16, 19, 22, which refer to Annas as high priest even though he had technically been deposed, see 111–12 and 135–38.

   This explanation of "chief priests" set out in this paragraph is the generally accepted one (see, for example, E. P. Sanders, *Judaism*, 327–32). For a slightly different view, see J. Jeremias, who suggests they were men who fulfilled specific roles in the temple, such as treasurers or temple administrators (*Jerusalem*, 175–81).

8. On the basis of a textual variant in the Greek text of *Antiq* 18.26, M. Stern suggests that Annas was the brother of Joshua b. See, who was appointed by Archelaus in *Antiq* 17.231 ("Aspects," 606). This, however, is purely conjectural.

9. See note 15 below.

10. On the Roman separation of "state" and "religion," see D. R. Schwartz, *Studies*, pp. 13–14, 29–43, 199–200.

11. D. W. Rooke, *Zadok's*; J. S. McLaren, *Power*, 202–3.

12. *Antiq* 20.251. He goes into more detail in *Against Apion*: "Could there be a finer or more equitable polity than one which sets God at the head of the Universe, which assigns the administration of its highest affairs to the whole body of priests, and entrusts to the supreme High Priest the direction of the other priests? ... Could God be more worthily honoured by such a scheme, under which religion is the end and aim of the training of the entire community, the priests are entrusted with the special charge of it, and the whole administration of the state resembles some sacred ceremony?" (2.185, 188, translated by H. St. John Thackeray, *Josephus LCL* I 367–68). The trustworthiness of Josephus's description here is questionable. His rosy picture of a harmonious nation united under the leadership of the priests is probably colored partly by his own priestly descent and partly by the fact that his readers would think there was something particularly honorable about an ancient priestly leadership. For this last point, see M. Hengel and R. Deines, "Sanders," 67.

13. See above, 62–63, n. 15.

14. For a discussion of the cultural values of the ancient Mediterranean world, see B. J. Malina, *New Testament World*, esp. 58–79. Malina notes that there was always a latent conflict between the powerful and the powerless, but in a competitive and agonistic culture, there was little chance of the powerless uniting against the powerful. The powerless simply did not see themselves as a "class" as we would understand the term today.

15. Prior to the governorship of Pontius Pilate, Josephus records no incidents whatsoever. Since this was a critical period, during which the people were adapting to Roman rule, the lack of any recorded rebellion suggests that the aristocrats managed to keep the peace with some success. (The incidents during Pilate's term of office will be discussed in the chapter on Caiaphas, Pilate, and John the Baptist.) Similar positive assessments can be found in E. P. Sanders, *Judaism*, 329–32; J. S. McLaren, *Power*; and P. W. Barnett, "Under Tiberius."

   A number of scholars take a less positive view than that outlined in these paragraphs:

   1. M. Goodman, for example, argues that the aristocracy had suffered so much in the political upheaval of the last few decades that they were no longer

capable of maintaining the respect and trust of the nation they were expected to lead (*Ruling*). Although there were clearly factions and unrest between high priestly houses in the years running up to the revolt (see 2 and 3 below), there seems to me to be little evidence for this in the quieter, early phase of Roman rule; see also P. A. Brunt, "Josephus."

2. Several scholars (including J. Jeremias, *Jerusalem*, 195–96; R. Bauckham, "Jesus," 79–80; and T. Rajak, *Josephus*, 22–23) cite a rhyme from the Talmud as evidence for widespread disaffection with the high priesthood in the time of Jesus:

> Woe unto me because of the house of Boethus;
> Woe unto me for their lances!
> Woe unto me because of the house of Hanin (Ananus),
> Woe unto me for their whisperings!
> Woe unto me because of the house of Kathros;
> Woe unto me because of their reed pens!
> Woe unto me because of the house of Ishmael b.Phiabi;
> Woe unto me because of their fist!
> For they are high priests and their sons are Treasurers
> And their sons-in-law are temple overseers
> And their servants smite the people with sticks.
> (b.Pesahim 57a, trans. J. Jeremias, *Jerusalem*, 195–96)

The problem here, however, is its *date*. The only period when reference to all four priestly families makes sense is in the later part of the first century, in the run-up to the revolt (high priests from the house of Kathros make an appearance in the 40s, while Ishmael b. Phiabi was high priest in 49–62). The passage, then, is a good illustration of the tensions within the high priesthood later in the century but tells us little about conditions prior to the reign of Agrippa I, when the high priesthood was dominated by the house of Annas. For a similar view, see E. P. Sanders, *Judaism*, 331.

3. It is also common to cite *Antiq* 20.204–10 as evidence for hatred between the high priestly aristocracy and ordinary people. According to this passage, the high priest Ananias sent his servants to steal the ordinary priests' tithes from the threshing floor; other high priests acted in like manner, and some priests died of starvation as a result. Again, the story is set during the turbulent years of the procurator Albinus, when the country was quickly descending into revolt (62–64 C.E.). The passage can hardly be taken as evidence of *ordinary* high priestly behavior.

Virtually the same story was recorded earlier in 20.179–81, where it was prefaced by a note that Agrippa gave the high priesthood to Ishmael b.Phiabi, an event that led to gang warfare. Presumably we are dealing with two versions of the same incident. Josephus describes the same events in *War* 2.272–76, but without the antipathy toward the high priests. Consequently, D. R. Schwartz concludes that Josephus in *Antiq* 20 used a source written by a Jerusalem priest who hated both Agrippa and the high priests appointed by him, "κατα." We can only guess how the high priests themselves might have justified their actions.

4. Scholars often note that as soon as the rebel forces gained control of Jerusalem at the outbreak of the war with Rome, they burned both the house of Ananias the high priest and the city archives where the money lenders' bonds were lodged (*War* 2.426–27). Ananias escaped but was soon killed by a revolutionary named Menelaus (2.441). This, it is claimed, proves that the high priests

and their oppressive regime were hated by ordinary Jews (see for example, C. A. Evans, "Jesus," 426). Yet this is a rather one-sided reading of events. We could equally well note that, prior to this incident, the high priest was able to persuade the people to demonstrate their goodwill to Rome by greeting the troops from Caesarea (he could not have known that the troops would slaughter the crowds [*War* 2.318–32]). Or that it was the son of the high priest, Eleazar (the captain of the temple), who, along with other priests and temple staff, stopped offering the daily sacrifice on behalf of the emperor (*War* 2.409–10, 417). And that Eleazar himself led the revolution for a time and was joined both by certain high priestly factions and by insurrectionists (*War* 2.422–56). The revolt was extremely complex, both in its underlying causes and the way it progressed. Society was highly fragmented, with factions springing up all around, some more extremist than others. We cannot make a simple distinction between "the people" and "the rulers." It is clear that in the opening stages of the revolt many belonging to high priestly houses continued to act as national leaders (see, for example, the glorious career of the former high priest Ananus, son of Annas, *War* 2.563–64, 4.319–20).

16. John 18:13 is the only evidence for this connection, but—despite his theological interest in linking the two men (see 135–38)—it is not improbable. Luke also assumes a close link between the two priests: Luke 3:2, Acts 4:6.

17. Such marriages are referred to as "endogamous." The Herodian family tree shows several endogamous marriages, particularly between cousins, or an uncle and his niece. See K. C. Hanson and D. E. Oakman, *Palestine*, 34.

18. *On Duties*, 1.57.

19. These regulations can be found in Lev 21:7–8, 13–15 and were taken with the utmost seriousness. Later in the first century, the marriage of a high priest to a widow named Martha caused a great outcry (see T. Rajak, *Josephus*, 24).

20. Philo, *Special Laws* 110.

21. On Jewish marriage in this period, see T. Ilan, *Jewish*, 57–96.

22. Josephus tells us that the high priest lived in the Upper City during the revolt (*War* 2.426); presumably this was also the case one generation earlier. R. E. Brown suggests that the high priest lived in the Hasmonean palace (*Gospel*, 2:823), but this was probably reserved for visiting Herods, since Herod the Great's former palace was now used by the Roman governor (see my *Pontius*, 8). Furthermore, there is no indication in Josephus that a particular house was reserved for the high priest. For traditions relating to the precise location of Caiaphas's palace, see Appendix D below.

23. Mark 14:68, Matt 26:71.

24. Exod 20:4, Deut 5:16, 27:15.

25. More generally see Y. Yadin, *Jerusalem*; J. J. Rousseau and R. Arav, "Jerusalem, Upper City" in *Jesus*, 169–73; N. Avigad, *Discovering*; M. Avi-Yonah, "Jerusalem"; and M. Broshi, "Excavations." Although substantial houses dating to the Herodian era have been found, perhaps unsurprisingly no obvious contender for Caiaphas's palace has been identified. See further on Caiaphas's palace in Appendix D below.

26. Annas and his clan are often charged with nepotism. At first sight, there is some substance to this charge. In the course of the first century, not only did Annas himself serve as high priest, but so too did five of his sons, his son-in-law (Caiaphas), and a grandson. It is quite likely that the old man used his influence to promote members of his family to prominent positions in the temple from which, when the time came, they might be promoted to the high priesthood. But Annas's actions need to be judged in their *first-century context* rather than against our own more democratic expectations. In a society that set great store

by protecting one's kin group and by a priesthood that had in earlier times been hereditary, it was natural that other members of the family should be groomed for the job. All men of influence sought to fill important posts with members of their family—that is simply how things worked in an aristocratic leadership. A father who did not look after the interests of his sons would have been failing in his duty. Nepotism in this sense would have been rife at all levels of Jewish society, not simply among the high priests.

We might consider the example of the early Christians here. After Jesus' death, the new movement was led not by Peter but by Jesus' brother James (a man who, according to the Gospels, appears to have played very little role in Jesus' ministry). What singled James out for leadership was not just his piety (though later sources attest to this), but his blood relationship with Jesus (Gal 1:19 and Acts 12:17, 15:13; 1 Cor 9:5 refers to other relatives of Jesus and their wives). James himself was succeeded by another relative, this time a cousin (Eusebius, *Hist. eccl.* 3.2.1). All this is in a movement that seems to have been distinctively antidynastic (Mark 3:31–35)! We should not employ dual standards here; what was acceptable for the Jesus movement was acceptable for the high priestly families.

27. When it was their time to serve in the temple, however, they would have abstained from wine; see Lev 10:8–11 and Josephus, *Against Apion* 1.199.

4. Caiaphas the High Priest

1. His predecessors were Coponius (6–9 C.E.), Marcus Ambivulus (9–12), and Annius Rufus (12–15)—all of whom were appointed by Augustus, *Antiq* 18.34–35.

2. The four high priests/groups of high priests referred to in this paragraph are as follows: 1. Soon after becoming king, Herod was forced into appointing Aristobulus, the last of the Hasmoneans, as high priest. But when, at the Feast of Tabernacles, the young man—who was tall and handsome—came out in his high priestly regalia and the people made too great a show of their affection towards him, Herod knew that he had to act quickly and promptly had him drowned (*Antiq* 15.50–56). 2. Removal was also the fate of Matthias, who was high priest towards the end of Herod's reign. When Herod rebuilt the temple, he placed a gilded eagle above the gates. This eagle—as both a symbol of Rome and a contravention of the law against graven images—was not surprisingly a continual source of irritation among the people. Eventually, as the king lay dying, two rabbis stirred up a number of young men to tear down the eagle. But there was still life in the old king, and when he heard of it he had the main culprits burnt alive. Matthias was removed from the high priesthood on the grounds that he was "partly to blame for what had happened." The precise nature of Matthias's involvement is not clear from Josephus, but Herod clearly held him personally responsible for the breach of the peace (*War* 1.648–55, *Antiq* 17.149–63). 3. When Herod died, the high priest had been Joazar of the house of Boethus. This Joazar seems to have been particularly disliked, and the people begged Archelaus to remove him. Archelaus agreed to their request but seems later to have reinstated him. As high priest once again Joazar persuaded the reluctant Judeans to accept the census but was "overpowered by a popular faction" for his pains (*Antiq* 18.26). 4. In *Antiq* 15.322 Herod removed Jesus son of Phiabi in favor of Simon son of Boethus; in *Antiq* 17.78, he removed Simon in favor of Theophilus.

3. See M. Beard, J. North, and S. Price, *Religions*, 1:221.

4. *Antiq* 18.34.

5. See R. Bultmann, *Gospel*, 410. John's reference to Caiaphas's holding the high

priesthood "that year" has suggested to some that, under Rome, the post was yearly and that the holder had to be reappointed annually (see, for example, M. Beard, J. North, and S. Price, *Religions*, 1.341). But John may mean nothing more than "that particular year"; see 132.

6. For examples of the captain of the temple and his police force in action, see Acts 5:24, 26, and 4:1. Y.Yoma 3.41a.5 suggests a high priest had first to serve as the captain of the temple.

7. P. Gaechter, citing 2 Macc 11:3, suggests that the post was leased for an annual fee ("Hatred," 6–7). K. C. Hanson and D. E. Oakman suggest that the high priest guaranteed a certain tax revenue each year (*Palestine*, 115–16). While it is likely that the supervision of tax collection was in the hands of Jewish aristocrats, there is no evidence that the high priest himself was directly involved or that his position was linked to tax revenues. On the collection of taxes in Roman Judea, see F. Herrenbrück, "Wer waren" and "Vorwurf."

8. D. R. Schwartz, "Appointment," in *Studies*. Schwartz notes that it is usually more profitable to take bribes from a competitor than an incumbent (see, for example, 2 Macc 4:7–10).

9. The suggestion that Jews petitioned Germanicus comes from D. R. Schwartz, "Appointment," in *Studies*. (Schwartz goes on to suggest that Gratus was also removed and that Pilate was appointed in 19 C.E., an argument I find less convincing; see my *Pontius*, 1, n.1.) The difficulty with a *formal* ruling is that Josephus does not seem to know anything about it—though it could be that since he has not mentioned the Jewish request for tax reduction, he had no opportunity to mention it.

10. *War* 5.230. He was expected to pay for the morning and evening daily meal offering, which was offered with the daily burnt offering, but he did not have to offer it himself.

11. See C. T. R. Hayward, *Jewish*, 45 for references.

12. Josephus constructs a theology of the high priest's robes in *Antiq* 3.172–84, as does Philo in *On the Life of Moses* 2.117–21.

13. Josephus describes the process in *Antiq* 15.403–8 and 18.91–94.

14. Lev 21:11 and Philo, *Special Laws* 113.

15. *Antiq* 17.165–66. According to tradition, on another occasion the high priest Simon son of Camith (17/18 C.E.) was prevented from officiating because he was touched by an Arab's spittle (b.Yoma 47a).

16. This is suggested by J. Jeremias (*Jerusalem*, 153), who also suggests that the high priest might have had an understudy.

17. For discussion, see D. W. Rooke, *Zadok's*, 24.

18. The high priest's vestments are described in Exod 28:1–43, 39:1–31; Lev 8:5–9; Sir 45:9–12; *Antiq* 3.172–78; and *Aristeas* 96–99.

19. Sir 50.

20. The high priest's breastplate was called an "oracle" and shone forth to predict future events (*Antiq* 3.214–18). The precious stones set on the breastplate were closely bound up with the Urim and Thummim (Exod 28:30, Lev 8:8), a famous priestly oracle that directly communicated God's decisions to Israel (Num 27:21; see C. T. R. Hayward, *Jewish*, 70). Although some traditions maintained that prophecy had expired by time of Malachi (Ps 74:9, Dan 3:38, 1 Macc 4:46, 14:41), Josephus ascribes the gift of prophecy to certain high priests (*War* 1.68–69; *Antiq* 11.327, 13.299–300; see also tos.Sotah 13.5–6). Josephus himself, though only a priest, also claimed prophetic powers (*War* 3.351, 399–408). See C. H. Dodd, "Prophecy," and R. Gray, *Prophetic*, 7–34.

21. Sir 50:14–21. Much of the above discussion is dependent on E. P. Sanders, *Judaism*, 141–43.

22. The rite is recorded in Num 19. It is unlikely that Caiaphas was directly involved with this, since the priests who burned the cow and sprinkled people were themselves unclean for a day and had to launder their clothes and bathe themselves.

23. Archelaus: *War* 2.10–13, *Antiq* 17.213–18. Cumanus: *War* 2.224–27, *Antiq* 20.105–12.

24. For example, 2 Macc 1:1–9, 1:10–2.18; 2 Chr 30:1–9, Esth 9:20–32. In Acts 28:21 Jews in Rome were surprised they had not been informed about Paul. The letter of Acts 15 is probably modeled on such missives. See M. F. Whitters, "Observations," and R. Bauckham, "James." On the calendar, see A. Jaubert, *Date*, 31–66.

25. On Nicodemus and the wealthy Gurion family to which he belonged, see R. Bauckham, "Nicodemus." On the close working relationship between chief priests and Pharisees, see U. C. von Wahlde, "Relationships."

26. *Special Laws*, 116; *On Dreams* 1.215.

27. See, for example, Jer 2:8, 6:13, 7:11, 14:18, 23:11, 32:21–22, 33–34; 34:19; Isa 1:11, 28:7, 29:9–20; Mic 3:9–12; 6:6–7.

28. For criticims of the Hasmonean priest-kings and their Jerusalem priesthood in the Dead Sea Scrolls, see 1QpHab 8.8–13, 11.4–15, 12.1–10; 4Q169 1.5; CD 6.12–17, 4Q175 22–30; 1QS 5.5–6, 8.5, 8–9, 9.6. See further, D. R. Schwartz, "Two Aspects"; J. M. Baumgarten, *Studies*, 101–42; and S. Talmon, "Aspects," 162–99.

29. See *The Psalms of Solomon* 2, 8, 17 (see further, R. B. Wright, in J. H. Charlesworth, *Pseudepigrapha*, 2.639–70; D. Rooke, *Zadok's*, 320–21); *Testament of Levi* 14.1–17.11 (see further, H. C. Kee in J. H. Charlesworth, *Pseudepigrapha*, 1:775–80, 788–95), *Testament of Moses* 5–8 (see further, J. Priest, in J. H. Charlesworth, *Pseudepigrapha*, 1:919–34; J. Tromp, *Assumption*; G. W. E. Nicklesburg, *Studies*).

30. E. P. Sanders, *Judaism*, 331. On attitudes towards the high priests generally, see his article "Grand 'Christian' Abstractions."

31. Theudas, *Antiq* 20.97–99; "deceivers and imposters" *War* 2.258–60, *Antiq* 20.169–72; the Egyptian, *War* 2.261–63, *Antiq* 20.169–72, Acts 21:38; and an unnamed figure under Festus, *Antiq* 20.188. On these desert prophets, see R. Gray, *Prophetic*, 112–44; and for the suggestion that their movements implicitly challenged the temple, D. R. Schwartz, *Studies*, 29–43. John the Baptist's movement may also fit here; see 55–56.

5. Caiaphas, Pilate, and John the Baptist

1. I owe this suggestion to M. Goodman, *Ruling*, 8. For the expulsion of Jews from Rome (apparently for proselytism), see my *Pontius*, 68 n. 61.

2. See, for example, R. A. Horsley, "High Priests," 35–37; J. D. Crossan, *Revolutionary*, 136–37.

3. Josephus recounts it first in *War* 2.169–71 and later in *Antiq* 18.55–59. Although the later account is much more heavily biased against Pilate, the basic outline of events is the same.

4. See, for example, R. A. Horsley, "High Priests," 36–37; E. M. Smallwood, "High Priests," 22; and, in general terms, M. Goodman, *Ruling*, 29–50. For the view that the movement had leaders, see J. S. McLaren, *Power*, 84, and A. Vicent Cernuda, "Conversión," 53. See also N. H. Taylor, "Popular," whose work on the Caligula crisis shows how such movements tended to operate.

5. Josephus gives a detailed account of a passive Jewish protest following Gaius Caligula's threat to erect a statue of himself as Zeus in the Jerusalem temple (*War* 2.184–203); conversely, the tragic culmination of the Jewish revolt—the

burning of the temple—illustrates what happens when Jews resort to arms rather than trusting in God. It is highly likely that Josephus's description of events at Caesarea has been colored by these aims. For further discussion of all three incidents referred to here, see my *Pontius*, 79–85 (for standards), 85–89 (for the aqueduct), and 36–46 (for the shields).

6.   *War* 2.175–77, *Antiq* 18.60–62.
7.   M.Shekalim 4.2. The date of this ruling is uncertain, but it is possible that it, or a similar ruling, was in force in the first century.
8.   *Embassy to Gaius* 276–329.
9.   Many of the ideas in the following paragraphs are taken from R. L. Webb's useful survey article, "John the Baptist." See also D. C. Allison, "Continuity."
10.   Antipas had ruled over Galilee and Perea since the old king's death in 4 B.C.E. Although he owed his position to Roman goodwill, his territory was not under direct Roman rule. There were no Roman troops and no Roman prefects, and his subjects did not pay tribute to Rome.

6. Caiaphas and Jesus

1.   Jesus' eschatology is one of the most disputed elements of his teaching. Those who think Jesus expected a coming apocalyptic kingdom and that God would decisively break into Israel's history very soon include E. P. Sanders, P. Fredriksen, D. C. Allison, J. P. Meier, G. Vermes, and N. T. Wright. Those who argue for a non-eschatological Jesus preaching a "here-and-now" kingdom include J. D. Crossan and M. Borg.
2.   Jesus' lament over Jerusalem in Luke 13:34 may well hint at an earlier visit. For a thorough discussion, see J. P. Meier, *Marginal*, 1:372–433.
3.   The precise year of Jesus' death is still disputed. It probably occurred some time between 29 and 33 C.E., with 30 being the year favored by most scholars. For a full discussion, see E. P. Sanders, *Historical*, Appendix 1, 282–90.
4.   John 11:1, 12:1 (Mark 14:3).
5.   For further details and bibliography, see my *Pontius*, 95–96, and R. E. Brown, *Death*, 36–57.
6.   Crossan has expressed his views in a number of publications—*Historical Jesus* (and, in more popular form, *Revolutionary Biography*) and *Birth of Christianity*; his views on the passion stories are outlined in *The Cross that Spoke* and *Who Killed Jesus?*
7.   In support of this, Crossan claims that the earliest Christian works of which we know (the document used by both Matthew and Luke, referred to as Q, and the *Gospel of Thomas*) appear to have no passion narrative. Q is thought by several modern scholars to have come from mid-first-century Galilee; see the survey by J. S. Kloppenborg, "Sayings." Yet, even so, appeal to Q is dubious: it is a hypothetical document (no copy of Q has ever been found), and we cannot know that the people who read Q did not also have a document containing a passion narrative. Crossan maintains (against the majority of scholarly opinion) that the *Gospel of Thomas* had an early stage in the 50s/60s C.E. Yet, even if it did have an early origin, *Thomas* is a collection of sayings. There are no deeds, so why should we expect an account of Jesus' death?
8.   Crossan calls this process "prophecy historicized" and likes to contrast it with "history remembered," which is how he categorizes the traditional view. This distinction is catchy but rather misleading. As we have seen, the consensus view accepts that there are elements within the passion narrative that can be termed "prophecy historicized." For a useful critique of Crossan's contrast between prophecy historicized and history remembered, see M. Goodacre, "Prophecy."

The process Crossan describes may well have been true for the birth narratives, in which the accounts in Matthew and Luke have little in common with each other and clearly reflect the interests of each evangelist, but it is unlikely to be true for the events of the passion narrative, set in a crowded city in which a number of people were passionately interested in Jesus' fate.

If, for Crossan, Jesus' disciples knew virtually nothing of their master's last hours and the Gospel narratives are "prophecy historicized," what does he think about Caiaphas's involvement in Jesus' death? Crossan doubts that there would have been even an interrogation in front of the high priest:

> I do not presume at all any high-level consultations between Caiaphas or Pilate about or with Jesus. They would no doubt have agreed before such a festival that fast and immediate action was to be taken against any disturbances and that some examples of crucifixion might be especially useful at the start. I doubt very much if Jewish police and Roman soldiery needed to go too far up the chain of command in handling a Galilean peasant like Jesus. (*Revolutionary*, 152).

Crossan will accept that Jesus "was executed by some conjunction of Jewish and Roman authority" (*Who Killed?* 147) but no more. While Crossan is undoubtedly correct that there was no *necessity* for a Galilean peasant like Jesus to be tried prior to crucifixion, the unanimous testimony of the Gospels lends some weight to their general sequence of events.

9. For general critiques of Crossan's work, see B. Witherington, *Jesus*, 58–92; L. E. Keck, "Second"; M. A. Powell, *Jesus*, 93–110; L. T. Johnson, *Real*, 44–50; and R. E. Brown, "Peter." Crossan's views are supported by B. L. Mack, *Myth*, 249–312.

10. We shall look at this in more detail in the chapters in part 2.

11. Translation by L. H. Feldman, *Josephus LCL* IX 49, 51.

12. No manuscript of the *Antiquities* earlier than the eleventh century now survives, and all copies contain this paragraph. Useful discussions can be found in P. Winter, "Josephus"; G. Vermes, "Jesus"; J. P. Meier, "Jesus"; J. Carleton Paget, "Observations"; R. E. Van Voorst, *Jesus*, 81–104; and A. M. Dubarle, "Témoignage"—all of whom favor a neutral, reasonably sympathetic reconstruction such as that outlined below.

   Writing about 280 C.E., Origen could state quite categorically that Josephus did not believe Jesus to be the Christ (*Against Celsum* 1.47 and *Commentary on Matthew* 13.55)—something that would have been impossible had he had our present text in front of him. Eusebius, however, writing about 324 C.E., knew the passage in its present form. It looks, then, as if the text was altered by Christian copyists some time between 280 and 324 C.E. See L. H. Feldman, *Josephus LCL* IX 48–49 nn. a and b.

13. After discussing a tenth-century citation of the *Testimonium* by Agapius of Hierapolis in which there is no reference whatsoever to Jewish involvement in the death of Jesus, S. Pines suggests that there was no reference to "leading men" in Josephus's original text (*Arabic*). In reply, E. Bammel noted that (1) Agapius customarily abbreviates his sources, (2) he may have been influenced by the creed, which similarly omits any reference to Jewish involvement, and, most importantly, (3) the peculiarities of Agapius's text as a whole can be accounted for by the fact that it originated in the context of debate with his Islamic neighbors ("New Variant"). Pines's work was, however, taken up and developed (in the light of other tenth- to twelfth-century texts) by A. M.

Dubarle, who suggested that originally there was a reference to Jewish leaders not believing in Jesus, which was later changed to a Jewish accusation by a Christian editor who wanted to bring the *Testimonium* into line with the Gospels ("Témoignage," esp. 501, 506). The difficulty with this view is that the *Testimonium* refers to the Jewish leaders in quite a measured way—if it were a later addition, perhaps from the third century, we would expect it to reflect the much more negative picture of Jews in Christian texts from that time (such as the *Gospel of Peter*—for discussion of which, see R. E. Brown, "Peter," and C. Setzer, *Jewish*, 116–25).

14. For example, 17.81, 18.98, and 18.7 (specifically Jewish notables).

15. Haim Cohn, *The Trial and Death of Jesus* (which appeared in Hebrew in 1968 and English in 1971). For Cohn, Jesus was a law-observant Jew. The Jewish leaders heard that Jesus was to be arrested by Rome on Passover Eve, and, in an attempt to save him, the high priest sent officers of the temple police to the arrest and took Jesus into Jewish custody for the night. Jesus was taken to the high priest's mansion, where leaders of the Jews met, not for a trial, but "to prevent the crucifixion of a Jew by the Romans, and, more particularly, of a Jew who enjoyed the love and affection of the people" (114). Caiaphas hoped that in this way his standing and prestige would be enhanced among the people. But Jesus refused the Jewish leaders' offer of help, and preferred to go to his fate in a Roman court. The leaders met again the following morning, and tried to find another strategy to persuade Jesus to cooperate, but saw they could do nothing more and had to deliver Jesus up to Rome. Jesus pleaded guilty to Pilate and was sentenced to death. Later, the Gospels put a different slant on things, pinning guilt for Jesus' death not on Rome but on the Jewish leaders.

Josephus's testimony argues strongly against such a view, and is a difficulty for Cohn. He has to assume that Josephus deliberately wanted to assign credit for the crucifixion of Jesus to Jews and Romans in equal shares, because it was expedient to do so. Josephus, he suggests, wanted to show his Roman readers that Jews and Romans had worked together to eradicate this particular troublemaker (308–12). But if Josephus had such an apologetic aim, we would expect him to make more of it. He shows very little interest in Christianity, and if the above reconstruction of the *Testimonium* is anywhere near accurate, he was neutral if not even mildly sympathetic towards its founder. Cohn's work built on the similar, though much less extreme, reconstruction of another Jewish scholar, P. Winter, *On the Trial* (Winter does accept that the Jewish leaders handed Jesus over to Rome, though he tends to downplay the significance of this; for a fuller discussion of Winter's views, see 187 n. 7 below).

16. This is a modification of her views in her earlier work, *From Jesus to Christ*, where she suggested that it was the incident in the temple that led to Jesus' death (107–25) (I have taken this general view in the following chapter). In other respects, I find Fredriksen's arguments in *Jesus* compelling.

17. John, less plausibly, suggests that it was the raising of Lazarus (11:45–46); see 131.

7. Execution of a Galilean Holy Man

1. The accounts in Matthew (21:12–13) and Luke (19:45–46) are similar, though both occur directly after Jesus' triumphal entry, omit Jesus' reference to "all the nations," and fail to link the event explicitly with the resolve of the Jewish leaders to do away with Jesus. Luke's account is highly abbreviated, presumably because this evangelist has a particularly positive view of the temple and Jesus' relationship to it (as we shall see below, 113). John's account, however, has a num-

ber of differences. First, although he agrees that the incident occurred at Passover, John sets it much earlier in his Gospel, soon after the commencement of Jesus' ministry (2:13–17). Second, John's Jesus not only sets himself against the money changers and dove sellers but also drives out the sellers of sheep and oxen (along with their animals) with a whip made from cord (though it is highly question-able whether cows and sheep would have been sold in the temple court!). Third, Jesus' words are different: "Take these things out of here! Stop making my Father's house a marketplace!" at which Jesus' disciples remember Psalm 69:9: "Zeal for your house will consume me."

2. This point is made by P. Fredriksen, *Jesus*, 232.

3. Brandon suggests that Jesus preached a political kingdom in which the existing political and social order would be overthrown and God's sovereignty estab-lished. His action in the temple was a "messianic *coup d'etat*, aimed primarily at the sacerdotal aristocracy, whose policy and opposition were deemed obstacles to the conversion of Israel and the establishment of God's kingdom" (*Trial*, 146). The evangelists, Brandon believes, toned down the political side of the incident. See his *Jesus and the Zealots*, followed by *Trial of Jesus*, which makes many of the same points. (See also H. Maccoby, *Revolution*, 135, 139–40, who makes many similar points.) Critiques of Brandon's views are offered in several of the essays contained in E. Bammel and C. F. D. Moule (eds.), *Jesus*. See also D. R. Schwartz (*Studies*, 128–46), who notes that "Jesus as Revolutionary" has tended to give way to "Jesus as socio-economic reformer" in much recent literature.

4. Whatever the historicity of individual components in this tradition, it is signif-icant that Jesus is never shown as criticizing the temple (except for the sayings that will be considered in [3] below). For similar estimates of Jesus' view of the temple, see J. P. Meier, *Marginal*, 3.500; G. Vermes, *Religion*, 13; P. Fredriksen, *Jesus*, 197–214; N. T. Wright, *Jesus*, 432–37; and E. P. Sanders, *Historical*, 129. It is sometimes suggested that Jesus' Galilean background may well have made him less reverential toward the temple than his Judean neighbors. See, for exam-ple, R. A. Horsley, *Galilee*, who suggests that there were a large number of Israelites living in Galilee (people from the old northern kingdom of Israel), who had little time for the Jerusalem leadership and the temple, and who kept their own northern traditions alive. For opposing views, see S. Freyne, "Galilee-Jerusalem"; J. L. Reed, *Archaeology*; and P. Fredriksen, *Jesus*, 178–84. Given the distance from Galilee to Jerusalem, it would have been quite possible for certain Galileans to privilege the Torah over the temple, but the evidence for such a view is inconclusive (a fact admitted by Horsley, 147).

5. See 182 n. 24 below.

6. See above, 30.

7. Drawing on two talmudic traditions, V. Eppstein argued that Caiaphas himself introduced traders into the temple ("Historicity"). The first is the well-known assertion that "Forty years before the destruction of the Temple the Sanhedrin departed from/was expelled from the Chamber of Hewn Stone in the Temple to a place on the Mount of Olives called Hanuth" (b. Rosh Hashanah 31a, b.Shabbath 15a, b.Abodah Zarah 8b). The second is a less well-known tradition that the sons of Hanan sold doves and other ritually pure objects for temple sacrifice on the Mount of Olives (y.Taanith 4.8). From these two texts Eppstein concluded that the Sanhedrin was expelled from the temple by Caiaphas in 30 C.E. and was subsequently made welcome on the Mount of Olives by the sons of Hanan. In retaliation against the sons of Hanan, the "vindictive" Caiaphas allowed rival dove sellers to set up their stalls in the temple. (This, Eppstein believed, was what angered Jesus so much when he visited the temple that same Passover.)

There are at least three major problems with Eppstein's theory: (1) There are difficulties with the historicity of the tradition concerning the expulsion of the Sanhedrin and, even if it does contain historical truth, "forty years" is probably a round number (C. K. Barrett suggests that the tradition "lacks historical reliability" [*Acts*, 224]). (2) Even granting the historicity of the tradition, no rabbinic texts make a connection between the expulsion of the Sanhedrin and the inauguration of the selling of sacrificial animals within the temple precincts. (3) Zech 14:21 already mentions traders in the temple, so the practice cannot have started in 30 C.E. Even Eppstein accepted that his proposal was only a "tentative hypothesis" (57). Both C. A. Evans ("Jesus") and B. Chilton (*Galilean*, 17–18, and "Caiaphas," 805–6) distance themselves to some extent from Eppstein's arguments, but both similarly regard Jesus' actions as a "cleansing." One of the difficulties with this view is that there is no indication elsewhere in the Gospel record that Jesus was interested in reforming the temple; surely if he were so against commercial activity, he would have had more to say on the matter. R. Bauckham suggests that Jesus' demonstration was an expression of his disapproval of the temple tax, which he regarded as an improper burden on the poor ("Jesus"). Although this fits well with Jesus' general agenda, there is again no indication elsewhere that he was particularly concerned with the temple tax.

8. It is often claimed that the powerful clan of Annas exercised a monopoly over the sale of sacrificial animals in the temple, that they deliberately inflated prices, and that they creamed off the profits to swell their own coffers (see, for example, C. A. Evans, "Jesus"; B. Chilton, "Caiaphas"; and R. Bauckham, "Jesus"). There is, however, no evidence to support this. One commonly cited reference is the complaint of Simeon b. Gamaliel (who was active in Jerusalem before the revolt) that a pair of pigeons cost one gold dinar—twenty-five times the usual price (m.Kerithoth 1.7). This is often taken as evidence that the temple priests deliberately inflated prices in order to increase their profits from sacrifices. There is, however, no indication in the passage that the chief priests were responsible for the exorbitant price (as H. Cohn notes, it was in the interests of the priests to keep the prices down so that more sacrifices could be offered and the priestly share was maintained [*Trial*, 57]). There is no first-century evidence to corroborate this story (Josephus does not mention it), and, perhaps strangest of all, the account suggests that a Pharisee could determine who offered what sacrifice. All in all, it would be unwise to build too much on this story alone.

9. See, for example, Jer 13:1–11 (where a linen waistcoat is ruined on the rocks of the Euphrates); Jer 19 (where the prophet breaks an earthen flask); Jer 27 (where the prophet puts a yoke about his neck); Hos 1:2–9 (where the prophet marries a prostitute, who bears him three children), and Isa 20:1–6 (where the prophet walks naked and barefoot for three years). All of these signs symbolized God's judgment on the people.

10. On the attitude of these prophets towards the temple and its cult, see B. A. Levine, "Prophetic."

11. They could appeal here to texts such as Pss 46 and 48:8.

12. See, for example, Jer 7:12–15. If the saying recorded in Mark 11:17 is historical, Jesus himself seems to have made a connection between his actions and those of Isaiah/Jeremiah (if not, the connection was an obvious one for the early church to make).

Scholars are often tempted to pick out one specific injustice in Jesus' critique. J. D. Crossan, for example, suggests that Jesus exploded in indignation at the nonegalitarian, patronal, and oppressive nature of the temple and that his action was a "symbolic negation of all the temple (stood) for" (*Who Killed?* 64–65). M. Borg, on the other hand, sees it as an attack on the "politics of holiness" that was overrunning Jewish society (*Jesus*, 175) (Borg incorrectly thinks that the temple tax was paid in "holy" coins with no images, whereas, in fact, the Tyrian shekel contained images of both the pagan god Melkart and an eagle). And N. T. Wright suggests that Jesus prophesied the destruction of the temple because of Israel's large-scale commitment to national rebellion (though he does add to this a critique of the lack of justice in society, not least within the temple system itself) (*Jesus*, 405–28). Yet we should be wary of specifying any one particular injustice here; the signs performed by the Old Testament prophets usually covered a wide variety of social ills, see above, n. 9. Furthermore, there is no justification for assuming that Jesus' critique was directed specifically towards Israel's *leaders*; neither Mark's account nor the parallels in Jeremiah single them out for sole criticism. For an interpretation similar to that advanced here, see J. P. M. Swete, "House."

13. This, of course, is presented as a false charge, though perhaps we are to see an element of truth in it. See 106.

14. For this suggestion, see E. P. Sanders, *Jesus*, 77–90. These apocalyptic hopes expected God (or God's Messiah) to rebuild the temple sanctuary: Tob 13:10, 14:5, *1 Enoch* 90:28–29, 91:13; *Eth Sib Or* 3.657–60, 702, 772–74; 11Q Temple cols 30–45. All these texts, however, imagine a *real* temple; I think it more likely that Jesus imagined a metaphorical temple; see 68–69.

15. See the variety of responses to Jeremiah, particularly in Jer 26.

16. *War* 6.300–309. For a fuller discussion of this man, see R. Gray, *Prophetic*, 158–63.

17. For this view, see N. T. Wright, *Jesus*, 426; R. Bauckham, "James"; C. F. D. Moule, "Sanctuary," 38; M. Borg, *Jesus*, 140–41; C. S. Keener, *Matthew*, 515; and E. Schüssler Fiorenza, *Memory*, 192–98. Other (later) NT passages include Eph 2:20–22; Heb 9:11, 24, 13:15–16; 1 Pet 2:5, 4:17; Rev 3:12, 11:1–2. John 2:22 also reflects this understanding. On all these passages, see R. J. McKelvey, *Temple*.

18. On Jewish movements in the first century, see R. A. Horsley, "Popular Messianic" and "Popular Prophetic."

19. J. P. Meier, *Marginal*, 3.407.

20. N. T. Wright notes that the charge of leading Israel astray was cited by Justin Martyr (*Dialogue* 69.7), b.Sanh 43a, 107b, and is also perhaps implicit in *Antiq* 18.63–64. For further discussion of the charges against Jesus, see *Jesus*, 439–42. Caiaphas may well have regarded Jesus in the same way that Josephus looked at the messianic agitators who proliferated in the time of the governor Felix. Contrasting them with a group of assassins known as the sicarii, Josephus comments that they had "cleaner hands, but *more impious intentions*, who no less than the assassins ruined the peace of the city. Deceivers and imposters, under the pretence of divine inspiration fostering revolutionary changes, they persuaded the multitude to act like madmen and led them out into the desert under the belief that God would there give them tokens of deliverance" (*War* 2.258–60).

21. For some of the main arguments on each side of the debate and bibliography, see my *Pontius*, 15–16, and R. E. Brown, *Death*, 1:363–72.

22. R. E. Brown takes a similar view (*Death*, 1:372) (see also his historical reconstruction, 557–59). Brown notes too that crucifixion would have placed Jesus under the curse of Deut 21:23 and would thus have discredited him among other Jews.

23. John suggests Pharisees were involved in this meeting (11:46, 47). There is, however, no indication in the Synoptics that Pharisees were involved in Jesus' death. Although Jesus interacted with them during his ministry, "the earliest strata of the Gospel traditions supply no basis for thinking that Jesus' clashes with the

Pharisees were the major reason why he was put to death" (J. P. Meier, *Marginal*, 3:339). The expansion of the role of the Pharisees in the Gospels of Matthew and John is due to their particular historical contexts. See also E. P. Sanders, *Historical*, 265, and D. Flusser, "Caiaphas," who goes so far as to claim that Pharisees saw the handing over of a Jew to a foreign authority as a sin that could not be forgiven!

24. It is possible that Roman troops also participated in the arrest (as John 18:3, 12 implies). Pilate's cooperation had been presumably assured before the arrest. See, further, my *Pontius*, 197.

25. Those who follow John's dating and think that Jesus died on Passover Eve include R. E. Brown, *Death*, 1351–73; J. P. Meier, *Marginal*, 1:395–401; G. Theissen and A. Merz, *Historical*, 37; and J. D. Crossan, *Who Killed?* 100. Alternatively, those who follow the Synoptic dating and think that Jesus died on the day of Passover include J. Jeremias, *Eucharistic*, 20–33, and C. S. Keener, *Matthew*, 622–33.

26. For Mark, see B. Chilton, "James," 150–54; for John, see D. Moody Smith, *Theology*, 117.

27. For example, the third-century *Didascalia* 21 and Epiphanius's *De fide* 22. For fuller discussion of the chronology of Jesus' arrest and death, see A. Jaubert, *Date*. Jaubert suggests the early Christians used a different calendar from that of the official lunar one and that in their calendar Passover began at sundown on the Tuesday.

28. For example, Justin Martyr, *Dialogue* 16; Origen, *Against Celsus* 1.47, 4.73, *Commentary on the Gospel of Matthew* 10.17; Eusebius, *Hist. eccl.* 2.23.20.

29. For references, see D. R. Schwartz, *Studies*, 245 n.6.

30. F. G. B. Millar suggests that "both as regards the narrative of Jesus' life and the culminating story of how he met his death, we should give our preference to John" ("Reflections," 376). See also P. Fredriksen, *Jesus*, 221–25; G. Theissen and A. Merz, *Historical*, 36; R. E. Brown, *Death*, 1:363, 425–26, 557; and E. P. Sanders, *Historical*, 72.

31. On the confused question of the identity of the high priest in Luke 3:2 and Acts 4 and 5, see 111–12. There are a number of theological themes at work in John 18:19–23 (see 135–38); yet, even so, the prominence given to Annas may rest on historical tradition.

32. For further details on the trial in front of Pilate, see my *Pontius*, 198–202.

8. Caiaphas and the Earliest Christians

1. See, for example, P. Gaechter, "Hatred," esp. 14–34; J. D. Crossan, *Birth*, 508–11; G. Theissen, *Gospels in Context*, 173; and, to a lesser extent, R. E. Brown, *Death*, 1:409.

2. The treacherous Judas was quickly replaced by Matthias (Acts 1:15–26).

3. On the centrality of the Jerusalem community for early Christianity, see Paul's references to the city in Gal 1:18–19, 2:1–3, 2:11; 1 Cor 16:1–4, 2 Cor 8–9; and Rom 16:25–6. For Jerusalem in Jewish thought, see *Jub.* 8.19, *1 Enoch* 26.1, Rev 20:8–9. References to the gathering of Jews in the eschatological age can be found in Isa 11:12, 43:5–6 and to Gentiles in Isa 2:2–3; Zech 8:20–23, Tobit 13:11–13. For fuller discussions see R. Bauckham, "James," and R. L. Brawley, *Luke–Acts*, 124–30.

4. On Luke's theology, see J. Jervell, *Theology*, and J. C. O'Neill, *Theology*. On the historical value of Acts, see M. Dibelius, *Studies*, 102–8; G. Lüdemann, *Early*, 1–23; and M. Hengel, *Acts*, *Between*, and *Property*. On Luke's sources, see J. Dupont, *Sources*, and C. J. Hemer, *Book*, 308–68.

5. Pharisees appear more favorable to Christianity than Sadducees in the early chapters of Acts (see, for example, 4:1 and 5:17), but even they will gradually join the opposition. For a fuller discussion of Luke's treatment of Jewish people and their leaders, see 109–11, 116–18.

6. See, for example, Acts 4:8. For a fuller discussion of this theme, see R. J. Cassidy, *Society*, 45–46.

7. Passages such as Luke 9:24–26, 9:43 and 12:8–12 seem to reflect some kind of persecution. For discussion, see E. Haenchen, *Acts*, 289–90; J. B. Green, *Theology*, 108–9; and J. T. Sanders, *Jews*, 306–13.

8. In Acts 4:2–3 the disciples are arrested because they are *preaching* the resurrection, while later they seem to be on trial for *healing* the lame man (4:7–9). It is also odd that the authorities know that the disciples are associated with Jesus in vv. 2 and 10, yet it seems to come as a surprise to them in v. 13!

9. H. Conzelmann, *Acts*, 41. The angelic rescue, of course, is new, but even this is a pale shadow of the rescues in 12:7–12 and 16:23–34. The fact that the rest of the scene does not refer to it again suggests that Luke has added the rescue himself; see G. Lüdemann, *Early*, 69.

10. Gamaliel is made to refer to the uprising of Theudas, an event which occurred over a decade later than the events of Acts 5 (Theudas was active during the time of the procurator Fadus, who came to the province in 44 C.E. [*Antiq* 20.97–98]). It is difficult not to conclude with C. K. Barrett that the "paragraph as a whole may be regarded as a piece of Luke's own composition . . . designed to conclude . . . the first section of his book" and that Gamaliel's speech is Luke's own composition (*Acts*, 1:281–82). See also G. Lüdemann, *Early*, 72–73, and H. Conzelmann, *Acts*, 31–33, 41–43.

11. For a fuller discussion of this text, see 111–12.

12. The majority of manuscripts read "John" here. I follow a textual variant in the fifth/sixth-century Western Text (Codex Bezae) which refers to this man as Jonathan. Since Luke clearly notes that all these men are part of the family of Annas, and since Jonathan would have been quite influential by this time, I think it more likely that the original text read Jonathan (or that, even if the original did call him John, it is Annas' son Jonathan who is meant). See also J. Jeremias, *Jerusalem*, 197, and P. Gaechter, "Hatred," 10–11, 14. D. Barag and D. Flusser see this as a reference to John son of Theophilus ("Ossuary," 39–44).

13. So also J. S. McLaren, *Power*, 103–9. G. Lüdemann does not find any historical traditions lying behind Acts 3:1–4.31 but suggests that Luke's "general knowledge" is of historical value: "his depiction of the conflict between the earliest community and the priestly nobility rests on correct historical assumptions" (*Early*, 60).

14. The word here is *zēlos*, which can have the more positive sense of "zeal" or "ardor." Given Luke's hostility towards the priestly rulers, however, it is unlikely that he has this more favorable sense in mind. On envy, see further, 104.

15. On historical traditions behind Acts 1–2, see G. Lüdemann, *Early*, 19–49.

16. See J. S. McLaren, *Power*, 109.

17. The chronology for this early period is difficult to reconstruct, as Luke's narrative provides us with no firm dates. A number of scholars put Stephen's death shortly after Pilate's removal in 37 C.E. or early in the reign of Agrippa I; it is only in such exceptional circumstances, it is argued, that Stephen could be tried by a high priest and stoned to death without any recourse to the Roman governor. See, for example, P. Gaechter ("Hatred," 19), who suggests that Stephen was stoned between Tabernacles 36 and Passover 37 and that the high priest was now Jonathan; J. D. Crossan (*Birth*, 508), who suggests late 30s and that the high priest was either Jonathan or his successor, Theophilus; and D. R. Schwartz

(*Agrippa I*, 71–73), who suggests some time between 39 and 41 and that the high priest was Simon Cantheras. These reconstructions, however, are too literal in their reading of Acts and do not take enough notice of Luke's desire to emphasize official Jewish responsibility. We shall see later in this discussion that both the presentation of the high priest and the semiformal stoning of Stephen are Lukan additions. When this is appreciated, there is no reason why Stephen's death should not have happened within a few years of Jesus' own death when Caiaphas was still high priest. M. Hengel suggests 32–34 C.E. (*Between*, 11), and J. S. McLaren suggests mid or late 30s (*Power*, 110).

18. Luke's construction here is rather awkward. While 6:9 could refer to *five* separate synagogues, it is more probably only one, as is suggested by C. K. Barrett, *Acts*, 1:323; F. F. Bruce, *Acts*, 187; B. Witherington, *Acts*, 253; and R. Riesner, "Synagogues," 204–5. It is possible that we even have inscriptional information relating to this synagogue: a famous inscription found in Jerusalem in 1913/14 refers to a synagogue founded by Theodotus son of Vettenus and refers to its members as "those who came from abroad." For discussion of the archaeological evidence and date of this inscription, see R. Riesner, "Synagogues."

19. Luke does not specifically say that Stephen was a member of this synagogue, but the narrative seems to imply it (see R. Riesner, "Synagogues," 206). In Acts 6:1–6 Luke reports the election of seven Hellenist (or Greek-speaking) deacons. Though he suggests that their purpose was to help in the distribution of food, it is clear from the rest of his narrative that their purpose was rather to act as missionaries and preachers to Greek speakers while the twelve went to Aramaic speakers.

20. For stoning as a Jewish punishment, see Lev 24, Num 15:35, and m.Sanhedrin 6.1. On the complicated issue of whether Jewish courts could execute at this period, see note 21 on 179 above. (If Stephen's death was not a judicial execution, however, but a mob lynching—as I shall argue below—then the legal niceties of Roman rule are irrelevant.)

21. On the parallels, see B. Witherington, *Acts*, 252–53.

22. On Luke's theology here, see J. D. G. Dunn, *Acts*, 88; E. Haenchen, *Acts*, 298; and J. C. O'Neill, *Theology*, 81. It is clear from 21:20 that Luke still holds out some hope for a Jerusalem mission, but the city as a whole has lost its chance. On the trial of Jesus in Mark, see 98–108.

23. This view is held by M. Hengel, *Pre-Christian*, 20; H. Conzelmann, *Acts*, 61; C. K. Barrett, *Acts*, 1:380–82; G. Lüdemann, *Early*, 92; and C. C. Hill, *Hellenists*, 28–31.

24. Luke's Gospel begins and ends in the temple (Luke 2:21–39, 41–51, 24:53), and the early chapters of Acts show the early Christians worshiping there (Acts 2:46, 5:42). Luke stresses that Paul was always obedient to the law: 21:17–26, 25:8, 28:17. As C. K. Barrett notes: "It is part of Luke's overall scheme to portray the first Christians as devout and observant Jews, maintaining Jewish practices and frequenting synagogue and temple till forced out of them" (*Acts*, 1:177). (There may, however, be some truth in Luke's account—the saying preserved in Matthew 5:23–24 presupposes that at least some early Christians continued to offer sacrifices in the temple.) For further discussion of Luke's attitude towards the temple and an analysis of Stephen's speech, see the chapter on Caiaphas in Luke–Acts below.

25. A. Loisy, cited by J. C. O'Neill, *Theology*, 75. The truth of this is borne out by Stephen's vision of the Son of Man at the right hand of God (7:56), a validation of Christian claims (see E. Haenchen, *Acts*, 295). For further discussion of this passage, see J. C. O'Neill, *Theology*, 74–75.

26. Despite Luke's claim that the charges were false, many scholars think that

Stephen *was* speaking against the temple and the law. See, for example, M. Hengel, *Between*, 22–24; H. Conzelmann, *Acts*, 47–58; and G. Lüdemann, *Early*, 85, 93. He is often thought to have been a representative of the "Hellenists," who as a group were more critical of the temple and the law than the "Hebrews"; see below, n. 29.

27. B. Witherington, *Acts*, 277.

28. See the useful discussion by C. C. Hill, "Acts 6:1–8:4," 137.

29. It has become customary in recent discussions to assume that this persecution involved only the "Hellenists," because of their critical attitude towards the temple and the law. Advocates of this view include M. Hengel, *Between*, 24–26; G. Lüdemann, *Early*, 90–93; and J. D. G. Dunn, *Acts*, 104–5. This, however, is not supported by Acts 8:1b, which suggests that the *whole* Jerusalem church (*tēn ekklēsian tēn en hierosolymois*) was persecuted and that all were scattered, *except the twelve apostles*. Nowhere does Luke make a distinction between the theology of the "Hellenists" and that of the "Hebrews." The specific reference to "the twelve" in 8:1b both shows the boldness of the apostles and serves to keep them at the head of the Jerusalem church. For a full (and persuasive) discussion of this, see C. C. Hill, "Acts 6:1–8:4" and *Hellenists*.

30. J. D. G. Dunn, *Acts*, 105–6. See also the discussions of Paul's activities in E. Haenchen, *Acts*, 297, and C. C. Hill, *Hellenists*, 39. For a rather different view, M. Hengel, *Pre-Christian*, 63–86, and S. Légasse, "Paul's," 379–89.

31. Herod the Great was the only sovereign allowed the exceptional privilege of extraditing a fugitive from a state outside his jurisdiction (Josephus, *War* 1.474). A letter in 1 Macc 15:16–21 from the Roman consul Lucius to King Ptolemy requesting him not to harm his Jewish neighbors and asking him to return to Simon the high priest any "pestilent men" who were hiding in his own country reads like a single request rather than evidence for high-priestly powers of extradition. Despite attempts to suggest that such powers were confirmed by Julius Caesar in 47 B.C.E. (F. F. Bruce, *Acts*, 223, and S. Applebaum, "Legal," both drawing on *Antiq* 14.192–95), it seems highly unlikely that a high priest would have possessed any such legal authority. Nor is the matter resolved by the suggestion that Damascus was under the control of Aretas IV of Nabatea at this point and that Caiaphas took advantage of a power vacuum in the city (F. G. B. Millar, *Roman*, 56–57).

   How Christianity came to Damascus is unknown. Perhaps the new faith was brought back by people who encountered it at one of the festivals in Jerusalem. It is unlikely that the community there had fled from persecution in Jerusalem: (1) as we have seen, Luke's report in Acts 8:1b is exaggerated, and (2) in Acts 9:13 Ananias had only *heard* of Paul's persecuting activity, not experienced it firsthand, a fact that suggests that he at least had not fled from Jerusalem.

32. Beheading was a punishment often associated with political offenses; for discussions of the whole matter, see D. R. Schwartz, *Agrippa I*, 119–24, and C. K. Barrett, *Acts*, 1:568–78.

33. J. Blinzler, for example, suggested that James was executed on the Sanhedrin's orders on the charge of being a false teacher ("Rechtsgeschichtliches"); P. Gaechter ("Hatred," 27–29) that it was at the prompting of the high priest Matthias; and R. J. Cassidy that the high priests and Agrippa had an "understanding" (*Society*, 47–48). All these scholars have been too much influenced by Luke's attempt to heighten high-priestly opposition in the early chapters of Acts.

   According to Luke, the death of James—and presumably the rest of the persecution—"pleased the Jews" (12:3). Who were these "Jews"? The house of Annas? (so J. D. Crossan, *Birth*, 508; R. J. Cassidy, *Society*, 48) Or the Jewish people? (G. Lüdemann, *Early Christianity*, 140; D. R. Schwartz, *Agrippa I*, 124

n. 70). By Acts 12, the portrayal of Jews and Jerusalem tends to be rather negative, and Luke probably intends us to think of these "Jews" as the Jewish people generally. Whether the Jerusalemites were genuinely happy about Agrippa's actions is more difficult to say.

34. J. S. McLaren, "Ananus." As McLaren notes, the common view that Ananus's opponents were Pharisees has no basis in the text (6–14); it is more likely that the opponents were "other priests, wealthy laity, and Herodians" (13). See also C. C. Hill, *Hellenists*, 183–91, who makes some of the same points. For the view that this episode demonstrates the hatred of the house of Annas towards Christianity, see P. Gaechter, "Hatred," 30–33.

9. Later Years

1. He is described as *epimelētēs*, a manager or overseer, in *Antiq* 18.89.
2. *Antiq* 18.85–89. For fuller discussion, see my *Pontius*, 89–93.
3. D. R. Schwartz, "Pontius," 203; E. M. Smallwood, "Date," 15.
4. E. M. Smallwood, "Date." Smallwood suggests December or January for this first visit. Less persuasively, H. Hoehner (*Antipas*, 313–16) and J. P. Lémonon (*Pilate*, 243–44) suggest that Vitellius's first visit was Passover 37 and that the second was Pentecost, which was celebrated early that year on May 11. Even with an early date, however, it seems unlikely that the news of Gaius's death would take so long to reach Vitellius.

    For a completely different solution to the problem of Vitellius's visits, see D. R. Schwartz, "Pontius." Taking a source-critical approach, Schwartz argues that Vitellius made only *one* visit to Jerusalem, at Passover 37. *Antiq* 18.90–95 gives an account of this visit from the point of view of the Jerusalem priesthood, while 18.109–26 describes it from a Roman perspective (as also does the account in 15.403–8). Although ingenious, the difficulty with this reconstruction is that Josephus has a different high priest deposed at each visit. Schwartz has to assume that Josephus added the notices about the change of high priests at a later stage in the composition of his work and forgot that Vitellius had made only one visit. Schwartz himself suggests that Vitellius fired Caiaphas at the same time that he suspended Pilate. The difficulty with this, however, is that Josephus, who knows a fair amount about Pilate and describes his governorship in some detail, does not connect his deposition with that of Caiaphas. The Samaritan complaint seems to have been directed against Pilate alone; there is no connection with Caiaphas.
5. E. M. Smallwood, "Date," esp. 17–18. Did Vitellius need to write to Tiberius? The legate possessed exceptional authority in the East (Tacitus, *Annals* 6.32), and D. R. Schwartz argues that he would not have needed to write. Schwartz attributes Josephus's presentation in 15.405 to the historian's apologetic desire to involve the emperor himself in the protection of Judea ("Pontius" 204 n. 9). Yet even if Vitellius was competent to grant the request, it is not improbable that he would have referred the whole matter to the emperor, particularly since the emperor was currently reviewing the situation in Judea. After the death of Agrippa I, when Fadus ordered the priests to deposit the vestments once again in the Antonia Fortress, the Jewish leaders successfully took their petition not to the Syrian legate but to the Emperor Claudius himself (*Antiq* 20.6–14).
6. See, for example, J. D. Crossan, who writes: "It is not unfairly cynical to presume that there was close co-operation between Caiaphas and Pilate, that it often offended Jewish sensitivities, and that eventually it became necessary to break up that co-operation in Rome's best interests" (*Who Killed?* 148). D. R. Schwartz also suggests a friendship may have developed between them ("Pontius," 213 n.

35). P. Gaechter suggests that Caiaphas was accused by the same people who accused Pilate or, less likely, a group of Pharisees ("Hatred," 17).

7. See the discussion above, 50–55.

8. The Greek is *kai tauta praxas epi euergesia tou ethnous kai ton archierea Iōsēpon ton Kaïaphan epikaloumenon apallaxas tēs hierōsynēs Iōnathēn kathistēsin Avavou tou archiereōs huion.* The structure of the whole passage and the way in which the notice about Caiaphas seems to be rather artificially tagged onto what precedes it supports D. R. Schwartz's general theory that Josephus is combining sources here ("Pontius," 212–13).

9. See above, 42, on the post of captain of the temple.

10. A. Vicent Cernuda, "Conversión."

11. A. Vicent Cernuda is correct to note the reticence with which the Gospel writers refer to Caiaphas ("Conversión," 62–69), yet, as the later chapters of my study show, this reticence can be explained differently.

12. The only trace of an early tradition in which Caiaphas is thought to have become a Christian is found among twelfth-century Syrian Jacobites (see Vicent Cernuda, "Conversión," 69–70, and above, 11). This "Christianizing," however, is probably part of the same movement that also turned Pilate into a supporter of Jesus, rather than an authentic historical tradition.

13. At the beginning of the reign of Herod the Great's son Archelaus in 6 C.E., the people similarly asked for "the removal of the taxes that had been levied upon public purchases and sales and had been ruthlessly executed" (*Antiq* 17.205). Presumably here too the people put their requests through their leaders.

14. *Antiq* 18.237. A number of scholars assume that Marullus here is to be identified with Vitellius's friend Marcellus who was already acting as interim prefect (e.g., S.L. De Laet, "Successeur," 418–19, and E. M. Smallwood, "Date," 14). However, as L. H. Feldman notes, there is no confusion in the manuscripts between the two names and Josephus specifically says that Gaius "dispatched" (*ekpempei*) Marullus, which would be an odd expression to use of someone already in the province (*LCL* IX, 143–44, n. f).

    D. R. Schwartz suggests that Marullus (and his predecessor Marcellus) was not an independent governor and that, following Pilate's departure, Judea was annexed to Syria until 41 (*Agrippa 1*, 62–66).

15. On the role of Jewish aristocrats in this incident, P. W. Barnett, "Under Tiberius," 570.

16. *War* 2.185–203; *Antiq* 18.261–308; Philo, *Embassy to Gaius* 207–333; (Tacitus, *History* 5.9). On this incident see E. M. Smallwood, "Philo"; N. H. Taylor, "Popular"; and J. S. McLaren, *Power*, 114–26.

17. *Antiq* 19.314.

18. *Antiq* 20.162.

19. P. W. Barnett, "Under Tiberius," 570, suggests that Annas died in 35 C.E., but offers no evidence for this.

10. The Gospels in Context

1. See above, 158–59.

2. This was presumably one of the earliest explanations—see Acts 3:17, 13:27 and perhaps 1 Cor 2:6–8 (W. Carr, "Rulers," 25–26).

3. The earliest Christian works are Paul's letters. Although Paul was much more interested in the *theological* significance of Jesus' death than outlining its historical causes, it is clear from his references to Jesus' last evening and betrayal (1 Cor 11:23–25), sufferings (Phil 3:10), crucifixion (Gal 2:20, 3:1, 1 Cor 1:23) and burial (1 Cor 15:3, Rom 6:4) that he—and his readers—knew the general course

of events. (See J. Fitzmyer, *Luke*, 1360; J. T. Carroll and J. B. Green, *Death*, 113–32.) Apart from 1 Thess 2:14–16, however, Paul shows no interest in identifying the people responsible for Jesus' death (for different views on this passage, see B. A. Pearson, "1 Thessalonians," and K. P. Donfried, "1 Thessalonians"). Paul's virtual silence on this issue may be because he was writing for predominantly Gentile audiences, for whom Jesus' rejection by Jewish religious leaders was less of a problem.

4. Tacitus, *Histories* 5.9.
5. On the causes of the war, see P. W. Barnett, "Under Tiberius," 565–66, and M. Goodman, *Ruling*. Josephus provides us with a full description of the war itself in *War*, esp. books 2–7; see also E. M. Smallwood, *Jews*, 293–330; E. Schürer, *History*, I:484–513; and J. Price, *Jerusalem*.
6. Josephus's description of conditions during the siege feeds into one of his major points in the *Jewish War*—the stupidity of revolt against Rome. Yet there can be no doubt that his descriptions rest to a large extent on historical fact.
7. The tax (known as the *fiscus Iudaicus*) was now payable not only by adult males (as formerly) but by all Jews, between the ages of three and sixty. On the tax, the coins, and anti-Jewish prejudice at this time, see M. Goodman, "Diaspora." For a vivid account of the triumph, see Josephus, *War* 7.123–57.
8. See E. Schürer, *History*, I:514–34.
9. On this process see the essays in J. D. G. Dunn, ed., *Jews and Christians*, and J. D. G. Dunn, *Parting*; R. Bauckham, "Parting"; and A. F. Segal, *Rebecca's*, 115–181. It is important not to overestimate rabbinic authority at this early period. It was not until the third century that rabbinic Judaism became dominant even within Palestine, and even longer before it became established in the Diaspora (P. S. Alexander, "Parting," 21–22).
10. W. Horbury, "New Wine," 38. Josephus always writes of the temple cult in the present tense, perhaps reflecting his hope that it would soon be reinstated (see E. Schürer, *History*, I:521–23). As R. Bauckham notes, one of the main aims of the Palestinian-based and widely supported Bar Kochba rebellion of 132–135 was to rebuild the temple; see R. Bauckham, "Parting," 145–46.
11. For the importance of the temple in Jewish-Christian controversy of the period, see R. Bauckham, "Parting."
12. Although the separation between the two faiths was largely complete by the second century, followers of Jesus were found in Jewish synagogues until at least the fifth century; see W. A. Meeks, "Breaking," 114.

11. Caiaphas in Mark

1. See M. Hooker, *Gospel*, 5–8; P. Fredriksen, *From Jesus*, 50. For fuller discussion and bibliography, see my *Pontius*, 94–95.
2. Eusebius, *Hist. eccl.* 2.15.2 links the Gospel to Rome. For more detailed arguments for a Roman provenance, see M. Hengel, *Studies*, 28–30, and R. H. Gundry, *Mark*, 1026–45. For Syria, see B. Mack, *Myth*, 11–12, 315–18; for Galilee, see W. Marxsen, *Evangelist*, 54–116. Perhaps all we can say with any confidence is that the Gospel was composed in a large Hellenistic city of the eastern empire (so M. Hooker, *Gospel*, 8).
3. Eusebius cites Papias, who claimed that Mark was the "interpreter (or translator) of Peter," *Hist. eccl.* 3.39.15.
4. This is suggested by Mark's inclusion of the phrase "all nations" at significant points in the narrative: the temple is to be a house of prayer for "all the nations" (11:17), and the gospel must be preached to "all nations" (13:10), even "the whole world" (14:9). The cycle of stories in 7:1–8:26 take the message to

Gentiles, and it is a Gentile centurion who is the first to recognize that the crucified Jesus is indeed "God's Son" (15:39). The Gospel preserves the vestiges of recent church-synagogue disputes over purity and Sabbath observance (for example, 2:16, 3:2, 7:1–19) and the Mosaic law (1:44, 3:4, 7:8–13, 10:19, 12:29–31). But these disputes seem to be in the past: the Markan community are the new cloth that cannot be sewn onto the old cloth of the Jewish synagogue, the new wine that is fit only for new skins (2:21–22).

5. The importance of the passion narrative can be seen from Mark's use of "immediately" (*euthys* in Greek). Throughout most of the Gospel, events follow one another in quick succession, giving the impression that events are rushing towards their climax. With the beginning of the passion narrative in chapter 14, however, this climax is reached: the word "immediately" is used much more sparingly. Mark tells us the precise day, and as events unfold, even the hour becomes important. This literary device helps to focus our attention on Jesus' dramatic last few hours.

6. S. Mason similarly comments on the peculiarity of the fact that Mark knows the name of Pilate but "does not disclose the name of the one truly responsible, the High Priest," (*Josephus*, 128).

7. This is the view of Paul Winter in his monumental work *On the Trial of Jesus*, 49–50. Central to Winter's thesis is the assumption that there never was a formal, Jewish trial such as we have in Mark 14:53–65. Winter does accept a certain amount of high-priestly involvement in Jesus' execution: he suggests that a meeting of chief priests expressed their unease at Jesus' activity and decided to hand him over to Pilate (rather like John 11:47–53). The trial narrative in Mark 14, however, is a Markan creation. Since the high priest's involvement in Jesus' execution had been only minimal, the Christian traditions that Mark inherited did not preserve his name, so Mark had no choice but to refer to him as simply "the high priest." It was left to later evangelists to work out—and to add—the appropriate name.

    Although I have a great deal of sympathy for Winter's thesis on a historical level, I do not find his explanation for Mark's silence persuasive. Even on Winter's reading of events, the involvement of the high priest was not all that minimal. If the high priest had had *any* involvement in handing Jesus over to Pilate, I find it very difficult to imagine that early Christian tradition did not preserve his name. Furthermore, as I have already suggested, the passion narratives had a much longer and more complex background than Winter will allow. There must have been a great deal of speculation right from the beginning as to what went on in front of the high priest, a fact that makes it difficult to imagine that none of the earlier traditions preserved his name.

8. G. Theissen, *Gospels*, 172–73. As Theissen notes, the fact that Mark can write simply of "*the* rebels" and "*the* insurrection" (15:7) also suggests that he expects his readers to be familiar with the story he has to tell (both Matthew and Luke change these references) (183).

9. R. Pesch, *Markusevangelium*, 2:1–27. On Caiaphas's deposition, see above, 188–95.

10. G. Theissen, *Gospels*, 189–99.

11. G. Theissen, *Gospels*, 166–74; the quotation is from 173. Theissen's proposal is followed by C. S. Keener, *Matthew*, 610. Theissen also suggests that Mark is more interested in Caiaphas's function as high priest than his name, and that—contrary to historical reality—the Sanhedrin receives a greater share of "blame" because of the experiences of the early Christian community in Palestine after Jesus' death, where conflicts were generally with Jewish officials (172). This insight will be developed in my own reading of the Gospel below.

12. See notes 1 and 2 above.
13. R. E. Brown, *Gospel*, 821.
14. Noted by D. Juel, *Messiah*, 65.
15. On the parallelism, see C. Myers, *Binding*, 370–71, and J. D. Crossan, *Who Killed?* 106–8.
16. In fact, Matthew seems to prefer to refer to Pilate as "the governor" and uses the term where we might have expected him simply to refer to Pilate by name (e.g., 27:11, 15). He seems to have had a particular interest in Pilate *as a Roman governor*; see my study of this in *Pontius*, 135–36. Following Mark, Luke refers to Pilate only by name within the trial narrative, though he formally introduces Pilate as "governor of Judea" in his introductory paragraph of 3:1.
17. On the characterization of Pilate in this scene, see my *Pontius*, 103–19.
18. G. Theissen, *Gospels*, 170–73.
19. As A. C. Hagedorn and J. H. Neyrey observe: "The narrative strategy in portraying Jesus envied seems to serve the basic rhetorical aim of the gospel, namely the praise of Jesus and the acknowledgement of him as Christ, Prophet, and Lord—that is, the most honourable person in the cosmos next to God" ("Envy," 40). Although their article focuses on the use of envy in Mark's Gospel, the authors claim to have unearthed *historical* reasons for the death of Jesus (56). However, while envy works well as a literary device within the Gospel, I find it less plausible on a historical level. Men in the ancient world envied only their *peers*; the gulf between the Galilean peasant and the anointed priestly leaders, however, was huge. The chief priests may well have been alarmed at Jesus' public recognition and popularity and may have feared that he would bring down the wrath of Rome on the nation, but it is unlikely that they really saw him as a significant competitor for their own privileged position. For a fuller discussion of envy, see B. Malina, *New Testament*, 108–33.
20. D. Juel, *Messiah*; M. D. Hooker, *Mark*, 354–57.
21. As we saw earlier (31 above) there were two temple veils, one outside the sanctuary and one covering the entrance to the holy of holies. Which does Mark have in mind? D. Juel, *Messiah*, 140–42, suggests the outer veil, and that its tearing symbolizes the end of the temple. M. D. Hooker, *Mark*, 377–78, however, argues that Mark means the inner veil, in which case its tearing would suggest that God's presence is no longer to be found primarily in the holy of holies but is available to all—including Gentiles.
22. M.Sanhedrin. The problem is that in very many respects Mark's Jewish trial flouts these procedures. For lengthy discussions of legal problems, see, for example, H. Cohn (*Trial*, 357–59) and R. E. Brown, *Death*, 1:357–63.
23. C. Myers, *Binding*, 370–74 (Myers describes Mark's scene as "grimly comic"); D. Juel, *Messiah*, 59–64; M. D. Hooker, *Mark*, 357.
24. Perhaps Mark saw this mockery as a fulfilment of Isa 50:6.
25. 11:15–19. Mark helps his readers to understand by linking this incident with another one, the story of Jesus cursing the fig tree. The first part of the fig tree story is narrated before the temple incident. Jesus went to a fig tree looking for fruit; when he found none, he cursed it (11:12–14). After the temple incident the story of the fig tree is picked up again; the tree is now withered (11:20–21). This "sandwiching" technique is common in Mark, and it is clear that the author intends the two stories to be read together so that the meaning of one influences the meaning of the other. Here the juxtaposition of these two stories suggests that Jesus' actions prophesy nothing less than the destruction of the temple.
26. For a similar interpretation of the temple charge, see D. Lührmann, "Markus." For a full discussion, see R. E. Brown, *Death*, 1:438–54, and R. J. McKelvey, *Temple*, 67–74.

27. D. Juel, *Messiah*, 93–95; M. D. Hooker, *Gospel*, 273–78. The words are from Ps 110:1 and Dan 7:13.
28. This fits with chapter 13 and the eschatology of the Gospel generally.
29. On the range of meanings covered by "blasphemy" in the first century, see R. E. Brown, *Death*, 1:520–47. This understanding of the use of blasphemy here is shared by E. P. Sanders, *Historical*, 273. For an alternative view, see D. Bock, *Blasphemy*, who argues that the blasphemy charge is historical and that Jesus' application of Ps 110:1 and Dan 7:13 to himself led to his condemnation.
30. Mark's insistence on the complicity of the whole council here makes the later actions of Joseph of Arimathea rather difficult to account for (15:42–46). While Mark does not suggest that Joseph was a believer (unlike later evangelists), his presentation of events indicates that Joseph was at least favorably disposed toward Jesus. The tension here stresses once again that historical concerns were not uppermost in Mark's mind as he penned his account of the trial.
31. P. Fredriksen, *Jesus*, 46.
32. B. Mack, *Myth*, 295.

12. Caiaphas in Luke–Acts

1. Scholars doubt that Luke was a Jew because he seems unclear about Jewish practices at 2:22–24, Acts 18:18 and 21:24–26 (see, for example, E. Trocmé, "Jews," 147). The paragraphs that follow owe a great deal to the following works: S. Mason, "Chief Priests"; E. Trocmé, "Jews"; J. D. G. Dunn, "Anti-Semitism"; J. T. Carroll and J. B. Green, *Death*, 60–81; C. Tuckett, *Luke*, 50–71; P. J. Tomson, *If This Be*, 214–54; J. Jervell, "Future"; L. T. Johnson, "Luke–Acts"; and A. George, "Israël."
2. For further discussion, see my *Pontius*, 138–39.
3. For a discussion of the setting of Agrippa's persecution within the book of Acts, see D. R. Schwartz, *Agrippa I*, 150–56.
4. Acts 13:46, 18:6, and, most dramatically of all, 28:28. Yet even if Luke knew that the future lay with the Gentile mission, he has not turned his back completely on the synagogues. Pharisees (who, as we have seen, were emerging as the leaders of Judaism at this period) are portrayed positively in Luke's work. In the Gospel, they do not plot to do away with Jesus (unlike Mark 3:6), nor are they involved in Jesus' death. Jesus is often invited to their homes, where he engages them in heated debates (7:36–50, 11:37–53, 14:1). Furthermore, Paul, the hero of Acts, is himself presented as a law-observant and devout Pharisee. As J. D. G. Dunn suggests, this may well "betoken a greater openness on Luke's part to continuing dialogue between the synagogue and the church, albeit marked by blunt talking on both sides, rather than a complete closing of the door" ("Anti-Semitism," 195). He is puzzled and distressed that so many Jews continue to reject Jesus but is still open to Jews joining what he regards as the true Israel.
5. This technique was used already in 1:5 and 2:1–7 and will be used again in Acts 11:28 and 18:2.
6. This was argued by P. Winter (*Trial*, 44–47), though he rather curiously suggests that the Annas to whom Luke referred was Ananus II, the high priest who was responsible for the death of James.
7. A man like Annas, who had held the office for some time himself and still retained influence through his family, might well have continued to enjoy the title high priest well after he had technically been deposed by a Roman governor (some people, indeed, may have refused to recognize such a deposition).
8. For views similar to those expressed in this paragraph, see R. E. Brown, *Gospel*,

820, and S. Mason, *Josephus*, 129–30. Did Luke's first readers realize that both men were high priests? Perhaps they did. Yet, as Luke–Acts was read and copied in the Gentile world, that fact would have quickly been lost. Anyone reading the two volumes without a knowledge of broader Jewish-Christian traditions would be forgiven for assuming that *Annas* was the acting high priest and that Caiaphas was simply the most prominent member of the remaining high-priestly family. This ambiguity is left unresolved by Luke's Jewish trial, which, as we shall see, assigns no specific role to either Annas or Caiaphas.

9. The differences between Luke and Mark have suggested to some that Luke drew on other sources and traditions at this point (see, for example, I. H. Marshall, *Gospel*, 845; D. Bock, *Luke*, 1776; and J. Fitzmyer, *Gospel*, 1365–66), or even an alternative continuous passion account (see, for example, J. Nolland, *Luke*, 1105). However, while it is certainly possible that there were other passion accounts and traditions in existence, there is nothing in Luke that necessitates the use of another source (or sources). A number of recent investigations have shown that Luke is working only with his Markan text. See in particular the detailed treatment of this theme by J. M. Harrington, who concludes that "Mark has continued to guide Luke in the Passion Narrative" (*Lukan*, 804). Harrington shows that even the trial in front of Herod (which is unique to Luke) can be accounted for as a Lukan creation, based on material about Herod in Mark. See also the detailed studies by F. J. Matera ("Luke 22,66–71," and "Death"), who similarly finds that the differences with Mark can be explained in the light of Luke's redactional activity.

10. Useful discussions of Luke's Jewish trial can be found in the commentaries (particularly J. Fitzmyer, I. H. Marshall, and J. Nolland); also see the detailed studies of F. J. Matera ("Luke 22,66–71") and A. Neagoe (*Trial*, 62–90).

11. On the temple in Luke, see F. D. Weinert, "Luke, the Temple" and "Luke, Stephen"; F. J. Matera, "Luke 22,66–71," 528–29; D. D. Sylva, "Temple"; J. B. Green, "Demise"; and E. Larsson, "Temple-Criticism."

12. On this, see in particular D. D. Sylva, "Temple."

13. F. J. Matera, "Luke 22,66–71," 525. See also A. Neagoe, *Trial*, 48–49.

14. The word for "blasphemy" is used in the mockery scene: v. 65 is literally "and they spoke many other words against him, blaspheming him."

15. Luke has toned down the animosity of the Jewish leaders earlier when they plot to do away with Jesus (22:1–2): no longer do they plan to "arrest him by stealth," and their intention to "put Jesus to death" (using the verb *anaireō*) is not as strong as Mark's "kill" him (*apokteinō*). Although the Jewish leaders engineer Jesus' death, Luke presents them in a less hostile manner than his Markan source. Furthermore, as the narrative progresses, it becomes clear that not all the councillors are against Jesus: Joseph of Arimathaea, for example, is described as "a good and righteous man, who, though a member of the council, had not agreed to their plan and action" (23:50–51), and later Gamaliel speaks up for Jesus' followers (Acts 5:34–39). Luke's use of Satan as Jesus' archenemy and the force that ultimately sends Jesus to the cross may also ameliorate the actions of the Jewish leaders at this point (Luke 4:13, 22:3, and 22:31).

16. F. J. Matera, "Luke 22,66–71," 520, n. 15. S. Mason suggests Luke knew that trials were conducted in a special chamber ("Chief Priests," 146). *Synedrion* also seems to be a place in Acts 4:15; 5:27, 34; 6:12, 15; 23:6, 20, 28; 24:20.

17. As S. G. F. Brandon notes, Luke's presentation gives the impression that the only notable thing to happen in the house of the high priest was Peter's denial (*Trial*, 118).

18. C. Tuckett, *Luke*, 44; J. Fitzmyer, *Gospel*, 1463; see Luke 9:51, 24:26, Acts 1:11; 2:30, 33–36; 3.20. Mark's "you will see" has also dropped out. This is perhaps

because Luke has toned down the apocalyptic nature of the phrase, perhaps too because "seeing" is an important theme in Luke's Gospel—only a believer will be able to see Jesus in his exalted state (see, for example, Stephen's vision in 7:55–56) (Fitzmyer, *Gospel*, 1467; J. Knight, *Luke's*, 161–62).

19. The Herod story also allows Luke to transfer several unsavory features from the Roman trial to Herod's court, particularly the mocking by the soldiers and the dressing up in mock-royal clothes.

20. Verse 17 is a later scribal gloss, presumably aimed at harmonizing Luke with the other *Gospels*. See B. M. Metzger, *Textual*, 179–80.

21. Moses: Luke 9:35 (Deut 18:5); Acts 3:22–23 (Deut 18:15, 18–19). Elijah: Luke 24:51–53, Acts 1:9–11, 2:1–13 (2 Kgs 2:1–14). Elijah and Elisha: Luke 7:1–16 (1 Kgs 17:17–25, 2 Kgs 5:1–14).

22. For fuller discussion of the scenes in front of Pilate, see my *Pontius*, 152–62.

23. Even those advocating Luke's use of an alternative source here (e.g., J. Nolland, *Luke*, 1105) have to explain why Luke preferred to use a version with no reference to the high priest over Mark's narrative.

24. This is suggested by S. Mason, "Chief Priests," 146, and D. Bock, *Luke*, 1782.

25. See the earlier discussion, 109–11.

26. L. T. Johnson, "Luke–Acts," 412. Throughout this and the following paragraphs, I am indebted to many of Johnson's insights on 411–12.

27. The divide between the actions of the high-priestly leaders and the will of God is apparent in 5:19–20; it comes out quite explicitly in Peter's speech of 5:29–32 and is highlighted even by Gamaliel, one of their number, who warns that by opposing the new movement they may find themselves opposing God (5:33–39).

28. L. T. Johnson, "Luke–Acts," 415.

29. See above, 77–79.

30. For useful discussions of Stephen's speech, see D. R. Schwartz, *Studies*, 119–21, and F. D. Weinert, "Luke, Stephen."

31. On the historical events here, see above, 70–72.

13. Caiaphas in Matthew

1. For various scholarly suggestions and bibliography, see my *Pontius*, 120–22.

2. 4:23 or 23:34 refer to "their" or "your" synagogues, which distances the author from the Jewish assemblies; references to persecution can be found in 5:11–12, 44; 10:17–22, 28, 34–39; and 24:9–14.

     Useful discussions of Matthew's relationship to the synagogue and his particular social setting can be found in: P. Fredriksen, *From Jesus*, 36–43; W. A. Meeks, "Breaking"; S. Freyne, "Vilifying"; G. Stanton, "Matthew's Christology"; A. F. Segal, *Rebecca's*, 117–62; J. D. G. Dunn, "Anti-Semitism," 203–10; P. J. Tomson, "*If This Be*," 263–89; L. M. White, "Crisis"; and U. Luz, *Theology*, 11–21.

3. Matthew's Jewish-Christian community presumably expects these Gentile converts to keep the Jewish law; see U. Luz, *Theology* 16–17.

4. On the Jewish leaders in Matthew, see J. D. Kingsbury, "Plot"; D. R. Bauer, "Major Characters," 363–66; and E. Buck, "Anti-Judaic."

5. Throughout the passion narrative, it will be these men, the chief priests and "elders of the people" (rather than Mark's "scribes") who lead the opposition against Jesus. The phrase "of the people" perhaps for Matthew underlined the representative nature of these men.

6. See above, 188 n. 25.

7. Positive references to the temple can be found at 5:23–24 (a passage that

suggests Matthew's community continued to worship in the temple prior to 70 C.E.); 17:24–27; and 21:13. On the temple incident, see especially D. Catchpole, "Answer."

8. On the genuine nature of Judas's repentance, see W. D. Davies and D. C. Allison, *Critical*, 3:261–63).

9. Pilate's hand-washing (an act that draws on Deut 21:1–9, 2 Sam 3:28, and Ps 26:6), his wife's dream, and the words of "all the people" are not contained in any other Gospel and are hardly likely to be historical. Instead, they reflect Matthew's social setting and theological outlook. On the scene before Pilate, see my *Pontius*, 120–37.

10. Precisely what is meant by "seal the tomb" is uncertain—perhaps it meant putting a wax seal on the stone, or surrounding the tomb with a cord to which was attached a seal. The precise meaning, though, probably does not matter very much, since the whole episode is clearly legendary. For discussion, see W. D. Davies and D. C. Allison, *Critical*, 3:655–56. The story probably arose to counter stories that the disciples had carried Jesus' body away and fabricated the story of the resurrection. The reference to Pharisees here is presumably an addition intended to implicate the pharisaic leaders of Matthew's own day; for a similar device in John, see 132.

11. Detailed discussion of Matthew's redaction of Mark can be found in D. Senior, *Passion*, 9–27, 157–91.

12. Matthew incorporated Mark's three passion predictions at 16:21, 17:22 and 20:18–19. The lack of specific references here suggests that the saying is a Matthean creation.

13. This early, *formal* meeting of the council has some similarities with John 11:47–53. The fact that Matthew (unlike John) seems to have no real information about what happened at this meeting, however, suggests that the evangelist did not derive the idea of a formal trial from a shared Johannine tradition but has inserted it instead for literary effect.

14. The Greek word *aulē* can mean either a palace or a courtyard; the former is more likely here. On the location of Caiaphas's palace, see Appendix D below.

15. On Matthew's penchant for referring to characters by name, see D. Senior, *Passion*, 25 with references. The evangelist, however, does not usually add names to his narrative, as R. Bauckham ("Eyewitnesses") points out. Apart from adding the name of Jesus' father, Matthew tends either to follow Mark's names or even to eliminate them—compare for example Mark 5:22 with Matt 9:18, or Mark 10:46 with Matt 20:30.

16. W. D. Davies and D. C. Allison suggest that the name was simply part of Matthew's common tradition, as it was of John's (*Critical*, 3:426).

17. Mark's rather messy opening (14:53) has been pared down, and his vague reference to "chief priests" eliminated; instead, Jesus is led "to Caiaphas the high priest, in whose house the scribes and the elders had gathered" (26:57). R. E. Brown also notes that Matthew's editing serves to heighten Caiaphas's role (*Death*, 1:402).

18. Deut 17:6–7, 19:15. Matt 18:16 shows that this law was still current within Matthew's own community.

19. This point is also made by D. Catchpole, "Answer." W. D. Davies and D. C. Allison also note that Matthew mutes the hostility against the temple (*Critical*, 3:525–26).

20. Mark has "the high priest stood up before them" (14:60), reminding the reader of the presence of other councillors; Matthew, however, has simply "the high priest stood up" (26:62).

21. Why did Matthew feel the need to alter Mark's unambiguous "I am"? D. Catch-

pole suggests it is a Semitic idiom meaning yes but "modified only by the important fact that more is needed for a complete understanding of Jesus, which indeed the kingly Son of Man saying immediately provides" ("Answer," 221). Matthew's alteration brings Jesus' words here into line with his words to Judas (26:25) and later to Pilate (27:11).

22. *Chitōn* occurs only twice in Matthew, *himation* twelve times. See D. Senior, *Passion*, 184.

23. This is suggested by C. S. Keener, *Commentary*, 642; see also W. D. Davies and D. C. Allison, *Critical*, 3:533. Mark's word *chitōn* is also used of the high-priestly garments in some texts (see below, 197 n. 38), though the earlier evangelist does not seem to see any particular significance in the high priest's actions (other than, perhaps, to signal the end of the cult). Josephus regularly uses another word—*stolē*—to refer to the vestments (*Antiq* 15.405–9, 18.90–95). The word for "rend" in both Matt 26:25 and Lev 21:10 is the same: *dierrēxen* (from *diarrēgnymi*).

24. Given the high priest's role as mediator between God and humanity, and his central importance within the temple, this was perhaps a natural development. Already in the Jewish Scriptures, Ps 110 combined messianic kingship with an ideal priesthood "after the order of Melchizedek," the mysterious priest-king of Gen 14:17–24. And Zech 4:14, the Greek translation of Ezek 21:30–32, and Sir 45:24–25, 50:1–21 moved in a similar direction. But it was in the first century B.C.E. that the priestly facet of the messiah really flourished, perhaps in response to (or as a reaction against) Israel's Hasmonean rulers, who themselves combined both royal power and priestly authority. The *Testament of Levi*, for example, expected God to raise up a "new priest" (17.2–11, 18.2–9). (On the difficulties of this text, see G. S. Oegema, *Anointed*, 73–81; and R. A. Stewart, "Sinless," 128–29.) Certain Qumran texts distinguished between a priestly and a royal messiah—the messiah of Aaron and the messiah of Israel—with the priestly messiah being superior to the royal one; others seem to imagine both roles in the same person. See, for example, 1QS 9.10–11; CD 12.22–23, 13.20–22, 14.19, 19.11, 20.1; 1Qsa 2.11–23; K. G. Kuhn, "Two Messiahs"; G. S. Oegema, *Anointed*, 86–102, 108–127; W. Horbury, *Jewish*, 59–63; W. H. Brownlee, "Messianic Motifs"; and J. Gnilka, "Erwartung," 396–405. For a discussion of the heavenly warrior (but apparently not high-priestly) figure of Melchizedek in 11Q Melchizedek, see M. de Jonge and A. S. van der Woude, "11Q Melchizidek" and J. A. Fitzmyer, "Further." Finally, Josephus, in his praise of John Hyrcanus, may well have been drawing on messianic categories when he claims that the king was "deemed by God worthy of the highest three honours—sovereignty, high priesthood, and prophetic office—for the divine was with him" (*Antiq* 13.299).

There is evidence, then, to support O. Cullmann's view that "Judaism knew of an ideal priest who, as the one true priest, should fulfil in the last days all the elements of the Jewish priestly office" (*Christology*, 86; see also R. Longenecker, *Christology*, 114, and J. Gnilka, "Erwartung," 405–8. For an opposing view, see A. J. B. Higgins, "Priestly").

25. U. Luz, *Theology*, 30; see also Matt 9:6, 8; 18:21–35; 26:28.

26. On Jesus as high priest in Matthew, see O. Cullmann, *Christology*, 104, and G. Friedrich, "Beobachtungen" (though the latter tends to overstate his case).

27. See J. Gnilka, "Erwartung," 418–21; O. Cullmann, *Christology*, 89–104; P. D. Duerksen, "Images"; M. C. Parsons, "Son"; R. A. Stewart, "Sinless"; and F. L. Horton, *Melchizedek*, 152–72.

28. On 1 Peter, see O. Moe, "Priestertum," col. 2271; for Revelation, see W. H. Brownlee, "Messianic," 207–8, and J. Gnilka, "Erwartung," 435.

29. A point made by C. F. D. Moule ("Sanctuary," 39).
30. For example, Gerrit von Honthorst's "Christ before the High Priest" (ca. 1617) and Matthias Stom's "Christ before Caiaphas" (early 1630s) which both condense the trial scene to two major characters (Christ and Caiaphas) and two background ones.

14. Caiaphas in John

1. On the date and provenance of the Gospel, see my *Pontius*, 163–65. For authorship, see the detailed discussion in R. E. Brown, *Gospel*, lxxxvii–ci (who favors John Zebedee as both the enigmatic Beloved Disciple and the author of the work); R. Schnackenburg, *Gospel*, 75–104, and C. K. Barrett, *Gospel*, 100–34 (who both opt for a disciple of the Beloved Disciple); and B. Lindars, *Gospel*, 28–34 (who argues that we simply do not know who wrote the Gospel).
2. John's distinctive presentation has raised the question of whether he knew the Synoptics. Some scholars think he had no connection and that he used independent sources (see for example C. H. Dodd, *Historical*, part 1a; R. E. Brown, *Gospel*, xlvi; and Lindars, *Gospel*, 25–28). Others suppose that he knew and used Mark, Luke, or all of the Synoptics (see for example C. K. Barrett, *Gospel*, 15–21, and F. Neirynck, *John*). My own view is that John knew at least Mark but had a number of his own traditions and deliberately chose to write his Gospel quite differently. For this reason, I shall not discuss Johannine redaction of Mark, though similarities with Mark's portrayal of "the high priest" will be noted where appropriate.
3. Compare, for example, Prov 8:23–36; Wis 7.22–8.1; 9.1–10.
4. On "the Jews" in John, see U. C. von Wahlde, "Johannine," and J. D. Crossan, "Anti-Semitism," 193–99 (both of whom regard "the Jews" within the text as Jewish leaders), and the range of views put forward by R. A. Culpepper, S. Motyer, J. Lieu, and A. Reinhartz, in R. Bieringer, D. Pollefeyt, and F. Vendecasteele-Vanneuville, eds., *Anti-Judaism*.
5. On the relationship between John's Gospel and Judaism, see J. D. G. Dunn, "Anti-Semitism"; D. Moody Smith, *Theology*, 48–56; A. F. Segal, *Rebecca's*, 156–58; P. Tomson, "*If This Be*," 290–332; W. A. Meeks, "Breaking"; S. Freyne, "Vilifying"; and the essays in R. Bieringer, D. Pollefeyt, and F. Vendecasteele-Vanneuville, eds., *Anti-Judaism*. Although "the Jews" are cast in a negative role, Israel is used in a positive sense throughout the Gospel: 1:47, 31, 49; 3:10; 12:13 (D. Moody Smith, *Theology*, 89), a feature that supports J. D. G. Dunn's suggestion that John's Gospel reflects a "dispute over the heritage of pre-70 Jewish religion" ("Anti-Semitism," 100).
6. Similarities with the formal setting of Matt 26:1–5 are particularly strong. Yet, as pointed out in the chapter on Matthew, it is unlikely that they shared a common source. Matthew's scene is quite different from John's and contains nothing which could not have been derived from Mark. See above, 192 n. 13.
7. On the historical questions raised by this scene, see above, 70.
8. For my historical reconstruction, see above, 67–72. A similar feature occurs in Matthew, 192 n. 10.
9. The precise meaning of "holy place" is not entirely clear; the Greek has only "place" (*ho topos*), but it is highly likely that it is the temple that is meant (so R. E. Brown, *Gospel*, 439). As Brown points out, 1 John 4:20; Acts 6:13, 7:7; and 2 Macc 5:19 refer to the temple in the same way. Less likely is the suggestion of P. Winter that *topos* is to be translated as "office" or "position" and that Caiaphas

was worried that Rome would take away the rights of individual members of the Sanhedrin to sit in assembly (*Trial*, 39). Some textual variants omit "nation" (*ethnos*) here, but as C. K. Barrett points out, there is no reason to doubt its authenticity (*Gospel*, 407).

10. See the historical discussion on 67–70 above.

11. The expression is used again in 11:51 and 18:13. The explanation offered here goes back as early as Origen and is supported by most major commentators. See, for example, R. E. Brown, *Gospel*, 440; C. K. Barrett, *Gospel*, 406; and B. Lindars, *Gospel*, 406. The designation also serves to distinguish Caiaphas, the actual high priest, from his father-in-law, Annas, who, we shall see, is also referred to as "high priest" in 18:19, 22. C. H. Dodd, however, remains unconvinced: "attempts to evade this implication [that John thought the high priesthood changed annually] I find more ingenious than convincing" ("Prophecy," 141 n. 3).

12. See above, 45. As C. H. Dodd observes, this fact shows that John's Gospel took shape in a circle in which the Jerusalem priesthood still held some of its mystique ("Prophecy," 140).

13. As R. E. Brown notes, "Caiaphas foresees the Roman destruction of the holy place; but he does not foresee that in the new temple that will replace it all the prophetic dreams of the gathering of the nations will be fulfilled" (*Gospel*, 443). The "prophetic dreams" refer to passages such as Isa 2:3, 60:6, and Zech 14:16, which imagine Gentiles coming to God's holy mountain at the end of time. I am also indebted to T. Nicklas, "Prophetie" for some of the ideas in these paragraphs.

14. The Greek word is *aulē*, which can mean either the palace itself or the outer courtyard. Since Peter's betrayals seem to take place outside, "courtyard" seems the best translation here.

15. It is not clear from the Greek whether it is the disciple or the slave girl who leads Peter inside. John is the only evangelist to specify that it was Peter who cut off the ear of the high priest's slave, an addition that adds tension to the narrative, particularly when Peter meets the man's relative in 18:26.

16. 13:23, 19:26, 20:3–10, 21:20–24. F. Neirynck offers a full survey of scholarship on the identity of this figure. Although he favors the Beloved Disciple, he accepts that "in recent studies . . . there is a remarkable evolution and Johannine scholars show a tendency to abandon the traditional identification" ("Other Disciple," 114). The matter is complicated by the fact that the Beloved Disciple is often identified with John Zebedee, and scholars who hold this view find it difficult to imagine a Galilean fisherman on intimate terms with Caiaphas (so C. K. Barrett, *Gospel*, 526, and R. Schnackenburg, *Gospel*, 3:235).

17. This is the conclusion of C. K. Barrett after an examination of the word's usage in the LXX (*Gospel*, 525–26). The constructions are slightly different in the two verses—in v. 15 *gnōstos* is used with a dative, in v. 16 with a genitive—but the meaning seems the same.

18. Nicodemus is referred to as a council member in 7:50; for Joseph of Arimathea, however, we need to turn to Mark 15:43 and Luke 23:50–51. E. A. Tindall suggests Nicodemus ("John xviii.15"), while R. Schnackenburg goes for Joseph of Arimathea, who in 19:38 was described as a "secret" disciple (*Gospel*, 235).

19. For a useful discussion of this whole question, see J. H. Charlesworth, *Beloved*, 336–59. Charlesworth opts for Judas as the most likely candidate here; so too does E. A. Abbott ("Notes") and T. L. Brodie (*Gospel*, 529), who notes that Judas is often grouped with Peter (6:68–71; 13:1–11, 21–30).

20. J. Charlesworth (*Beloved*, 353) comes to a similar answer. R. E. Brown, rather surprisingly, sees no theological significance to this character (*Gospel*, 841).

21. Is there perhaps a deliberate contrast between Jesus' odd declaration in 10:7 and 9 that he is the "door" [NRSV "gate"] (*thura*) through which any who enter will be saved, and the "door" (*thura*) in 18:16?

22. Peter is, of course, reinstated after the death of Jesus when he runs to the empty tomb with "the other disciple" (here, the Beloved Disciple), and chapter 21 (which most scholars consider an addition) clearly allows him to atone for his threefold denial (21:15–19). Yet John's omission of any immediate repentance in 18:27 is striking.

23. See R. E. Brown, "Incidents," 149–52. More generally, see A. E. Harvey, *Jesus*, and A. T. Lincoln, "Trials."

24. Although Jesus is taken away from Caiaphas's palace in v. 28, it is not entirely clear where John thinks the earlier hearing before Annas took place. Does he imagine Jesus was first taken to Annas' residence? Or does he think they live in the same place?

25. R. Schnackenburg, *Gospel*, 236.

26. E. Haenchen, *John*, 168.

27. On this scene, see R. E. Brown, *Gospel*, 817–36; F. J. Matera, "Jesus"; R. L. Brodie, *Gospel*, 530–31; I. de la Potterie, *Hour*, 62–79; E. Haenchen, *John*, 168–69; J. Lieu, "Temple"; and, esp. B. Escaffre, "Pierre," 52–54, 58–61, 63–67. The ideas in the following paragraphs owe a great deal to these studies.

28. For a similar use in Luke, see 112.

29. The following put v. 24 after v. 13: an early twefth-century MS known as 1195, the margin of the Harclean Syriac, codex A of the Palestinian Syriac lectionary, and Cyril of Alexandria. All, however, repeat v. 24 again in its present place. A later twelfth-century MS known as 225 brings v. 24 into the middle of v. 13. Another manuscript (the Sinaitic Syriac) is even bolder and changes the order of the text quite radically, so that it reads: v. 13 (Jesus taken to Annas), v. 24 (Jesus taken to Caiaphas), vv. 14–15 (notes on Caiaphas and Peter's entry to the high priest's palace), vv. 19–23 (interrogation by the high priest Caiaphas), and vv. 16–18, 25–27 (Peter's denial). Martin Luther also—quite independently—proposed a similar order. For discussion of the MS evidence here, see B. M. Metzger, *Textual*, 251–52. Metzger himself, along with the committee that published the third edition of the UBS Greek text, is certain that none of these emendations is original. All seem to be trying to correct what appeared to them to be an error in the account.

    In a similar vein, P. Winter argued that the source behind John 18:12–28a referred only to Annas, and that the references to Caiaphas in vv. 13b, 14, and 24 were inserted (either by the evangelist or an "ecclesiastical redactor") as a "correction," and that in v. 28a Caiaphas was substituted for Annas. The reference to Caiaphas in 11:47–53 is also, he claims, a secondary insertion (*Trial*, 35–38; see also W. Grundmann, "Decision," 303–4). This is all part of Winter's attempt to suggest that the name of the high priest was not passed down among the early Christians, a fact that, for Winter, proves the high priest had little part in the proceedings against Jesus (39). See further above, 187 n. 7.

30. Scholars who see the high priest here as Annas include R. E. Brown, *Gospel*, 820–21; G. R. Beasley-Murray, *John*, 323–24; D. A. Carson, *Gospel*, 581; T. L. Brodie, *Gospel*, 529; C. H. Dodd, *Fourth*, 235; and R. Schnackenburg, *Gospel*, 3:236. Those who see him as Caiaphas include G. H. C. MacGregor, *Gospel*, 327–29; B. F. Westcott, *Gospel*, 257; J. Schneider, "Komposition"; and D. F. Strauss, who took the verb in v. 24 as a pluperfect (rather than an aorist) and so translated the phrase parenthetically as "Annas had sent Jesus to Caiaphas," that is, before the events recounted in vv. 19–23 (noted by R. E. Brown, *Gospel*, 827)—a strategy also adopted by the AV. Noting the "impossibility of combin-

ing the statements made about the high priest," C. K. Barrett also tentatively identifies Jesus' interrogator with Caiaphas (*Gospel*, 523–25).

31. The first was the conclusion of R. Bultmann, *Gospel*, 643; the second has been the verdict of a number of scholars; see, for example, C. H. Dodd, *Historical*, 93–94.

32. See B. Escaffre ("Pierre," 58–61), who makes a similar case.

33. Isa 45:19; Prov 8:2–3, 9:3; Wis 6:14, 16.

34. This is noted by T. L. Brodie, *Gospel*, 529.

35. See above, 45.

36. This idea is developed in 1 John 2:1; see also Rom 8:34 and Heb 8–10.

37. Similar ideas can be found in Heb 2:11 and 10:10 (a document in which Jesus' high-priestly identity is explicit; see above, 127).

38. See above, 45. The Greek version of both Exod 38:4 and Lev 16:4 use the same word as John (*chitōn*) to refer to the high priest's robe. John's reference to the robe here should not surprise us—Jewish writers were quick to see allegorical significance in the high-priestly robes (see above, 172 n. 12). Interestingly, in what is probably no more than a parallel development, Philo linked both the seamless robe (*On Flight and Finding* 110–12) and the high priesthood (*On the Giants* 52, and *On the Migration of Abraham* 102) with the Logos (John 1:1). R. E. Brown (*Gospel*, 920–22), C. K. Barrett (*Gospel*, 550), and J. Gnilka ("Erwartung," 423) are open to the possibility that the high-priestly robes are referred to here; B. Lindars, however, rejects the suggestion, on the grounds that Jesus has nowhere else been identified with the high priest in John (*Gospel*, 577–78). It is my contention that this identification lies behind the interrogation of 18:19–23.

39. On Jesus as the high priest in John, see O. Cullmann, *Christology*, 105–6; R. Longenecker, 114; O. Moe, "Priestertum," col. 338; and J. Gnilka, "Erwartung," 421–25. W. H. Brownlee goes much further: drawing on the Messiah of Aaron at Qumran, who presides over the eschatological banquet, he suggests that when Jesus provides wine for the wedding at Cana, he is substituting for the bridegroom whose resources have been exhausted and so shows himself to be the true bridegroom, the priestly Messiah. Furthermore, the priestly Messiah was expected to be particularly active at holy seasons, and, as Brownlee notes, it is preeminently at these times that Jesus reveals himself in his messianic mission, "Messianic," 206.

40. For a fuller discussion of this scene, see my *Pontius*, 166–93.

41. C. K. Barrett opts for Judas here (*Gospel*, 543). Caiaphas is preferred by R. E. Brown, *Gospel*, 568–69; C. H. Dodd, *Historical*, 107; and G. H. C. MacGregor, *Gospel*, 341. R. Bultmann (*Gospel*, 662 n. 6) and B. Lindars (*Gospel*, 569) take the singular participle as "the Jews" generally.

42. W. A. Meeks, *Prophet*, 77; E. P. Sanders, *Judaism*, 135.

Appendix B: High Priests of Judea

1. On the house of Boethus, see E. M. Smallwood, "High Priests," 32–34.

2. Joazar seems to have been reappointed some time later since he was overpowered by a popular faction and deposed by Quirinius in 6 C.E. (*Antiq* 18.27).

3. On the possible relationships between Simon Cantheras, Elionaeus b. Cantheras, and the house of Boethus, see 164 n. 3.

4. Ananias is usually thought to have continued as high priest until 60 C.E., despite being sent in chains to Rome in 49 (*War* 2.243, *Antiq* 20.131). D. R. Schwartz, however, argues persuasively that Ishmael was appointed in the spring of 49 (*Studies*, 218–42).

Appendix C: Was Caiaphas a Zadokite??

1. See, for example, J. Le Moyne, *Sadducéens*, 63–67, 387–99; R. Meyer, "Saddoukaîos," 35–54; G. Baumbach, "Sadducees," and, more cautiously, J. P. Meier, *Marginal*, 3:447–48 n.16.
2. See, for example, P. Gaechter, "Hatred," 3-6; M. Goodman, *Ruling*; and the standard works of E. Schürer, *Jesus*, 1:297; J. Jeremias, *Jerusalem*, 181–82; M. Stern, "Aspects," 2:565; and E. P. Sanders, *Judaism*, 26.
3. See, for example, J. D. Crossan, *Who Killed?* 52–53, and C. Thoma, "High Priesthood."
4. Translated by H. St. John Thackeray, *Josephus, LCL III*, 45–49.
5. This is acknowleged by E. P. Sanders, *Judaism*, 26, and J. Jeremias, *Jerusalem*, 193. M. Parah 3.5 refers to Ananel as an "Egyptian," which suggests to R. Meyer that he was a Zadokite priest from Leontopolis in Egypt, "Saddoukaîos," 45.
6. This is suggested by R. Meyer, " Saddoukaîos," 45; and G. Baumbach, "Sadducees," 183.
7. On Roman practice in these matters, see M. Goodman, *Ruling*, 109–16.

Appendix D. The Location of Caiaphas's Palace

1. Discussions of the location of Caiaphas's palace are found in J. Finegan, *Archaeology*, 242–45; G. H. Dalman, *Sacred*, 328–31; W. Sanday, *Sacred*, 54 n. 2, 87–88; P. W. L. Walker, *Holy*, 289–93; and J. Wilkinson, *Egeria's* and "Christian." References to the texts mentioned here can be readily found in most of these works. On the Madaba Map, see H. Donner, *Mosaic*, and for pilgrimage in medieval times, H. F. M. Prescott, *Jerusalem*.
2. *Topography*, 40–45; translated by F. E. Peters, *Jerusalem*, 157.
3. For details of these excavations, see J. Gerner-Durand, "Maison," and E. Power, "Church" and "House."
4. L. H. Vincent, "Saint-Pierre."
5. For details of these excavations, see M. Broshi, "Excavations."
6. M. Broshi, "Excavations," 58; N. Avigad, *Discovering*, 150. One of the difficulties here is that we do not know how strict first-century Jews were in keeping the commandment against graven images. Images set up by pagans and/or used in religious contexts would certainly cause offense. But decorative images of natural scenes may have been perfectly acceptable to many—even the Jerusalem temple contained representatives of cherubim, and the temple tax was payable in Tyrian shekels with images of the god Melkart and an eagle. On the other hand, Herod Antipas's palace in Tiberias was destroyed early in the Jewish revolt, supposedly because it contained decorative animal scenes (Josephus, *Life* 64–67). See discussion in E. P. Sanders, *Judaism*, 242–47.
7. Eusebius, *Hist. eccl.* 3.5.2–5.
8. A similar skepticism is shared by the following: J. J. Rousseau and R. Arav, *Jesus*, 136–39; G. H. Dalman, *Sacred*, 330; R. E. Brown, *Gospel*, 823; and P. W. L. Walker, *Holy*, 290–92. The last notes the strange silence of the Caesarean Eusebius, who although he refers four times to Jesus' trial before Caiaphas, never indicates that he knew the site. As Walker notes, this *could* point to a certain degree of skepticism concerning the site. J. Murphy O'Connor, however, writing about the Cenacle (the location of the Upper Room), is more trusting of the ancient sources and suggests ways in which an unbroken tradition might have been passed down within early Christian circles ("Cenacle").

Bibliography

Abbot, E. A. Referred to under "Notes of Recent Exposition." *Expository Times* 25 (1913/14): 149–50.

Abbott, G. F. "The Report and Death of Pilate." *JTS* 4 (1903): 83–86.

Alexander, P. S. "'The Parting of the Ways' from the Perspective of Rabbinic Judaism." In *Christians and Jews*, edited by J. D. G. Dunn, 1–25.

Alexander, P. S. "Rabbinic Judaism and the New Testament." *ZNW* 74 (1983): 237–46.

Allison, D. C., Jr. "The Continuity between John and Jesus." *JSHJ* 1 (2003): 6–27.

Applebaum, S. "The Legal Status of the Jewish Communities in the Diaspora." In *The Jewish People in the First Century*, edited by S. Safrai and M. Stern, 1:420–63.

Avigad, N. "The Architecture of Jerusalem in the Second Temple Period." In *Jerusalem Revealed*, edited by Y. Yadin, 14–20.

———. *Discovering Jerusalem*. Oxford: Blackwell, 1984. (Hebrew original, 1980.)

Avi-Yonah, M. "Jerusalem of the Second Temple Period." In *Jerusalem Revealed*, edited by Y. Yadin, 9–13.

Avni, G., Z. Greenhut, and T. Ilan. "Three New Burial Caves of the Second Temple Period in Aceldama (Kidron Valley)." In *Ancient Jerusalem Revealed*, edited by H. Geva, 206–18. Jerusalem: Israel Exploration Society, 1994.

Bahat, D., and M. Broshi. "Excavations in the Armenian Garden." In *Jerusalem Revealed*, edited by Y. Yadin, 55–56.

Bammel, E. "A New Variant Form of the *Testimonium Flavianum*." *Expository Times* 85 (1973/74): 145–47.

―――. "The Revolution Theory from Reimarus to Brandon." In *Jesus and the Politics*, edited by E. Bammel and C. F. D. Moule, 11–68.

―――. "Jewish Activity against Christians in Palestine according to Acts." In *The Book of Acts in Its First Century Setting*, edited by R. Bauckham, 357–64.

―――. "The Eyewitnesses and the Gospel Traditions." *JSHJ* 1 (2003): 28–60.

Bammel, E., and C. F. D. Moule, eds. *Jesus and the Politics of His Day*. Cambridge: CUP, 1984.

Barag, D. "The Temple Cult Vessels Graffito from the Jewish Quarter Excavations at Jerusalem." In *Ancient Jerusalem Revealed*, edited by H. Geva, 277–78.

Barag, D., and D. Flusser. "The Ossuary of Yehohanah Granddaughter of the High Priest Theophilus." *IEJ* 36 (1986): 39–44.

Barker, M. *The Gate of Heaven: The History and Symbolism of the Temple in Jerusalem*. London: SPCK, 1991.

Barnett, P. W. "Under Tiberius All Was Quiet." *NTS* 21 (1975): 564–71.

Barrett, C. K. *The Gospel according to St John*. 2d ed. London: SPCK, 1978.

―――. *The Acts of the Apostles*. International Critical Commentary. Vol. 1. Edinburgh: T. & T. Clark, 1994.

Bauckham, R. "Jesus' Demonstration in the Temple." In *Law and Religion: Essays on the Place of the Law in Israel and Early Christianity*, edited by B. Lindars. Cambridge: James Clarke & Co., 1988.

―――. "The Parting of the Ways: What Happened and Why?" *ST* 47 (1993): 135–51.

―――. "James and the Jerusalem Church." In *The Book of Acts in Its First Century Setting*, edited by R. Bauckham, 415–80.

―――. "Nicodemus and the Gurion Family." *JTS* 47 (1996): 1–37.

―――. "Josephus' Account of the Temple in Contra Apionem 2.102–9." In *Josephus' Contra Apionem: Studies in Its Character and Context with a Latin Concordance to the Portion Missing in Greek*, edited by L. H. Feldman and J. R. Levison, 327–47. Leiden: E. J. Brill, 1996.

Bauckham, R., ed. *The Book of Acts in Its First Century Setting*. Vol. 4: *Palestinian Setting*. Carlisle: Paternoster, 1995.

Bauer, D. R. "The Major Characters of Matthew's Story: Their Function and Significance." *Interpretation* 46 (1992): 357–67.

Baumbach, G. "The Sadducees in Josephus." In *Josephus, the Bible, and History*, edited by L. H. Feldman and G. Hata, 173–95.

Baumgarten, J. M. *Studies in Qumran Law*. Leiden: E. J. Brill, 1977.

Beadle, R., and P. King, eds. *York Mystery Plays*. Oxford: Clarendon Press, 1984.

Beard, M., J. North, and S. Price. *Religions of Rome*. Vol. 1: *A History*. Cambridge: CUP, 1998.

Beasley-Murray, G. R. *John*. Waco, Tex.: Word Books, 1987.

Best, E. *The Temptation and the Passion: The Markan Soteriology*. Cambridge: CUP, 1965.

―――. *Mark: The Gospel as Story*. Edinburgh: T. & T. Clark, 1983.

Bieringer, R., D. Pollefeyt, and F. Vandecasteele-Vanneuville, eds. *Anti-Judaism and the Fourth Gospel*. Louisville, Ky.: Westminster John Knox Press, 2001.

Beutler, J. "Two Ways of Gathering: The Plot to Kill Jesus in John 11.47–53." *NTS* 40 (1994): 399–406.

Bilde, P. *Flavius Josephus between Jerusalem and Rome: His Life, His Works, and Their Importance*. Sheffield: JSOT Press, 1988.

Blass, F., and A. Debrunner. *Greek Grammar of the New Testament and Other Early Christian Literature*, translated and revised by R. W. Funk. Chicago: Chicago University Press, 1961.

Blinzler, J. "Rechtsgeschichtliches zur Hinrichtung des Zebedaiden Jakobus." *NT* 5 (1962): 191–206.

Bock, D. L. *Blasphemy and Exaltation in Judaism and the Final Examination of Jesus: A*

Philological-Historical Study of the Key Jewish Themes Impacting Mark 14.61–64. Tübingen: Mohr Siebeck, 1998.

———. *Luke 9:51–24:53.* Baker Exegetical Commentary on the New Testament. Grand Rapids: Baker Books, 1996.

Bond, H. K. "The Coins of Pontius Pilate: Part of an Attempt to Provoke the People or to Integrate Them into the Empire?" *JSJ* 27 (1996): 242–62.

———. *Pontius Pilate in History and Interpretation.* Cambridge: CUP, 1998.

———. "New Currents in Josephus Research." *Currents in Research: Biblical Studies* 8 (2000): 162–90.

———. "Caiaphas: Reflections on a Jewish High Priest." *Expository Times* 113 (2002): 183–87.

Borg, M. J. *Jesus A New Vision: Spirit, Culture, and the Life of Discipleship.* San Francisco: HarperSanFrancisco, 1987.

Borland, A. *Personalities at the Crucifixion.* London: Pickering & Inglis, 1969.

Brandon, S. G. F. *Jesus and the Zealots: A Study of the Political Factor in Primitive Christianity.* Manchester: Manchester University Press, 1967.

———. *The Trial of Jesus of Nazareth.* London: B. T. Batsford, 1968.

Brawley, R. L. *Luke-Acts and the Jews: Conflict, Apology, and Conciliation.* Atlanta: Scholars Press, 1987.

Brody, R. "Caiaphas and Cantheras." In *Agrippa I,* D. R. Schwartz, 190–95.

Brodie, T. L. *The Gospel according to John: A Literary and Theological Commentary.* Oxford: OUP, 1993.

Broshi, M. "Excavations in the House of Caiaphas, Mount Zion." In *Jerusalem Revealed,* edited by Y. Yadin, 57–60.

———. "Jewish Jerusalem: A Quarter Century of Archaeological Research." *Israel Museum Journal* 7 (1988): 13–23.

Brown, R. E. "Incidents that Are Units in the Synoptic Gospels but Dispersed in St John." *CBQ* 23 (1961): 143–52.

———. *The Gospel according to John I–XII.* New York: Doubleday, 1966.

———. *The Gospel according to John XIII–XXI.* New York: Doubleday, 1970.

———. "The Gospel of Peter and Canonical Gospel Priority." *NTS* 33 (1987): 321–43.

———. *The Death of the Messiah: From Gethsemane to the Grave. A Commentary on the Passion Narrative in the Four Gospels.* 2 vols. New York: Doubleday, 1994.

———. "The Babylonian Talmud on the Execution of Jesus." *NTS* 43 (1997): 158–59.

———. *Introduction to the New Testament.* New York: Doubleday, 1997.

Brown, R. E., and J. P. Meier. *Antioch and Rome: New Testament Cradles of Catholic Christianity.* London: Chapman, 1983.

Brownlee, W. H. "Messianic Motifs of Qumran and the New Testament." *NTS* 3 (1957): 195–210.

Bruce, F. F. *The Acts of the Apostles: The Greek Text with Introduction and Commentary.* 3d ed. Grand Rapids: Eerdmans, 1990.

Brunt, P. A. "Josephus on Social Conflict in Roman Judaea." *Klio* 59 (1977): 149–53.

Buck, E. "Anti-Judaic Sentiments in the Passion Narrative according to Matthew." In *Anti-Judaism in Early Christianity,* edited by P. Richardson and D. Granskou, 1:165–80.

Bultmann, R. *The History of the Synoptic Tradition.* ET. Oxford: Blackwell, 1963.

———. *The Gospel of John.* ET. Philadelphia: Westminster Press, 1971.

Carleton Paget, J. "Some Observations on Josephus and Christianity." *JTS* 52 (2001): 539–624.

Carr, W. "The Rulers of This Age—1 Corinthians II.6–8." *NTS* 23 (1976/77): 20–35.

Carroll, J. T., and J. B. Green. *The Death of Jesus in Early Christianity.* Peabody, Mass.: Hendrickson, 1995.

Carson, D. A. *The Gospel according to John.* Grand Rapids: Eerdmans, 1991.

Cassidy, R. J. *Society and Politics in the Acts of the Apostles.* Maryknoll, N.Y.: Orbis, 1987.

Catchpole, D. R. "The Answer of Jesus to Caiaphas (MATT. XXVI. 64)." *NTS* 17 (1976/77): 213–26.

Charlesworth, J. H., ed. *The Beloved Disciple: Whose Witness Validates the Gospel of John?* Valley Forge, Pa.: Trinity, 1995.

———. *The Old Testament Pseudepigrapha.* 2 vols. New York: Doubleday, 1985.

Chilton, B. "Caiaphas." *ABD* 1:803–06.

Chilton, B. "James in Relation to Peter, Paul, and the Remembrance of Jesus." In *The Brother of Jesus: James the Just and His Mission,* edited by B. Chilton and J. Neusner, 138–60. Louisville: Westminster John Knox, 2001.

Chilton, B. *A Galilean Rabbi and His Bible: Jesus' Own Interpretation of Isaiah.* London: SPCK, 1984.

———. "Annas." *ABD* 1:257–58.

Chilton, B., and C. A. Evans, eds. *Jesus in Context.* Leiden: E. J. Brill, 1997.

———, eds. *Studying the Historical Jesus: Evaluations of the State of Current Research.* Leiden: E. J. Brill, 1994.

Cohen, S. J. D. *Josephus in Galilee and Rome: His Vita and Development as a Historian.* Leiden: E. J. Brill, 1979.

———. *From the Maccabees to the Mishnah.* Philadelphia: Westminster Press, 1987.

———. *The Beginnings of Jewishness: Boundaries, Varieties, Uncertainties.* Berkeley: University of California Press, 1999.

Cohn, H. *The Trial and Death of Jesus.* London: Weidenfeld & Nicolson, 1967.

Cohn-Sherbok, D. *The Jewish Messiah.* Edinburgh: T. & T. Clark, 1997.

Collins, A. Y. "The Genre of the Passion Narrative." *ST* 47 (1993): 3–28.

Collins, J. J. *Sibylline Oracles* (translation and introduction) in *Pseudepigrapha,* edited by J.H. Charlesworth. 1:317–472.

Collins, R. F. "From John to the Beloved Disciple: An Essay on Johannine Characters." *Interpretation* 49 (1995): 359–69.

Colson, F. H., translator. *Philo: The Embassy to Gaius. LCL* vol. X, London: Heinemann, 1962.

Conzelmann, H. *Acts of the Apostles.* German, 1972. ET. Philadelphia: Fortress, 1987.

Cook, M. J. *Mark's Treatment of the Jewish Leaders.* Leiden: E. J. Brill, 1978.

Crossan, J. D. "Anti-Semitism and the Gospel." *Theological Studies* 26 (1965): 189–214.

———. *Birth of Christianity: Discovering what Happened in the Years Immediately after the Execution of Jesus.* Edinburgh: T. & T. Clark, 1999.

———. *Cross that Spoke: The Origins of the Passion Narrative.* San Francisco: Harper & Row, 1988.

———. *Historical Jesus: The Life of a Mediterranean Jewish Peasant.* San Francisco: HarperSanFrancisco, 1991.

———. *Jesus: A Revolutionary Biography.* San Francisco: HarperSanFrancisco, 1994.

———. *Who Killed Jesus? Exposing the Roots of Anti-Semitism in the Gospel Story of the Death of Jesus.* San Francisco: HarperSanFrancisco, 1996.

Cullmann, O. *The Christology of the New Testament.* 2d ed. London: SCM, 1963.

Dalman, G. H. *Sacred Sites and Ways: Studies in the Topography of the Gospels,* translated by P. P. Levertoff. London: SPCK, 1935.

Davies, W. D., and D. C. Allison. *A Critical and Exegetical Commentary on the Gospel according to Saint Matthew.* Edinburgh: T. & T. Clark, 1988–1997.

De Jonge, M., and A. S. van der Woude. "11Q Melchizidek and the New Testament." *NTS* 12 (1965/66): 301–26.

De Laet, S. L. "Le Successeur de Ponce-Pilate." *Antiquité Classique* 8 (1939): 413–19.

De La Potterie, I. *The Hour of Jesus. The Passion and Resurrection of Jesus according to John: Text and Spirit.* ET. Slough: Middlegreen Publications, 1989.

Derrett, J. D. M. "The Zeal of the House and the Cleansing of the Temple." *Downside Review* 95 (1977): 79–94.

Dibelius, M. *Studies in the Acts of the Apostles*. London: SCM, 1956.

Dodd, C. H. *The Fourth Gospel*. Cambridge: CUP, 1953.

———. *Historical Tradition in the Fourth Gospel*. Cambridge: CUP, 1963.

———. "The Prophecy of Caiaphas (John xi 47–53)." In *Neotestamentica et Patristica*, 134–43. Leiden: E. J. Brill, 1962.

Domeris, W. R., and S. M. S. Long. "The Recently Excavated Tomb of Joseph Bar Caiapha and the Biblical Caiaphas." *Journal of Theology for Southern Africa* 89 (1994): 50–58.

Donfried, K. P. "1 Thessalonians 2.13–16 as a Test Case." *Interpretation* 38 (1984): 242–53.

Donner, H. *The Mosaic Map of Madaba*. Kampen: Kok Pharos, 1992.

Dostoevsky, F. *A Raw Youth*, translated by C. Garnett. London: Heinemann, 1916.

———. *The Notebooks for The Brothers Karamazov*, edited and translated by E. Wasiolek. Chicago: University of Chicago Press, 1971.

Dubarle, A. M. "Le témoignage de Josèphe sur Jésus d'après la tradition indirecte." *RB* 80 (1973): 481–513.

Duerksen, P. D. "Images of Jesus Christ as Perfect High Priest for God's People." *Quarterley Review* 14 (1994): 321–36.

Dunn, J. D. G. *The Acts of the Apostles*. London: Epworth, 1996.

———. *Christology in the Making: An Inquiry into the Origins of the Doctrine of the Incarnation*. 2d ed. London: SCM, 1989.

———. "The Question of Anti-Semitism in the New Testament Writings of the Period." In *Jews and Christians*, edited by J. D. G. Dunn, 177–211.

———. *The Partings of the Ways: Between Christianity and Judaism and their Significance for the Character of Christianity*. London: SCM, 1991.

———, ed. *Jews and Christians: The Parting of the Ways A.D. 70–135*. Tübingen: J. C. B. Mohr (Paul Siebeck), 1992.

Dupont, J. *The Sources of Acts: The Present Position*. London: Darton, Longman, and Todd, 1964.

Edwards, D. "The Socio-Economic and Cultural Ethos of the Lower Galilee in the First Century: Implications for the Nascent Jesus Movement." In *Galilee*, edited by L. I. Levine, 53–73.

Eisler, R. *The Messiah Jesus and John the Baptist*. London: Methuen, 1931.

Elliot, J. K., ed. *The Apocryphal Jesus: Legends of the Early Church*. Oxford: OUP, 1996.

———, ed. *The Apocryphal New Testament*. Oxford: Clarendon, 1993.

Engle, A. "An Amphorisk of the Second Temple Period." *PEQ* 109 (1977): 117–22.

Eppstein, V. "The Historicity of the Gospel Account of the Cleansing of the Temple." *ZNW* 55 (1964): 42–58.

Escaffre, B. "Pierre et Jesus dans la cour du grand prêtre (Jn 18, 12–27)." *RTL* 31 (2000): 43–67.

Evans, C. A. "Jesus' Action in the Temple: Cleansing or Portent of Destruction?" In *Jesus in Context*, edited by B. Chilton and C. A. Evans, 395–439.

Feldman, L. H. "Josephus." *ABD* 3: 981–98.

Feldman, L. H., and G. Hata, eds. *Josephus, Judaism, and Christianity*. Leiden: E. J. Brill, 1987.

Feldman, L. H., R. Marcus, and R. Wikgreen, translators. *Josephus: Jewish Antiquities*. LCL vols. IV–IX. London: Heinemann, 1930–65.

Fiensy, D. A. *Prayers Alleged to be Jewish: An Examination of the Constitutiones Apostolorum*. Chico, Calif.: Scholars Press, 1985.

———. "The Composition of the Jerusalem Church." In *The Book of Acts in Its First Century Setting*, edited by R. Bauckham, 213–236.

Finegan, J. *The Archaeology of the New Testament: The Life of Jesus and the Beginning of the Early Church*. Revised edition. Princeton: Princeton University Press, 1992.

Fitzmyer, J. A. "Further Light on Melchizedek from Qumran." *JBL* 86 (1967): 25–41.

————. *The Gospel according to Luke (X–XXIV)*. Introduction, translation, and notes. New York: Doubleday, 1985.

Flusser, D. ". . . To Bury Caiaphas, Not to Praise Him." *Jerusalem Perspective* 4 (1991): 23–28.

————. "Caiaphas in the New Testament." *'Atiqot* 21 (1992): 81–87.

Frank, G. "Popular Iconography of the Passion." *Publications of the Modern Language Association* 46 (1931): 333–40.

Fredriksen, P. *From Jesus to Christ: The Origins of the New Testament Images of Jesus*. New Haven: Yale University Press, 1988.

————. *Jesus of Nazareth: King of the Jews*. New York: Vintage Books, 1999.

Freyne, S. "Galilee-Jerusalem Relations according to Josephus' *Life*." *NTS* 33 (1987): 600–609.

————. "Vilifying the Other and Defining the Self: Matthew's and John's Anti-Jewish Polemic in Focus." In *To See Ourselves as Others See Us*, edited by J. Neusner and E. S. Frerichs, 117–43.

Friedrich, G. "Beobachtungen zur messianischen Hohepriestererwartung in den Synoptikern." *ZTK* 53 (1956): 265–311.

Gaechter, P. "The Hatred of the House of Annas." *Theological Studies* 8 (1947): 3–34.

Gardner, J. F., and T. Wiedemann. *The Roman Household: A Sourcebook*. London, New York: Routledge, 1991.

Garnsey, P., and G. Woolf. "Patronage of the Rural Poor in the Roman World." In *Patronage in Ancient Society*, edited by A. Wallace-Hadrill, 153–70. London: Routledge, 1989.

George, A. "Israël dans l'œuvre de Luc." *RB* 75 (1968): 481–525.

Gerner-Durand, J. "La Maison de Caïphe et l'Église Saint-Pierre a Jérusalem." *RB* 23 (1914): 71–94, 222–46.

Geva, H., ed. *Ancient Jerusalem Revealed*. Jerusalem: Israel Exploration Society, 1994.

Glasson, T. F. "The Reply to Caiaphas (Mark XIV. 62)." *NTS* 7 (1960/61): 88–93.

Gnilka, J. "Die Erwartung des Messianischen Hohenpriesters in den Schriften von Qumran und im Neuen Testament." *RevQ* 2 (1960): 395–426.

Goldstein, J. A. *1 Maccabees: A New Translation with Introduction and Commentary*. New York: Doubleday, 1976.

Goodacre, M. "Prophecy Historicized or History Scripturized? Reflections on the Origin of the Crucifixion Narrative." Paper given at the British New Testament Conference (Jesus Seminar), 2001.

Goodblatt, D. *The Monarchic Principle: Studies in Jewish Self-Government in Antiquity*. Tübingen: J. C. B. Mohr (Paul Siebeck), 1994.

————. "Judaean Nationalism in the Light of the Dead Sea Scrolls." In *Historical Perspectives from the Hasmonaeans to Bar Kockba in Light of the Dead Sea Scrolls*, edited by D. Goodblatt, A. Pinnick, and D. R. Schwartz, 3–27. Leiden: Brill, 2001.

————. "The Babylonian Talmud." *ANRW* 2/19/2, 259–336.

Goodman, M. *The Ruling Class of Judaea*. Cambridge: CUP, 1987.

————. "Diaspora Reactions to the Destruction of the Temple." In *Jews and Christians*, edited by J. D. G. Dunn, 27–38.

Gough, M. *The Early Christians*. London: Thames & Hudson, 1961.

Grabar, A. *The Beginnings of Christian Art: 200–395 A.D.* London: Thames & Hudson, 1967.

Grabbe, L. *An Introduction to First Century Judaism*. Edinburgh: T. & T. Clark, 1996.

Gray, R. *Prophetic Figures in Late Second Temple Jewish Palestine: The Evidence from Josephus*. Oxford: OUP, 1993.

Green, J. B. "The Demise of the Temple as Culture Centre in Luke–Acts: An Exploration of the Rending of the Temple Veil (Luke 22.44–49)." *RB* 101 (1994): 495–515.

————. *The Theology of the Gospel of Luke*. Cambridge: CUP, 1995.

Greenhut, Z. "Discovery of the Caiaphas Family Tomb." *Jerusalem Perspective* 4 (1991): 6–11.

———. "The 'Caiaphas' Tomb in the North of Jerusalem." *'Atiqot 21* (1992): 63–71.

———. "The Caiaphas Tomb in North Talpiot, Jerusalem." In *Ancient Jerusalem Revealed*, edited by H. Geva, 219–22.

Grundmann, W. "The Decision of the Supreme Court to Put Jesus to Death (John 11.47–57) in Its Context: Tradition and Redaction in the Gospel of John." In *Jesus and the Politics*, edited by E. Bammel and C. F. D. Moule, 295–318.

Gundry, R. H. *Mark: A Commentary on His Apology for the Cross.* Grand Rapids: Eerdmans, 1993.

Hachlili, R., and A. Killebrew. "Jewish Funerary Customs during the Second Temple Period, in the Light of the Excavation at the Jericho Necropolis." *PEQ* 115 (1983): 109–39.

———. "Was the Coin-on-Eye Custom a Jewish Burial Practice in the Second Temple Period?" *Biblical Archaeologist* 46 (1983): 147–153.

Haenchen, E. *The Acts of the Apostles: A Commentary.* German, 1965. ET. Oxford: Blackwell, 1971.

———. *John.* Vol. 2. ET. Philadelphia: Fortress, 1984.

Hagedorn, A. C., and J. H. Neyrey. "'It was out of envy that they handed Jesus over' (Mark 15.10): The Anatomy of Envy and the Gospel of Mark." *JSNT* 69 (1998): 15–56.

Hamilton, N. Q. "Temple Cleansing and Temple Bank." *JBL* 88 (1964): 365–72.

Hanson, K. C. "Blood and Purity in Leviticus and Revelation." *Listening: Journal of Religion and Culture* 28 (1993): 215–30.

Hanson, K. C., and D. E. Oakman. *Palestine in the Time of Jesus: Social Structures and Social Conflicts.* Minneapolis: Fortress Press, 1998.

Happe, P. *English Mystery Plays.* London: Penguin, 1975.

Harrington, J. M. *The Lukan Passion Narrative. The Markan Material in Luke 22,54–23,25. A Historical Survey: 1891–1997.* Leiden: E. J. Brill, 2000.

Harris, S. L. *Understanding the Bible.* 5th ed. Mountain View, Calif.: Mayfield, 2000.

Harvey, A. E. *Jesus on Trial: A Study in the Fourth Gospel.* London: SPCK, 1976.

Hayward, C. T. R. *The Jewish Temple: A Non-Biblical Sourcebook.* London: Routledge, 1996.

Heine, R., translator. *Origen, Commentary on the Gospel of John. Books 13–32.* The Fathers of the Church 89. Washington: Catholic University of America Press, 1993.

Hemer, C. J. *The Book of Acts in the Setting of Hellenistic History.* Tübingen: J. C. B. Mohr (Paul Siebeck), 1989.

Hengel, M. *Acts and the History of Earliest Christianity.* London: SCM, 1979.

———. *Between Jesus and Paul: Studies in the Earliest History of Christianity.* London: SCM, 1983.

———. *The Pre-Christian Paul.* London: SCM, 1991.

———. *Property and Riches in the Early Church: Aspects of a Social History of Early Christianity.* London: SCM, 1974.

———. *Studies in the Gospel of Mark.* London: SCM, 1985.

Hengel, M., and R. Deines. "E. P. Sanders' '"Common Judaism," Jesus, and the Pharisees.' A Review Article." *JTS* NS 46 (1995): 1–70.

Herrenbrück, F. "Wer waren die 'Zöllner'?" *ZNW* 72 (1981): 17, 8–94.

———. "Zum des Kollaboration des Zöllners mit Rom." *ZNW* 78 (1987): 186–99.

Higgins, A. J. B. "The Priestly Messiah." *NTS* 13 (1967): 211–39.

Hill, C. C., "Acts 6.1–8.4: Division or Diversity?" In *History, Literature, and Society in the Book of Acts*, edited by B. Witherington, 129–53. Cambridge and New York: Cambridge University Press, 1996.

———. *Hellenists and Hebrews: Reappraising Division within the Earliest Church.* Minneapolis: Fortress Press, 1992.

Hill, G. F. *Catalogue of the Greek Coins of Palestine (Galilee, Samaria, and Judaea)*. London: British Museum, 1914.

Hoehner, H. *Herod Antipas*. Cambridge: CUP, 1972.

Holzmeister, U. "Wann Was Pilatus Prokurator von Judaea?" *Biblica* 13 (1932): 228–32.

Hooker, M. D. *The Gospel according to St Mark*. Black's New Testament Commentaries. London: A. & C. Black, 1991.

Horbury, W. "The 'Caiaphas' Ossuaries and Joseph Caiaphas." *PEQ* 126 (1994): 32–48.

———. "Jewish-Christian Relations in Barnabas and Justin Martyr." In *Jews and Christians*, edited by J. D. G. Dunn, 315–45.

———. *Jewish Messianism and the Cult of Christ*. London: SCM, 1998.

———. "New Wine in Old Skins: IX—The Temple." *Expository Times* 86 (1974): 36–42.

Horsley, R. A. *Archaeology, History, and Society in Galilee: The Social Context of Jesus and the Rabbis*. Valley Forge, Pa.: Trinity Press, 1996.

———. "The Death of Jesus." In *Studying the Historical Jesus*, edited by B. Chilton and C. A. Evans, 395–422.

———. "High Priests and the Politics of Roman Palestine: A Contextual Analysis of the Evidence of Josephus." *JSJ* 17 (1986): 23–55.

———. "Popular Messianic Movements around the Time of Jesus." *CBQ* 46 (1984): 471–95.

———. "Popular Prophetic Movements at the Time of Jesus: Their Principal Features and Social Origins." *JSNT* 26 (1986): 3–27.

Horton, F. L. *The Melchizedek Tradition: A Critical Examination of the Sources to the Fifth Century A.D. and in the Epistle to the Hebrews*. Cambridge: CUP, 1976.

Hurtado, L. W. "A Taxonomy of Recent Historical-Jesus Work." In *Whose Historical Jesus?* W. A. Arnal and M. Desjardins, 272–95. Waterloo, Ontario: Wilfred Laurier University Press, 1997.

Hussey, M. *The Chester Mystery Plays*. London: Heinemann, 1975.

Ilan, T. "Notes on the Distribution of Jewish Women's Names in Palestine in the Second Temple and Mishnaic Periods." *Journal of Jewish Studies* 40 (1989): 191–92.

———. *Jewish Women in Greco-Roman Palestine*. Peabody, Mass.: Hendrickson, 1996.

———. *Integrating Women into Second Temple History*. Texts and Studies in Ancient Judaism 76. Tübingen: J. C. B. Mohr (Paul Siebeck), 1999.

Jaubert, A. *The Date of the Last Supper*. New York: Alba House, 1965.

Jeremias, J. *Jerusalem in the Time of Jesus: An Investigation into Economic and Social Conditions during the New Testament Period*. ET. London: SCM, 1969.

———. *The Eucharistic Words of Jesus*. London: SCM, 1966.

Jervell, J. "The Future of the Past: Luke's Vision of Salvation History and Its Bearing on His Writing of History." In *History, Literature and Society in the Book of Acts*, edited by B. Witherington III, 104–26. Cambridge: CUP, 1996.

Jervell, J. *Theology of the Acts of the Apostles*. Cambridge: CUP, 1996.

Johnson, L. T. "Luke-Acts." *ABD* 4:403–18.

———. *The Real Jesus: The Misguided Quest for the Historical Jesus and the Truth of the Traditional Gospels*. San Francisco: HarperSanFrancisco, 1996.

Juel, D. *Messiah and Temple: The Trial of Jesus in the Gospel of Mark*. SBL Dissertation Series 31. Missoula, Mont.: Scholars Press, 1977.

Karris, R. J. *Luke: Artist and Theologian: Luke's Passion Account as Literature*. New York: Paulist Press, 1985.

Keck, L. E. "The Second Coming of the Liberal Jesus?" *Christian Century* 111/24 (1994): 784–86.

Kee, H. C. *Testament of Levi* (translation and introduction) in *Pseudepigrapha*, edited by J.H. Charlesworth. 1:775–80, 788–95.

Keener, C. S. *Commentary on the Gospel of Matthew*. Grand Rapids: Eerdmans, 1999.

Kingsbury, J. D. *Conflict in Mark: Jesus, Authorities, Disciples*. Minneapolis: Fortress, 1989.

————. "The Plot of Matthew's Story." *Interpretation* 46 (1992): 347–56.

Klausner, J. *The Messianic Idea in Israel: From Its Beginning to the Completion of the Mishnah.* London: George Allen & Unwin, 1956.

Klijn, A. F. J. "Scribes, Pharisees, High Priests, and Elders in the New Testament." *NT* 3 (1959): 259–67.

Kloppenborg, J. S. "The Sayings Gospel Q: Recent Opinion on the People behind the Document." *Currents in Research: Biblical Studies* 1 (1993): 9–34.

Knight, J. *Luke's Gospel.* New Testament Readings. London: Routledge, 1998.

Koester, H. *Ancient Christian Gospels: Their History and Development.* London: SCM, 1990.

Kuhn, K. G. "The Two Messiahs of Aaron and Israel." In *The Scrolls and the New Testament,* edited by K. Stendahl, 54–64. London: SCM, 1958.

Lampe, G. W. H. "A.D. 70 in Christian Reflection." In *Jesus and the Politics,* edited by E. Bammel and C. F. D. Moule, 153–71.

————. "The Trial of Jesus in the *Acta Pilati.*" In *Jesus and the Politics,* edited by E. Bammel and C. F. D. Moule, 173–82.

Larsson, E. "Temple-Criticism and the Jewish Heritage: Some Reflexions on Acts 6–7." *NTS* 39 (1993): 379–95.

Légasse, S. *Trial of Jesus.* London: SCM, 1997.

————. "Paul's Pre-Christian Career according to Acts." In *The Book of Acts in Its First Century Setting,* edited by R. Bauckham, 365–90.

Lémonon, J. P. *Pilate et le gouvernement de la Judée: texts et monuments.* Études bibliques. Paris: Gabalda, 1981.

Le Moyne, J. *Les Sadducéens.* Paris: Gabalda, 1972.

Levine, B. A. "An Essay on Prophetic Attitudes toward Temple and Cult in Biblical Israel." In *Minhah le-Nahum: Biblical and Other Studies Presented to Nahum M. Sarna in Honour of his Seventieth Birthday,* edited by M. Brettler and M. Fishbane, 202–25. Sheffield: JSOT Press, 1993.

Levine, L. I., ed. *The Galilee in Late Antiquity.* New York and Jerusalem: Jewish Theological Seminary of America, 1992.

————. *Judaism and Hellenism in Antiquity: Conflict or Confluence?* Peabody, Mass.: Hendrickson, 1999.

Lietzmann, H., N. A. Bees, and G. Sotiriv. *Die griechisch-christlichen Inschriften des Peleponnes.* Athens, Greece: Christlich-Archäologische Gesellschaft zu Athen, 1941.

Lieu, J. "Temple and Synagogue in John." *NTS* 45 (1999): 51–69.

Lightfoot, R. H. *The Gospel Message of St Mark.* Oxford: Clarendon Press, 1950.

Lincoln, A. T. "Trials, Plots and the Narrative of the Fourth Gospel." *JSNT* 56 (1994): 3–30.

Lindars, B. *The Gospel of John.* London: Oliphants, 1972.

————. *Essays on John,* edited by C. M. Tuckett. Especially "The Passion in the Fourth Gospel," 67–85. Leuven: Leuven University Press, 1992.

Longenecker, R. N. *The Christology of Early Jewish Christianity.* London: SCM, 1970.

Lüdemann, G. *Early Christianity according to the Traditions in Acts: A Commentary.* London: SCM, 1989.

Lührmann, D. "Markus 14.55–64: Christologie und Zerstörung des Tempels im Markusevangelium." *NTS* 27 (1980/81): 457–74.

Luz, U. *The Theology of the Gospel of Matthew.* Cambridge: CUP, 1995.

MacAdam, H. I. "Quid Est Veritas? Pontius Pilate in Fact, Fiction, Film, and Fantasy." *Irish Biblical Studies* 23 (2001): 66–99.

Maccoby, H. *Revolution in Judaea: Jesus and the Jewish Resistance.* New York: Taplinger, 1980.

MacGregor, G. H. C. *The Gospel of John.* London: Hodder & Stoughton, 1928.

Mack, B. L. *A Myth of Innocence: Mark and Christian Origins.* Philadelphia: Fortress, 1988.

Magen, Y. "Jerusalem as a Center of the Stone Vessel Industry during the Second Temple Period." In *Ancient Jerusalem Revealed,* edited by H. Geva, 244–56.

Malbon, E. S. "The Jewish Leaders in the Gospel of Mark: A Literary Study of Marcan Characterization." *JBL* 108 (1989): 259–81.

Malina, B. J. *The New Testament World: Insights from Cultural Anthropology.* 3d ed. Louisville, Ky.: Westminster John Knox, 2001.

Marshall, I. H. *The Gospel of Luke. A Commentary on the Greek Text.* New International Greek Testament Commentary. Exeter: Paternoster, 1978.

Marxsen, W. *Mark the Evangelist.* Nashville: Abingdon, 1969.

Mason, S. N. "Chief Priests, Sadducees, Pharisees, and Sanhedrin in Acts." In *The Book of Acts in its First Century Setting,* edited by R. Bauckham, 115–77.

———. *Josephus and the New Testament.* Peabody, Mass.: Hendrickson, 1992.

———. "Priesthood in Josephus and the 'Pharisaic Revolution.'" *JBL* 107 (1988): 657–61.

Matera, F. J. "The Death of Jesus according to Luke: A Question of Sources." *CBQ* 47 (1985): 469–85.

———. "Luke 22,66–71. Jesus before the ΠΡΕΣΒΥΤΕRION." In *L'Evangile de Luc/The Gospel of Luke,* edited by F. Neirynck, 517–33. Leuven: Leuven University Press, 1989.

———. "Jesus before Annas: John 18.13–14, 19–24." *Ephemerides theologicae lovanienses* 66 (1990): 38–55.

McKelvey, R. J. *The New Temple: The Church in the New Testament.* Oxford: OUP, 1969.

McLaren, J. S. *Power and Politics in Palestine.* Sheffield: Sheffield Academic Press, 1991.

———. "Ananus, James, and Earliest Christianity. Josephus' Account of the Death of James." *JTS* 52 (2001): 1–25.

———. *Turbulent Times? Josephus and Scholarship on Judaea in the First Century C.E.* Sheffield: Sheffield Academic Press, 1998.

Meeks, W. A. "Breaking Away: Three New Testament Pictures of Christianity's Separation from the Jewish Communities." In *To See Ourselves as Others See Us,* edited by J. Neusner and E. S. Frerichs, 93–115.

———. *The Prophet King: Moses Traditions and the Johannine Christology.* Leiden: E. J. Brill, 1967.

Meeks, W. A., and R. L. Wilken, *Jews and Christians in Antioch. In the First Four Centuries of the Common Era.* SBL Sources for Biblical Study 13. Missoula, Mont.: Scholars Press, 1978.

Meier, J. P. "Jesus in Josephus: A Modest Proposal." *CBQ* 52 (1990): 76–103.

———. *A Marginal Jew: Rethinking the Historical Jesus.* Vols 1–3. New York: Doubleday, 1991–2001.

———. "Matthew, Gospel of." *ABD* 4: 622–41.

Merkel, H. "The Opposition between Jesus and Judaism." In *Jesus and the Politics,* edited by E. Bammel and C. F. D. Moule, 129–44.

Metzger, B. M. *A Textual Commentary on the Greek New Testament.* London: United Bible Societies, 1971.

Meyer, R. "Saddoukaîos." *TDNT* 7 (1971): 35–54.

Meyers, C. "Temple, Jerusalem." *ABD* 6:350–69.

Meyers, E. M. "Roman Sepphoris in Light of New Archaeological Evidence and Recent Research." In *Galilee,* edited by L. I. Levine, 321–38.

Millar, F. G. B. "Reflections on the Trials of Jesus." In *A Tribute to Geza Vermes: Essays on Jewish and Christian Literature and History,* edited by P. R. Davies and R. T. White, 355–81. Sheffield: Sheffield Academic Press, 1990.

———. *The Roman Near East, 31 B.C.–A.D. 337.* Cambridge, Mass.: Harvard University Press, 1993.

Mitchell, J. P. "Honour and Shame" and "Patrons and Clients." In *Encyclopaedia of Social and Cultural Anthropology,* edited by A. Barnard and J. Spenser, 280–81, 416–18. London: Routledge, 1996.

Moe, O. "Das Priestertum Christi im NT ausserhalb des Hebraeerbriefs." *TLZ* 72 (1947): cols. 335–38.

Moule, C. F. D. "Sanctuary and Sacrifice in the Church of the New Testament." *JTS* 1 (1950): 29–41.

Murphy O'Connor, J. "The Cenacle—Topographical Setting for Acts 2.44–45." In *The Book of Acts in Its First Century Setting*, edited by R. Bauckham, 303–21.

Myers, C. *Binding the Strong Man: A Political Reading of Mark's Story of Jesus*. Maryknoll, N.Y.: Orbis, 1988.

Naveh, J. "Nameless People." *IEJ* 40 (1990): 108–23.

Neagoe, A. *The Trial of the Gospel: An Apologetic Reading of Luke's Trial Narratives*. Cambridge: CUP, 2002.

Neirynck, F. *John and the Synoptics: 1975–90*. Paper given at the 39th Colloquium Biblicum Lovaniense (1990). Leuven: Leuven University Press, 1992.

———. "'The Other Disciple' in Jn 18.15–16." *Ephemerides theologicae lovanienses* 51 (1975): 113–41.

Neusner, J. *The Mishnah: A New Translation*. New Haven, Conn.: Yale University Press, 1988.

———. *From Politics to Piety: The Emergence of Pharisaic Judaism*. Englewood Cliffs, N.J.: Prentice-Hill, 1973.

Neusner, J., and E. S. Frerichs, eds. *To See Ourselves as Others See Us: Christians, Jews, Others in Late Antiquity*. Chico, Calif.: Scholars Press, 1985.

Nicklas, T. "Die Prophetie de Kajaphas. Im Netz johanneischer Ironie." *NTS* 46 (2000): 589–94.

Nicklesburg, G. W. E., ed. *Studies on the Testament of Moses*. SBL Septuagint and Cognate Studies 4. Cambridge, Mass.: SBL, 1973.

Nineham, D. E. *The Gospel of St Mark*. London: A. & C. Black, 1963.

Nolland, J. *Luke 18.35–24.53*. Word Biblical Commentary 35c. Dallas: Word Books, 1993.

Oegema, G. S. *The Anointed and His People: Messianic Expectations from the Maccabees to Bar Kochba*. Sheffield: Sheffield Academic Press, 1998.

O'Neill, J. C. *The Theology of Acts in Its Historical Setting*. London: SPCK, 1961.

Paffenroth, K. *Judas: Images of the Lost Disciple*. Louisville: Westminster John Knox, 2001.

Parker, P. "John the Son of Zebedee and the Fourth Gospel." *JBL* 81 (1962): 35–43.

Parsons, M. C. "Son and High Priest: A Study in the Christology of Hebrews." *Evangelical Quarterly* 60 (1988): 195–216.

Patrich, J. "The Structure of the Second Temple—A New Reconstruction." In *Ancient Jerusalem Revealed*, edited by H. Geva, 260–71.

Pearson, B. A. "1 Thessalonians 2.13–16: A Deutero-Pauline Interpolation." *HTR* 64 (1971): 79–94.

Peristiany, J.G., ed. *Honour and Shame: The Values of Mediterranean Society*. London: Weidenfeld & Nicolson, 1965.

———, ed. *Mediterranean Family Structures*. Cambridge: CUP, 1976.

Pesch, R. *Das Markusevangelium*. Herders Theologischer Kommentar zum Neuen Testament, vol 2. Freiburg: Herder, 1977.

Peters, F. E. *Jerusalem*. Princeton, N.J.: Princeton University Press, 1985.

Pines, S. *An Arabic Version of the Testimonium Flavianum and Its Implications*. Jerusalem: Israel Academy of Sciences and Humanities, 1971.

Piper, O. A. "God's Good News: The Passion Story according to St Mark." *Interpretation* 9 (1955): 165–82.

Pitt-Rivers, J. "Honour and Social Status." In *Honour and Shame*, edited by J. G. Peristiany, 19–77.

Porton, G. G. "Sadducees." *ABD* 5:892–95.

Powell, M. A. *The Jesus Debate: Modern Historians Investigate the Life of Christ*. Oxford: Lion Publishers, 1998.

Power, E. "The Church of St Peter at Jerusalem. Its Relation to the House of Caiphas and Sancta Sion." *Biblica* 9 (1928): 167–86.

———. "The House of Caiphas and the Church of St Peter." *Biblica* 10 (1929): 275–305, 394–416.

Prescott, H. F. M. *Jerusalem Journey: Pilgrimage to the Holy Land in the Fifteenth Century.* London: Eyre & Spottiswoode, 1954.

Price, J. J. *Jerusalem Under Siege: The Collapse of the Jewish State 66–70 C.E.* Leiden: E. J. Brill, 1992.

Priest, J. *Testament of Moses* (translation and introduction) in *Pseudepigrapha*, edited by J. H. Charlesworth. 1:919–934.

Publications of the Israel Numismatic Society, *The Dating and Meaning of Ancient Jewish Coins.* Numismatic Studies and Researches, vol. 2. Jerusalem: Schocken Publishing House, 1958.

Puech, E. "A-t-on redécouvert le tombeau du grand-prêtre Caïphe?" *Le Monde de la Bible* 80 (1993): 42–47.

Rabin, C., and Y. Yadin. *Scripta Hierosolymitana.* Vol. 4: *Aspects of the Dead Sea Scrolls.* Jerusalem: Hebrew University, 1958.

Rahmani, L. Y. "Ossuaries and Ossilegium (Bone-Gathering) in the Late Second Temple Period." In *Ancient Jerusalem Revealed*, edited by H. Geva, 191–205. Jerusalem: Israel Exploration Society, 1994.

———. *A Catalogue of Jewish Ossuaries in the Collections of the State of Israel.* Jerusalem: Israel Antiquities Authority, 1994.

Rajak, T. *Josephus. The Historian and His Society.* London: Duckworth, 1983.

Rappaport, U. "How Anti-Roman Was the Galilee?" In *Galilee*, edited by L. I. Levine, 95–102.

Reed, J. L. *Archaeology and the Galilean Jesus: A Re-examination of the Evidence.* Harrisburg, Pa.: Trinity Press International, 2000.

Reich, R. "Ossuary Inscriptions from the Caiaphas Tomb." *Jerusalem Perspective* 4 (1991): 13–21.

———. "Ossuary Inscriptions from the 'Caiaphas' Tomb." *'Atiqot* 21 (1992): 72–77.

———. "Ossuary Inscriptions of the Caiaphas Family from Jerusalem." In *Ancient Jerusalem Revealed,* edited by H. Geva, 223–25.

Reicke, B. "Judaeo-Christianity and the Jewish Establishment, A.D. 33–66." In *Jesus and the Politics,* edited by E. Bammel and C. F. D. Moule, 145–52.

Reifenberg, A. *Ancient Jewish Coins.* Jerusalem: Rubin Mass, 1963.

Riesner, R. "Synagogues in Jerusalem." In *The Book of Acts in Its First Century Setting,* edited by R. Bauckham, 179–211.

Rooke, D. W. *Zadok's Heirs: The Role and Development of the High Priesthood in Ancient Israel.* Oxford: OUP, 2000.

Rosenblatt, S. "The Crucifixion of Jesus from the Standpoint of Pharisaic Law." *JBL* 75 (1956): 314–21.

Rousseau, J. J., and R. Arav. *Jesus and His World: An Archaeological and Cultural Dictionary.* London: SCM, 1996.

Safrai, S., and M. Stern, in cooperation with D. Flusser and W. C. van Unnik. *The Jewish People in the First Century: Historical Geography, Political History, Social, Cultural, and Religious Life and Institutions.* I. 1–2. CRINT. Assen: Van Gorcum, 1976.

Safrai, Z. "The Roman Army in the Galilee." In *Galilee*, edited by L. I. Levine, 103–14.

Saldarini, A. J. *Pharisees, Scribes, and Sadducees in Palestinian Society: A Sociological Approach.* Wilmington, Del.: Michael Glazier, 1988.

Sanday, W. *Sacred Sites of the Gospels.* Oxford: Clarendon, 1903.

Sanders, E. P. *The Historical Figure of Jesus.* London: Penguin, 1993.

———. *Jesus and Judaism.* London: SCM, 1985.

————. "Judaism and the Grand 'Christian' Abstractions: Love, Mercy, and Grace." *Interpretation* 39 (1985): 367–68.

————. *Judaism: Practice and Belief 63 B.C.E.—66 C.E.* London: SCM, 1992.

Sanders, J. T. *The Jews in Luke-Acts.* London: SCM, 1987.

Schnackenburg, R. *The Gospel according to St John.* Vol. 3. ET. Kent: Burns & Oates, 1982.

Schneemelcher, W. *New Testament Apocrypha.* ET edited by R. McL. Wilson. Cambridge: James Clark and Co., 1991. Vol. 1: *Gospels and Related Writings.*

Schneider, J. "Zur Komposition von Joh 18,12–27. Kaiphas und Hannas." *ZNW* 48 (1957): 111–19.

Schreckenberg, H., and K. Schubert. *Jewish Historiography and Iconography in Early and Medieval Christianity.* CRINT. Assen: Van Gorcum, Fortress, 1991.

Schürer, E. *History of the Jewish People in the Age of Jesus Christ,* revised by G. Vermes and F. Millar. 3 vols. Edinburgh: T. & T. Clark, 1973–86.

Schüssler Fiorenza, E. *In Memory of Her: A Feminist Theological Reconstruction of Christian Origins.* London: SCM, 1983.

Schwartz, D. R. "κατὰ τοῦτου τὸν καιρὸν: Josephus on Agrippa II." *JQR* 72 (1981): 241–68.

————. *Agrippa I: The Last King of Judaea.* Tübingen: J. C. B. Mohr (Paul Siebeck), 1990.

————. "On Two Aspects of a Priestly View of Descent at Qumran." In *Archaeology and History in the Dead Sea Scrolls: The New York University Conference in Memory of Yigael Yadin,* edited by L. H. Schiffman, 157–79. Sheffield: Sheffield Academic Press, 1990.

————. "Pontius Pilate's Appointment to Office and the Chronology of Josephus' *Antiquities* Books 18–20." In D. R. Schwartz, *Studies in the Jewish Background of Christianity,* 182–201.

————. "Pontius Pilate's Suspension from Office: Chronology and Sources." In D. R. Schwartz, *Studies in the Jewish Background of Christianity,* 202–17.

————. Review of M. Goodman, *The Ruling Class of Judaea, IEJ* 40 (1990): 237–39.

————. *Studies in the Jewish Background of Christianity.* Tübingen: J. C. B. Mohr (Paul Siebeck), 1992.

Segal, A. F. *Rebecca's Children: Judaism and Christianity in the Roman World.* Cambridge, Mass.: Harvard University Press, 1986.

Senior, D. P. *The Passion Narrative according to Matthew: A Redactional Study.* Leuven: Leuven University Press, 1982.

Setzer, C. *Jewish Responses to Early Christians: History and Polemics, 30–150 C.E..* Minneapolis: Fortress Press, 1994.

Shutt, R. J. H. *Letter of Aristeas* (translation and introduction) in *Pseudepigrapha,* edited by J. H. Charlesworth. 2:7–34.

Sloyan, G. S. *The Crucifixion of Jesus: History, Myth, Faith.* Minneapolis: Fortress, 1995.

Smallwood, E. M. "The Date of the Dismissal of Pontius Pilate from Judaea." *Journal of Jewish Studies* 5 (1954): 12–21.

————. "High Priests and Politics in Roman Palestine." *JTS* 13 (1962): 14–34.

————. *The Jews under Roman Rule: From Pompey to Diocletian.* Leiden: E. J. Brill, 1976.

————. "Philo and Josephus as Historians of the Same Events." In *Josephus, Judaism,* edited by L. H. Feldman and G. Hata, 114–29.

Smith, D. Moody. *The Theology of the Gospel of John.* Cambridge: CUP, 1995.

Smith, S. H. "The Role of Jesus' Opponents in the Markan Drama." *NTS* 35 (1989): 161–82.

Stanton, G. N. "Matthew's Christology and the Parting of the Ways." In *Jews and Christians,* edited by J. D. G. Dunn, 99–116.

————. "The Communities of Matthew." *Interpretation* 46 (1992): 379–91.

Stemberger, G. *Jewish Contemporaries of Jesus: Pharisees, Sadducees, Essenes*. Minneapolis: Fortress, 1995.
Stern, M. "Aspects of the Priesthood." In *Jewish People in the First Century*, S. Safrai and M. Stern.
Stewart, R. A. "The Sinless High Priest." *NTS* 14 (1967/68): 126–35.
Swete, J. P. M. "The Zealots and Jesus." In *Jesus and the Politics*, edited by E. Bammel and C. F. D. Moule, 1–9.
———. "A House Not Made with Hands." In *Templum Amicitiae: Essays on the Second Temple presented to Ernst Bammel*, edited by William Horbury, 368–90. Sheffield: Sheffield Academic Press, 1991.
Sylva, D. D. "The Temple Curtain and Jesus' Death in the Gospel of Luke." *JBL* 105 (1986): 239–50.
———. "The Meaning and Function of Acts 7.46–50." *JBL* 106 (1987): 261–75.
Talbot Rice, D. *The Beginnings of Christian Art*. London: Hodder & Stoughton, 1957.
Talmon, S. "Aspects of the Dead Sea Scrolls." In *Scripta Hierosolymitana*, edited by C. Rabin and Y. Yadin, 4:162–99.
Taylor, N. H. "Popular Opposition to Caligula in Jewish Palestine." *JSJ* 32 (2001): 54–70.
Thackeray, H. St. J., translator. *Josephus: The Jewish War*. LCL vols.. II and III. London: Heinemann, 1927–8.
———, translator. *Josephus: The Life/Against Apion*. LCL vol. I. London: Heinemann, 1926.
Theissen, G. *The Gospels in Context: Social and Political History in the Synoptic Tradition*. Edinburgh: T. & T. Clark, 1992.
Theissen, G., and A. Merz. *The Historical Jesus: A Comprehensive Guide*. London: SCM, 1998.
Thoma, C. "The High Priesthood in the Judgement of Josephus." In *Josephus, Judaism, and Christianity*, edited by L. H. Feldman and G. Hata, 196–215.
Thomas, G. *The Trial: The Life and Inevitable Crucifixion of Jesus*. London: Bantam, 1987.
Tindall, E. A. "Jn xviii.15." *Expository Times* 28 (1916/17): 283–84.
Tomson, P. J. *'If this be from Heaven . . .' Jesus and the New Testament Authors in Their Relationship to Judaism*. Sheffield: Sheffield Academic Press, 2001.
Tovey, D. *Narrative Art and Act in the Fourth Gospel*. Sheffield: Sheffield Academic Press, 1997.
Trocmé, E. "The Jews as Seen by Paul and Luke." In *To See Ourselves as Others See Us*, edited by J. Neusner and E. S. Frerichs, 145–61.
Tromp, J. *The Assumption of Moses: A Critical Edition with Commentary*. Leiden: E. J. Brill, 1993.
Tuckett, C. M. *Luke*. New Testament Guides. Sheffield: Sheffield Academic Press, 1996.
Tzaferis, V. "The Burial of Simon the Temple Builder." In *Jerusalem Revealed*, edited by Y. Yadin, 71–72.
Van der Horst, P. W. "The Jews of Ancient Crete." *Journal of Jewish Studies* 39 (1988): 183–200.
VanderKam, J. *Dead Sea Scrolls Today*. London: SPCK, 1994.
Van Iersel, B. *Reading Mark*. Edinburgh: T. & T. Clark, 1989.
Van Voorst, R. E. *Jesus outside the New Testament: An Introduction to the Ancient Evidence*. Grand Rapids: Eerdmans, 2000.
Vermes, G. "The Jesus Notice of Josephus Re-Examined." In *Journal of Jewish Studies* 38 (1987): 1–10.
———. *The Religion of Jesus the Jew*. London: SCM, 1993.
———. *Complete Dead Sea Scrolls in English*. London: Allen Lane/Penguin, 1997.
Vicent Cernuda, A. "La Conversión de Caifás y el Hallazgo de sus Huesos." *Estudios Bíblicos* 54 (1996): 35–78.

Vincent, L. H. "Saint-Pierre en Gallicante." *RB* 39 (1930): 226–56.

Von Wahlde, U. C. "The Johannine 'Jews': A Critical Survey." *NTS* 28 (1982): 33–60.

———. "Relationships between Pharisees and Chief Priests." *NTS* 42 (1996): 506–22.

Walker, P. W. L. *Holy City, Holy Places? Christian Attitudes to Jerusalem and the Holy Land in the Fourth Century.* Oxford: Clarendon, 1990.

Wallace-Hadrill, A., ed. *Patronage in Ancient Society.* London: Routledge, 1989.

Weatherley, J. A. *Jewish Responsibility for the Death of Jesus in Luke–Acts.* Sheffield: Sheffield Academic Press, 1994.

Webb, R. L. "John the Baptist and His Relationship to Jesus." In *Studying the Historical Jesus*, edited by B. Chilton and C. A. Evans, 179–229.

Weinert, F. D. "Luke, the Temple, and Jesus' Saying about Jerusalem's Abandoned House (Luke 13:34–35)." *CBQ* 44 (1982): 68–76.

———. "Luke, Stephen, and the Temple in Luke–Acts." *BTB* 17 (1987): 88–90.

Werman, C. "The Sons of Zadok." In *The Dead Sea Scrolls: Fifty Years after Their Discovery*, edited by L. H. Schiffman, E. Tov, and J. C. VanderKam, 623–30. Jerusalem: Israel Exploration Society in cooperation with The Shrine of the Book, Israel Museum, 2000.

Westcott, B. F. *The Gospel according to St John.* London: John Murray, 1902.

White, L. M. "Crisis Management and Boundary Maintenance." In *Social History of the Matthean Community*, D. L. Balch, 211–47. Minneapolis: Fortress Press, 1991.

Whitters, M. F. "Some New Observations about Jewish Festal Letters." *JSJ* 32 (2001): 272–88.

Wilkinson, J. *Egeria's Travels.* London: SPCK, 1971.

———. "Christian Pilgrims in Jerusalem during the Byzantine Period." *PEQ* 108 (1976): 75–101.

Williams, M. H. "Palestinian Jewish Personal Names in Acts." In *The Book of Acts in Its First Century Setting*, edited by R. Bauckham, 79–113.

Winter, P. *On the Trial of Jesus.* 2d ed., rev. by T. A. Burkill and G. Vermes. Berlin: De Gruyter, 1974.

———. "Excursus II—Josephus on Jesus and James Ant xviii 3,3 (63–4) and xx 9,1 (200–2)." In *History of the Jewish People*, E. Schürer, revised, 428–41.

Witherington, B. *The Jesus Quest: The Third Search for the Jew of Nazareth.* Carlisle: Paternoster, 1995.

———. *The Acts of the Apostles: A Socio-Rhetorical Commentary.* Grand Rapids: Eerdmans, 1998.

———, ed. *History, Literature, and Society in the Book of Acts.* Cambridge: CUP, 1996.

Wright, D. P. "Unclean and Clean." *ABD* 6: 729–41.

Wright, N. T. *Jesus and the Victory of God.* London: SPCK, 1996.

Wright, R. B. *Psalms of Solomon* (translation and introduction) in *Pseudepigrapha*, edited by J. H. Charlesworth. 2:639–670.

Wroe, A. *Pilate: The Biography of an Invented Man.* London: Jonathan Cape, 1999.

Yadin, Y., ed. *Jerusalem Revealed. Archaeology in the Holy City 1968–1974.* Jerusalem: Israel Exploration Society/'Shikmona' Publishing Co., 1975.

Zias, J. "Human Skeletal Remains from the 'Caiaphas' Tomb." *'Atiqot* 21 (1992): 78–80.

Index of Modern Authors

Index of Subjects

CPSIA information can be obtained at www.ICGtesting.com
Printed in the USA
LVOW050508130612

285822LV00002B/56/P